STATE AND FAMILY

IN

EARLY ROME

BY

CHARLES W. L. LAUNSPACH

OF THE MIDDLE TEMPLE

BARRISTER-AT-LAW

Nach ewigen, ehernen
Grossen Gesetzen
Müssen wir Alle
Unseres Daseins
Kreislauf vollenden.
GOETHE.

Yet I doubt not thro' the ages one increasing purpose runs.
TENNYSON.

THE LAWBOOK EXCHANGE, LTD.
Clark, New Jersey

ISBN 978-1-58477-542-3

Lawbook Exchange edition 2005, 2022

The quality of this reprint is equivalent to the quality of the original work.

THE LAWBOOK EXCHANGE, LTD.
33 Terminal Avenue
Clark, New Jersey 07066-1321

*Please see our website for a selection of our other publications
and fine facsimile reprints of classic works of legal history:*
www.lawbookexchange.com

Library of Congress Cataloging-in-Publication Data

Launspach, Charles, W. L. (Charles William Louis)
 State and family in early Rome / Charles W.L. Launspach.
      p. cm.
 Originally published: London : G. Bell, 1908.
 Includes bibliographical references and index.
  ISBN 1-58477-542-4 (cloth : alk. paper)
   1. Constitutional history—Rome. 2. Rome—Social life and customs. 3.
Rome—History—To 510 B.C. I. Title.

JC83.L37 2005
937'.01—dc22   2004056798

Printed in the United States of America on acid-free paper

STATE AND FAMILY

IN

EARLY ROME

LONDON: GEORGE BELL AND SONS
PORTUGAL ST. LINCOLN'S INN, W.C.
CAMBRIDGE: DEIGHTON, BELL & CO.
NEW YORK: THE MACMILLAN CO.
BOMBAY: A. H. WHEELER & CO.

STATE AND FAMILY

IN

EARLY ROME

BY

CHARLES W. L. LAUNSPACH

OF THE MIDDLE TEMPLE

BARRISTER-AT-LAW

Nach ewigen, ehernen
Grossen Gesetzen
Müssen wir Alle
Unseres Daseins
Kreislauf vollenden.
                    GOETHE.

Yet I doubt not thro' the ages one increasing purpose runs.
                    TENNYSON.

LONDON

GEORGE BELL AND SONS

1908

CHISWICK PRESS: CHARLES WHITTINGHAM AND CO.
TOOKS COURT, CHANCERY LANE, LONDON.

FOREWORD

THE present treatise deals only with Rome in its infancy and adolescence. A considerable portion of that period is prehistoric. Its reconstruction—faulty at the best—demands a strong effort of synthesis; and whilst the subject is calculated to stimulate the imagination, the paucity of the available authentic material has lent itself to many interpretations provocative of controversy. The central idea that has furnished my text is that the early Roman State was a conscious imitation of the ancient Gens or ancient Family, that its theory of Government was founded upon the relations existing between kinsmen, and that these, again, were determined by religious notions which later became transformed through developments within the City and external influences. To call such a State, in its earliest days, either a democracy, an autocracy, or an aristocracy might be verbally true; but it would be substantially false. It is not explainable without reference to the religious notions of the Romans before they came under the direct influence of the Greek theogony. How largely the religious element underlies what on the surface appear to be purely political and economic controversies, has been shown by M. Fustel de Coulanges. Without some such key, the struggles of the patrician and plebeian orders, for instance, are to my mind merely bewildering. But when we perceive how self-interest is buttressed or antagonized by traditional, though doubtless obsolescent, religious prejudices, politics and economics drop into their proper perspective, and we may impartially respect the standpoints of all parties.

Such struggles could only have been waged without mutual destruction in a community of considerable political maturity, which could appreciate the nature of civic freedom and dignity. There was no law-giver of transcendent genius to guide, and few peoples have owed less to the teaching of their leaders. If we would enumerate the men of surpassing intellect who flourished under the Republic, our tale (unless we include the " Uebermensch " Sulla) must begin with the great Julius and end with his august nephew, both of whom belong to a decadent age. For earlier examples of eminence we are thrown back upon splendid mediocrities like the persevering Cunctative Fabius, the well-intentioned Camillus, and the highly respectable Cato. Probably the development of the Roman people was exceptional. Owing perhaps to the strategic accident of

its position, Rome started almost at the outset of
its career as a conquering State; and before the
regal or oligarchical power had time to become
hereditary and despotic, as was probably the case
with most of the older Cities, the compulsory and
voluntary influx of plebeians into the rising community leavened the old burgher stock with immigrants who valued their hard-won rights as free
citizens in proportion to the trouble they had been
at to obtain them. Had the patriciate been less
profuse of its blood upon the battle-field, and the
new-comers less numerous or less mettlesome, the
former might have retained its privileges, or at most
grudgingly dispensed them upon a graduated scale,
and a caste-system, rigid and baleful, might, as in
Hindustan, have determined the development of
the later civilization.

It is for this reason that the history of early Rome
contrasts so strikingly with that of the ensuing ages.
The first epoch may be said to have closed on the
day—in the year of the City 490 (264 B.C.)—when
a fleet conveyed Roman troops across the Straits
of Messina, inaugurating a new era of extra-Italian
conquest. Theretofore the citizen-soldier had encountered, in peace and war, men whose habits, institutions and civilization in the main resembled
his own. It was not difficult to absorb, or at least to
manage, subject communities which presented so

many points of contact; and so long as Roman expansion was confined to the Peninsula, domestic
strife and external warfare only developed and emphasized the national character. Very different were
the effects of the wars beyond seas. The Roman-
izing process in Italy was seriously disturbed by
the irruption of Hannibal, and the first two Punic
Wars exercised a disintegrating influence upon the
old-Roman system itself. The ensuing rapid expansion brought about economic changes which transformed the conditions of national life, whilst the
exotic elements crowding eagerly to the metropolis
assisted to modify and degrade the native character.
The home-keeping population was weaned from the
hardening process of war, but it did not appreciably
progress in the arts of peace. The leading class of
the Optimates found, indeed, unlimited opportunities
of enrichment, legitimate and otherwise. But the
stolid good sense of the humbler citizen was from
the beginning hopelessly outclassed by the nimble
brain and facile commercial morals of Greek, Syrian,
Egyptian, African, and Jew. A wise oligarchy would
have endeavoured by drastic measures to protect the
solid elements upon which the national greatness had
been reared. But politics had sunk to an unworthy
rivalry of coteries, which successively maintained
their power by flattering and bribing the populace at
the expense of the Commonwealth. It was to the

convenience of all the parties contending for popular favour that the individual citizen should be shallow, improvident, unambitious, and consequently easily led or cheaply purchasable. The franchise, in the absence of representative government, was in practice confined to those of the electorate who either resided within Rome, or had means and leisure to travel thither upon occasion. To govern and speculate at will the Optimates needed but to buy the favour of the few effective voters, and the resident citizen was amused with shows, and fed at the expense of worthier populations. The inevitable consequence was the extinction of the middle class, and a widening of the gap between the higher and lower orders. Never had the old-time patricians and plebeians found themselves at such opposite poles as now stood "Known" and " Unknown "—" Nobiles " and " Ignobiles."

It must not be supposed that the Roman nation had become utterly worthless. The Marian and Sullan proscriptions might decimate the leading houses, and economic pressure drive the farmer off the land; the places of the former largely fell to adventurers, whilst hordes of slaves occupied what had been the homesteads of a free peasantry. Yet there survived sufficient administrative talent, honesty of purpose, and dignity of character to save the Republic, if only they could have had free play in public life. But the process of pauperizing the urban electorate had acquired a momentum which the best elements were powerless to check, and the citizen who lightly surrendered his liberty for free tickets and free food had small heed for those who offered only hard truths and unpalatable advice. Respectable men of the wealthier classes, disgusted, held aloof from politics. The sturdier and more independent of the poorer orders, finding no employment at home, either emigrated or joined the legions.

The early Roman Populus had been both Army and People, and only levies of allied and kindred communities had fought side by side with Roman troops. Frequent and protracted employment of large expeditionary forces now necessitated a standing army, partly recruited from non-citizen, and even non-Italian elements. What remained of Roman virtue was found beneath the eagles, where the linesman's steady bravery still repaired the general's blunders, the short sword still pierced its way to victory over Asian dart and Keltic claymore. The Warrior became distinct from the Burgher, and the time-honoured form of address: Quirites! was degraded to a term of reproach to lash self-respect into a mutinous legion. The professional soldier had neither cause nor will to disguise his scorn of the shiftless civilian populace. He yielded obedience not to any civil power but to his own military leaders, and scantily supplied the quality of disciplined patriotism by a gladiator-like *esprit de corps*.

As the moral fibre of the civilian citizen weakened, the Constitution fell into contempt, and in the tumultuous assemblies of the people legislation was carried as much by violence as by vote. From the rioter's bludgeon to the soldier's sword is facile transition, and mob rule passes easily through the disorder of faction to a military dictatorship. The reign of law was in the end restored. An all-powerful Administration re-established decent government, sheltered property and the amenities of life, and permitted commerce, arts, science, and philosophy to flourish with unheard-of splendour. But it was at the price of freedom, which could no longer co-exist with order and was willingly surrendered by a distracted nation. The Gabinian and Manilian Laws had rehearsed the stratocracy of the first Triumvirate; and after the renewed convulsions which followed Caesar's murder the world gladly found refuge in Octavian's ordered despotism.

Antiquity records struggles only outwardly dissimilar from those in constant operation around us— political and economic collisions between races blindly working out their destiny, domestic conflicts between privileged and unprivileged, rulers and ruled, rich and poor, which at this distance of time we are able to review without passion, remembering that every huge controversy, it has been well said, is not so much between Right and Wrong, as between Right and Right. I am conscious that the present-day proneness to compare modern with ancient civilization must be indulged with caution. In all ages long periods of prosperity and luxury are attended with similar resultant evils; but, to say nothing of the influence of religion (with us happily still an active force), the leading nations of to-day are several, and their unwholesome tendencies are largely repressed by mutual contemplation and a self-consciousness denied to the Roman-Greek world. Nevertheless, a study of the rise and decline of the Roman Commonwealth suggests reflections and conclusions which may be applied to many present-day conditions, and in dealing with some problems which now vex us, ancient history provides warning, if not counsel.

All systems of human association have their day, and yield to others. Back to the infancy of mankind, which the mists of time conceal from mortal view, we may imagine that every social institution, however ancient, has at one time displaced a yet older. Yet though Change be the Law, even where Stability seems greatest, it is evident that the standard of speed differs enormously. The Western world, during its comparatively brief career, has witnessed repeatedly the rise, spread, and then the gradual destruction, of supposedly durable institutions, whilst

highly organized societies of Asia and backward
races of Africa have resembled each other in remaining only slightly affected by the passage of
time. Judged from a cosmopolitan standpoint, the
development of European culture, however excel-
lent in itself, has proceeded upon abnormal lines,
and the resulting uncertainty of its future affords
additional reason for careful scrutiny of its past.
Change is not necessarily identical with what we
call Progress, and even a real reform in one age
may survive to work havoc in the next. Moreover,
progress and retrogression appear to have co-existed
at every stage of European history; and although
human life nowadays is probably, upon balance,
more tolerable than at any known preceding period,
there is little to indicate whether we are still heading
towards perfection or already treading the backward
sweep of an enormous circle.

C. W. L. L.

PLOWDEN BUILDINGS, TEMPLE,
    May, 1908.

CONTENTS

TABLE OF ABBREVIATED REFERENCES

THE BIBLE. Genesis; Exodus; Deuteronomy; Samuel; Kings; Jeremiah; Matthew; Luke; Acts of the Apostles.

BACHOFEN, J. J. Das Nexum, die Nexi und die Lex Petillia. (Bâle, 1843.)

BLACKSTONE, SIR WILLIAM. Commentaries on the Laws of England. (Dublin, 1771.)

BOUCHÉ-LECLERCQ, AUGUSTE. Manuel des Institutions Romaines. (Paris, 1886.)

BRYCE, JAMES. Studies in History and Jurisprudence. (Oxford, 1901.)

CAESAR, C. JULIUS. De Bello Gallico.

CATO, M. PORCIUS (CENSORIUS). De Re Rustica.

CATULLUS, C. VALERIUS. Carmina.

CICERO, M. TULLIUS. De Divinatione. De Natura Deorum. Pro Domo Sua. De Legibus. De Republica. De Officiis. De Oratore. Pro L. Murena. In Q. Caecilium.

CLARK, E. C. Early Roman Law. The Regal Period. (London, 1872.)

COHN (CONRAT), MAX. Beiträge zur Bearbeitung des römischen Rechts.

COULANGES, FUSTEL DE. La Cité Antique. (Paris, 1903.)

CUQ, EDOUARD. Les Institutions juridiques des Romains (L'Ancien Droit). (Paris, 1904.)

CZYHLARZ, CARL VON. Lehrbuch der Institutionen des römischen Rechtes. (Prague, 1889.)

DIONYSIUS (of Halicarnassus). French translation by Bellanger. (Paris, 1807.)

FERRERO, GUGLIELMO. The Greatness and Decline of Rome. (Zimmern's translation, London, 1907.)

FESTUS, SEXTUS POMPEIUS. De Verborum Significatione.

FLORUS, L. ANNAEUS. Epitome Rerum Romanarum.

b

FOWLER, W. WARDE. Roman Festivals of the Period of the Republic.

FRIEDLAENDER, LUDWIG. Darstellungen aus der Sittengeschichte Roms. (Leipzig, 1888.)

GAIUS. Institutes. (Poste's edition, 1904.)

GELLIUS, AULUS. Noctes Atticae.

GIBBON, EDWARD. Decline and Fall of the Roman Empire.

GIDE, PAUL. Etude sur la condition privée de la femme. (Paris, 1867.)

GIRARD, PAUL FRÉDÉRIC. Manuel élémentaire de Droit Romain. (Paris, 1901.)

GLADSTONE, RT. HON. W. E. Juventus Mundi. The Gods and Men of the Heroic Ages. (London, 1869.)

HAECKEL, ERNST. Natürliche Schöpfungsgeschichte. (Berlin, 1879.)

HALLAM, HENRY. Europe during the Middle Ages. (Fourth edition.)

HOELDER, EDUARD. Die Stellung des römischen Erben.

HOLMES, O. W., JUNR. The Common Law. (London, 1882.)

Q. HORATIUS FLACCUS. Carmina. Satirae.

HUNTER, W. A. A Systematic and Historical Exposition of Roman Law. (London, 1903.)

IHERING, RUDOLPH VON. Entwickelungsgeschichte des römischen Rechts. (Leipzig, 1894.) Geist des römischen Rechts auf den verschiedenen Stufen seiner Entwickelung. (Leipzig, 1852.) Vorgeschichte der Indo-Europäer. (Leipzig, 1894.)

IHNE, WILHELM. Forschungen auf dem Gebiete der römischen Verfassungsgeschichte. (Frankfort-on-Maine, 1847.)

JUSTINIAN. Codex. (Krueger, Berlin, 1877.) Digest. (Mommsen, Berlin, 1870.) Institutes. (Moyle, 1903; Sandars, 1898.)

JUVENALIS, DECIUS JUNIUS. Satirae.

KARLOWA, OTTO. Römische Rechtsgeschichte. (Leipzig, 1885.)

KLEINEIDAM, FEODOR. Die Personalexecution der XII Tafeln. (Breslau, 1904.)

LECKY, W. E. H. History of European Morals from Augustus to Charlemagne. (London, 1892.)

LEONHARD, RUDOLF. Institutionen des römischen Rechts. (Leipzig, 1894.)

T. LIVIUS PATAVINUS. Historiae ab Urbe Condita.

MACROBIUS, AMBROSIUS THEODOSIUS. Commentarius in Somnium Scipionis. Saturnalia.

MAINE, SIR HENRY SUMNER. Ancient Law. (London, 1907.) The Early History of Institutions. (London, 1893.) Dissertations on Early Law and Custom. (London, 1891.)

MOMMSEN, THEODOR. Römische Forschungen. (Berlin, 1864.) Römische Geschichte. (Berlin, 1903.) Römisches Staatsrecht. (Leipzig, 1887.)

MUIRHEAD, JAMES. Historical Introduction to the Private Law of Rome. (London, 1899.)

NIEBUHR, B. G. Römische Geschichte. (Berlin, 1853.)

P. OVIDIUS NASO. Amores. Fasti. Metamorphoses.

ORTOLAN, J. L. E. Explication historique des Instituts de l'Empereur Justinien. (Paris, 1870.)

PICTET, ADOLPHE. Les Origines Indo-Européennes. (Paris, 1859.)

C. PLINIUS SECUNDUS. Historia Naturalis.

PLUTARCH. Quaestiones Romanae. Vitae parallelae.

POTHIER, R. J. Traités de Droit Civil et de Jurisprudence françoise. (Traité du Mariage.)

PRELLER, LUDWIG. Römische Mythologie. (Berlin, 1858.)

RENAN, ERNEST. Histoire du Peuple d'Israël.

ROSSBACH, AUGUST. Untersuchungen über die römische Ehe. (Stuttgart, 1853.)

SCHJØTT, P. O. Studien zur alten Geschichte. (German text, Dybwad, Christiania, 1903.)

SMITH'S DICTIONARY OF GREEK AND ROMAN ANTIQUITIES. (London, 1890.)

SOHM, RUDOLPH. Institutionen des römischen Rechts. (Leipzig, 1884.)

SOLTAU, WILHELM. Ueber die Entstehung und Zusammensetzung der altrömischen Volksversammlungen. (Berlin, 1880.) Die Gültigkeit der Plebiscite. (Berlin, 1884.)

SPENCER, HERBERT. Principles of Sociology. (London, 1876.)

SUETONIUS TRANQUILLUS. Vitae XII Caesarum.

TACITUS, C. CORNELIUS. Annales. Germania. Vita Julii Agricolae.

ULPIANUS, DOMITIUS. Fragmenta.

VALERIUS MAXIMUS. Facta dictaque memorabilia.

VARRO, MARCUS TERENTIUS. De Lingua Latina.

P. VERGILIUS MARO. Aeneid. Georgics.

VOIGT, MORITZ. Die XII Tafeln (1883). Römische Rechtsgeschichte. (Leipzig, 1892-1902.)

WESTERMARCK, E. Human Marriage.

WHITNEY, W. D. Life and Growth of Language.

WOODS HUTCHINSON. Evolutionary Ethics of Marriage and Divorce. (Contemporary Review, September, 1905.)

STATE AND FAMILY IN EARLY ROME

CHAPTER I

ORIGIN OF THE ROMANS

THE principles underlying the primitive polities of Greece and Italy are borrowed essentially from the domestic system which appears to have prevailed among Aryan [1] peoples for many ages be-

[1] By "Aryan" I mean throughout collectively the great racial group which embraces Keltic, Scandinavian, Teutonic, Graeco-Italic, Slavic, Iranian and Hindu members. The name (said to be derived from the Sanskrit Arya = lord, land-lord), though frequently used on the Continent to designate only the Asiatic wing of the family, is appropriately applied to the whole group of nations whose most prominent members have so long controlled the world's destiny. The denomination "Indo-Germanic" was once preferred by German scientists, "for no other assignable reason," says Whitney (Life and Growth of Language, p. 180), "than that it contains the foreign appellation of their own particular branch, as given by their conquerors and teachers, the Romans." It is not more, indeed it is less, justified than "Indo-Keltic," and is now generally discarded on the Continent for "Indo-European." But even the latter term labours under the objection that it appears to exclude some races (e.g., Persians) which it is intended to embrace, and to include others (e.g., Magyars and Finns) which are racial strangers. Haeckel, Natürliche Schöpfungsgeschichte, Vortrag xxiii, divided the "Mediterranean" or "Indo-Atlantic"

fore Athens and Rome had been heard of. Inasmuch as the State was a reflex of the Clan or the Family, later radical changes in the body politic almost necessarily reacted upon those root-ideas of domestic association on which the framework of society rested. The internal political development of Rome during the first centuries of its existence was at once the outcome of institutions which had become unsuitable to the growing Commonwealth, and the driving-power which in the end modified those institutions almost beyond recognition. Consequently, the study of Roman history—certainly of early Roman history—is most usefully coupled with an examination of the primitive rules and customs (the expression "law" is somewhat premature) which governed domestic relations among the most remarkable people of antiquity.

For many centuries later, European culture was dominated almost exclusively by classical influences. And naturally so, for the European system, as gauged by the standard of to-day, lagged far behind the vanished Graeco-Roman civilization, until an assertive middle class brought to a world impatient of feudal trammels the same emancipation which the restlessness of the Romanized plebs had accomplished two thousand years previously for hide-bound ancient

species chiefly into "Indo-Germans" and "Hamosemites," subdividing the former into "Slavo-Germans" and "Ario-Romans," and restricting the term Aryan to Iranians and Hindus. See also Pictet, Origines Indo-Europ., i, 27 ff.

Latium. Yet only the modern world, relying less upon brilliant hypothesis than upon patient research, has bestowed upon ancient principles an amount of analytical attention at all commensurate with their importance. Without some understanding of the internal working of archaic societies, ancient history becomes (what, indeed, modern history, as taught in schools, likewise and for a similar reason tends to become) a string of highly-coloured biographies, interspersed with more or less apocryphal accounts of personal exploits and adventures. Every one has heard of the Horatii and Curiatii, but few can appreciate the habit of mind which rendered the fable credible and intelligible to succeeding generations. And whilst every schoolboy is familiar with the battles of Poictiers and Azincourt, few adults have reviewed the economic causes of the Hundred Years' War, for which Edward's claim to the French throne formed a convenient pretext.

For the purpose of this treatise it is sufficient to confine it in point of time mainly to the epoch preceding the great Carthaginian struggle, and in point of topic to the internal, domestic and constitutional developments of Rome during that epoch. With the deliberate knowledge that I am thereby alienating the sympathy of all those who, to use Mérimée's phrase, " n'aiment dans l'histoire que les anecdotes," I purpose to rigidly exclude as irrelevant the merely picturesque and dramatic. Further, I am constrained to almost entirely disregard foreign politics, military conquests, colonizations, biographical matter, and various episodes of tradition or quasi-history which bulk so largely in the Roman chronicles, and have received from modern writers certainly not less than their due share of attention. Some general knowledge of Rome's history is therefore necessarily imputed to the reader.

Beginning with the question of the origin of the Roman people, I accordingly dismiss unnoticed the romantic legends with which poets and historians of after-times, writing in the glamour of a splendid Empire, sought to explain the gradual transformation of a ring of rustic habitations around the Palatine Hill into the pivot of Occidental civilization and the world's centre of gravity. The foundation of Rome was not a marvellous, not even an unusual event; the first Romans, springing from the same stock and living under the same conditions as their neighbours, surpassed the latter in intellect[1] and physique[2] as little as they could claim superiority by virtue of divine dispensation.

[1] Mommsen, Römische Geschichte, i, 304: "Das ganze römische Wesen lief darauf hinaus, die Bürger durchschnittlich zu tüchtigen Männern heranzuziehen, geniale Naturen aber nicht emporkommen zu lassen."

[2] Probably the Latins were slighter men than the Etruscans, "obesus Etruscus" (Catullus, Carm. 39). The huge forms of the barbarian invaders are frequently alluded to in literature: "Plerumque omnibus Gallis prae magnitudine corporum suorum brevitas nostra contemptui est" (Caesar, Bell. Gall., ii, 30); cf. Juvenal, Sat. viii, speaking of the slaughtered Cimbri.

At some remote period, the approximate date of which it is hazardous to estimate, one great branch of the Aryan race, urged possibly by the progressive desiccation of the country, betook itself from its central Asian home westwards into Europe. An offshoot, now called the Graeco-Italic family, separated, in the course of its wanderings, from its Keltic, Slav, and Teutonic kinsmen, and, deflecting southwards, finally occupied what are now the Balkan and Italian peninsulas.[1]

At the dawn of history we discern in what, for convenience, we will call Italy, although that name was originally confined to the southern extremity of the peninsula,[2] three racially distinct groups of inhabitants: the Japigians, the Etruscans or Tyrrhenians, and the tribes of Central Italy, which latter

---

[1] The Greeks and the Italians (applying the latter term prematurely to all the tribes of Central Italy) are generally deemed sister nations, a view supported by affinities of language and institutions. But the Kelts are by some considered more closely allied to the Graeco-Italic race than Slavs or Teutons, and to stand (despite very divergent characteristics) in closer relationship to the Italic tribes than even the Greeks. See Haeckel's Stammbaum der Indo-germanischen Rasse in his Natürliche Schöpfungsgeschichte, xxiii. Vortrag. Cf. Mommsen's Römische Geschichte, i, 327. It is of course possible, and even probable, that the Aryan races known to us had been preceded by others, whom the later invaders exterminated or absorbed.

[2] The term "Italy" was gradually extended to include the centre of the peninsula. Under Augustus, Italy was created an official administrative unit, divided into eleven regions. It then corresponded very nearly with the present Kingdom, plus Istria and minus Sicily and Sardinia.

we are justified in collectively denominating the
Italic race. The vexed question of the "aboriginal"
inhabitants has no bearing upon our subject, and
need not detain us. Neither are we concerned with
the Japigians, who at a comparatively early period
became absorbed in the powerful Greekish communities established by immigration from beyond
the sea. The origin and exact position in the Aryan
family of the Etruscans[1] (= Ras-na or Rasena),
long the leading power in the peninsula, are still
doubtful. Our information of the Central Italic
tribes is less unsatisfactory, and with them alone we
are immediately concerned. They may be divided
into a Western (Latin) and an Eastern (Umbrian)
group, including, to the South, the powerful Samnite
nation, destined to become Rome's chief rival for
the supremacy over Italy. Language, customs,
political and religious institutions point to close
racial affinity between the Italiot communities, and
to the similarity of their social systems. A number
of individuals owning obedience to a common (real
or reputed) kinsman, generally long-deceased and
not always ascertainable, constituted a Gens, having
community of cult, sanctuary, altar, and festivals. The

---

[1] Cf. Preller, Römische Mythologie, i, 12. As to the high
probability that the Etruscan language belonged to the Indo-
European group, see Whitney, The Life and Growth of Language, p. 188. Mommsen, Römische Geschichte, i, 118-119, is
less positive. Schjøtt, Studien zur alten Geschichte, holds that
the Etruscans were racially allied with the Phoenicians; cf.
Tacitus, Ann., iv, 55.

exigences of a defensive policy, or the imperceptible action of economics, sometimes produced coalitions of gentes which, if they endured, evolved into civitates or cities. Offshoots of these frequently arose through voluntary or compulsory emigration of some members of a community into the outside world, to fare as the gods might direct. Most of those emigrants probably perished; the remnant, following any indication which imagination might construe as a sign from above, set up altars over sods of earth brought from the old home, founded new settlements, and under propitious circumstances emerged as new communities, cherishing the institutions of the parent stock and generally maintaining some connection with it.

Although the notion of kinsmanship was at the bottom of all institutions which bound men together, the conventional basis of solidarity was not Kin nor Race, but Ritual. The more frequently any two persons found themselves associated in religious observances, the closer was the bond between them. Members of the same gens daily worshipped the manes of their common ancestors. When the gentes began to break up into families, relations between gentiles became subordinated to the tie which claimed each man's first duty for his actual living ancestor and his more immediate forbears; but their association with each other remained more intimate than with members of other gentes, whom they joined in periodically worshipping the tutelary deities of a common city. Finally, a common cult, performed periodically though at infrequent intervals, held most of the cities of Latium (= the " Broad Plain ") in a loose connection, which facilitated intermarriage and contractual intercourse among the members, and in times of common danger might induce united action.[1]

As presiding head and ritual-centre of the loose Latin federation, Alba Longa (the " Long White Town," or, as we should have said in England, " Long Whitton ") stood towards the other tinier States of Latium in the relation of a mother city to its colonies. To Alba repaired periodically representatives of the federated cities for the joint celebration of the feriae Latinae, and in all probability also for the discussion of temporal matters of common interest. During these times, peace reigned throughout Latium, and the cities granted each other's members safe conduct: but otherwise, the federal bond neither prevented individual cities from warring together, nor, apparently, necessarily obliged them to act as one in a federal campaign against an external enemy.

Among the youngest of the Latin cities was Rome,[2] to whose settlement three separate tribes, the Ramnians, Titians, and Luceres, are said to have contributed. Ancient writers claim for them, respectively, a

---

[1] Mommsen, Staatsrecht, iii, c. Der latinische Stammbund.
[2] Cf. Livy, ii, 45. The taunt "upstart" would naturally sting a community which asserted religious as well as political supremacy over older subject cities.

Latin, Sabine, and Etruscan origin, apparently upon the assumption that the astonishing development of the Roman Commonwealth, almost from its very commencement, required the concentration in the new nation of characteristics of the sturdiest races. The theory might appeal to Englishmen, who trace their own descent from the fiercest and worthiest peoples of the North, but the evidence supporting it is distinctly inconclusive, and our positive knowledge of the earliest Romans points in the contrary direction, namely, to a remarkable racial homogeneousness. That the Ramnians were Latins is almost universally admitted, and as they gave their name to the City, they may be safely regarded as the predominant element. The Sabines belonged to the Eastern, or Umbro-Sabellian, wing of the Italic race, and differed from the Latins less, probably, than the Danish invaders from Alfred's Saxons. The Latin origin of the Luceres is not less likely than any other: the evidence of their immigration from Etruria is uncertain, and not very probable. In point of race, language, and ritual, Etruscans diverged widely from Latins and Sabellians, and although the commercial intercourse existing from time immemorial between the two sides of the Tiber left numerous traces, there is nothing to denote unmistakably the presence of any important Etruscan element in the budding Roman nation.[1]

---

[1] Cf. Mommsen, Römische Geschichte, i, c. 4: "die unverstän-

It is most probable that long before Rome existed, the progenitors of its founders lived as colonists or clients of Alba along the south bank of the Tiber, and engaged in rude commerce (the chief export being cattle) as well as in agriculture. Such a population would naturally include the usual complement of women and children. The theory of the foundation of Rome by bands of male adventurers is inherently improbable, and discredited by circumstances. The legend of the rape of the Sabine women, when analyzed, falls to the ground as historically unnecessary and contrary to prevailing contemporary notions.[1]

The generally received date of the foundation of Rome is the year B.C. 753. In reality, it would perhaps be difficult, if we knew the whole of the facts, to assign any one year to the event. Rome was not built in a day—nor in a year. A central position, desirable from the point of view both of mercantile convenience and of hygiene, attracted and united the shrewd and thrifty riparian dwellers of Latium.

dige Meinung dass die römische Nation ein Mischvolk sei "; Soltau, Altrömische Volksversammlungen, i, § 2. Ethnologically, the vicus Tuscus can no more count as evidence than Hanover Square or the Promenade des Anglais can determine the racial constituents of England or Provence. Schjøtt would have it that Rome was an Etruscan colony. Yet there is no certain instance on record of an Etruscan gens having been received into the Roman populus (like the Claudii and the Alban gentes) as we should expect to find if kinship had existed.

[1] Fustel de Coulanges, Cité Antique, 429.

Upon the Palatine Mount, wattled and mud-daubed habitations, sufficiently roomy to harbour numerous inmates, sheltered cattle breeders and agriculturists, who in certain seasons found it dangerous to dwell in the swampy and fever-stricken plains. The settlement developed on the normal lines of similar associations, evolved a common cult, and emerged as a new addition to the cities ·of Latium. As the community advanced in importance and dignity, offshoots or suburbs of the City were established on the neighbouring heights. An important accession of political strength was derived from the coalescence with the Palatine inhabitants of those occupying the eminence afterwards known as the Quirinal Hill. It may be that the union was not at first voluntary, but the consequence of conquest by Sabine neighbours.[1]

Agriculture, the economic mainstay of most non-barbarous peoples, had been known to the Italic races before their migration into the Peninsula, and the Latin language contains many indications, some of which are discernible in modern speech, of the extent to which husbandry entered into the daily life of the people. But it would seem that from the earliest period commerce, which, before the advent of coined money, must have been mostly barter, was also actively pursued in Rome, and the presence from time immemorial of an important trading element which might or might not also engage in husbandry, is

[1] Ihne, Forschungen, 25, 33 ff.

proved by the comparatively large number of citizens capable of bearing arms in a territory comprising but a few score square miles. Possessed from very early times of a seaport at the mouth of the Tiber, the City itself lay sufficiently inland to be protected against piratical incursions: the kindred Latin cities lay to the south and east,[1] and the Tiber, whilst affording a fairly effective barrier against Etruscan aggression, yielded a convenient vehicle of intercourse with Etruscan trade and civilization. Commercial activity, with its concomitants, a spirit of enterprise and self-confidence, a steady influx of wealth and population, and a progressing standard of civilization, contributed largely to secure to Rome in process of time the hegemony of Latium, the supremacy over Italy, the conquest of the world. But commercial advantages alone would not have availed, if unaccompanied by the qualities of an imperial race. The first impetus to the predominancy of Rome over the rest of Latium may, indeed, have been given by geographical accident. The hills successively occupied by the new city clustered too closely to admit permanently of separ-

---

[1] "Friendly" Latium, however, despite religious, racial, commercial, and social ties, was much more frequently than Etruria the objective of the early Roman military expeditions. Excepting Veii, with which the Romans waged constant war until its destruction 358 urbis, we find no important Etruscan town on the Tiber in proximity to Rome. It is even doubtful whether the inhabitants for some distance north of the Tiber were not themselves Latins living under Etruscan overlords.

ate settlements, and when united, the Roman community appears to have been larger and more powerful than any of its neighbours. This result the shrewd farmers and cattle-dealers could hardly have foreseen. But they were not slow to discern the economic advantages of the situation, once created, and history during the ensuing centuries was moulded by the recognition by all classes that the general prosperity was best defended and extended by military superiority. It was an anticipation (in an unscrupulous and remorseless form) of the modern doctrine that Trade follows the Flag. The rise and progress of the Roman State appeals to us as essentially a victory of national character, due not to the genius of a few talented statesmen, but to the high standard of the average citizen. "Moribus antiquis stat res Romana virisque." Inferior in brilliancy of imagination and intellectual power to many of the peoples whom he ultimately enslaved,[1] the Roman owed his triumphs first and foremost to a deliberate blending of his private interest with that of the State. The individual citizen was merely a stone added to the cairn of empire. Hence his steadfastness of purpose, his sobriety of judgement, his sense of discipline reinforced by his family sys-

[1] "Ueberall ist die römische Staatskunst mehr ausgezeichnet durch Zähigkeit, Schlauheit und Konsequenz, als durch eine grossartige Auffassung und rasche Ordnung der Dinge, worin ihr vielmehr die Feinde Roms von Pyrrhos bis auf Mithradates oft überlegen gewesen sind." Mommsen, Römische Geschichte, p. 570.

tem, and that moral strength which refuses to believe in failure.[1] For the better appreciation of these qualities it is now desirable to examine the conditions of life amid which they evolved.

---

[1] "Les Romains ont eu au plus haut degré cette vertu maîtresse, la fermeté de caractère, tempérée par une autre vertu non moins précieuse, l'esprit de mesure." Cuq, Institutions juridiques des Romains, p. 74.

CHAPTER II

I N proceeding to investigate the primary institutions of Rome, we must detach ourselves from many habits of thought which we usually bring to bear when considering modern, but which mislead when applied to ancient, conditions. Within the memory of middle-aged men, Europe has witnessed two great national consolidations,[1] but neither presents any true analogy with the development of the Roman State. At bottom, the modern instinct of nationality and patriotism mainly represents a widening of the sentiment of kinsmanship, operating as an emotional force to consecrate, as it were, an already existing, more or less intimate community of material interests. But in Rome's early days the widening process had scarcely commenced, and, having commenced, it proceeded less upon a theory of racial affinity than that of a common allegiance to and worship of determinate, special, and (later) national gods. The Nation was essentially an extension of the Gens, and the basis of gentile organization was religious, or at least ritualistic. Strangers in blood were brothers if they worshipped

[1] The Kingdom of Italy and the German Empire.

15

at the same house-altar; brothers by blood became strangers when one was banished from it. And again, men were fellow citizens when and so long only as they adored the same City gods; the exile, excluded from the cult of his City, thereby forfeited his citizenship.

Long before Rome was founded, the Aryan races, at least those of Greece and Italy, had progressed beyond the cruder stages of barbarism, and their maturing intellect, though as yet untrained and in-experienced, had already found time and strength for those speculations which, with endless diversity, colour and obscure their cults.

So far as we are able to discern, the religious system of the Aryan races, appears under the three-fold aspect of Ancestor-worship, Hero-worship, and Nature-worship. It seems highly probable that the first prompted the second. Whether the cult of the Ancestor preceded that of Nature, or contrariwise, we are not called upon here to decide.[1] The com-

---

[1] According to the Spencerian theory, all religions derive from Ghost-worship, this being based upon the supposed existence of a man's "other self," as manifested by dreams, insanity, disease, or by involuntary movements, as sneezing or convulsions. To the ghosts the savage will ascribe every abnormal and unexplained occurrence, whether boon or misfortune, and he will desire to placate them, as he himself would be placated, by offerings and flattery. Out of ghost-worship in general there grew up a worship of ancestral ghosts, to whom, under patriarchism, religious rites became restricted. According to Spencer, Nature-worship itself had no other origin. "The conclusion warranted by the facts is that Nature-worship, like each of the worships previously

mon origin of the three worships, if it ever existed, is concealed in the mists of remote antiquity. Certainly the connection is no longer distinguishable in the religious system of Rome.[1] It is therefore justifiable to treat the latter under the separate heads of State or Public Religion, apparently founded upon Nature-worship, and Family or Private religion, which was equivalent to Ancestor-worship. Roman notions, which claimed all the dead, however illustrious and however humble, for the family cult alone, rejected the adoration, so common in Greece, of heroes, or deified mortals, whose posthumous renown had induced after-generations to associate them with the public gods. The Romans never elaborated any extensive cult of heroes, and such beginnings as later ages introduced belong to a

analyzed, is a form of ancestor-worship, which has lost, in a still greater degree, the external characters of its original. Partly by confounding the parentage of the race with a conspicuous object marking the natal region of the race, partly by literal interpretation of birthnames, and partly by literal interpretation of names given in eulogy, there have been produced beliefs in descent from mountains, from the sea, from the dawn, from animals which have become constellations, and from persons once on earth who now appear as moon and sun. Implicitly believing the statements of forefathers, the savage and semi-civilized have been compelled grotesquely to combine natural powers with human attributes and histories, and have been thus led into the strange customs of propitiating these great terrestrial and celestial objects by such offerings of food and blood as they habitually made to other ancestors " (Sociology, § 193).

[1] F. de Coulanges, Cité Antique, c. 4.

different period from that under review.[1] For present purposes, hero-worship may be neglected.

The roots of the ancient Aryan belief must have lain deep down in the human race. The infinity of gods active for good and evil, the man's double or shadow, the sacrifices, oracles, divination by signs and portents, the shadowy after-life without adequate provision for the reward of righteousness and punishment of guilt, none of these is exclusively Aryan; and ancestor-worship is to this day practised by peoples so far apart, racially, intellectually, and geographically, as the Japanese and the Bantu tribes of Damaraland. Even the later development of cult discloses parallelisms among Europeans and Semites in their evolution from patriarchism to civilization. Ancestor-worship, indeed, is not a feature of Hebrew religion as it appears in the Bible. But the tradition of human sacrifice, the use of flint knives for religious purposes long after weapons of metal were in vogue, the custom of purification, the ritualistic dance, the absence, in the pastoral stage, of temples and professional sacerdocy, which then grew up spontaneously under the influences of settled life, the gradual transformation of the primitive deities from moral abstractions into corporeal beings to behold or to embrace whom is death to mortals,[2]

[1] Preller, Römische Mythologie, i, 3; Mommsen, Römische Geschichte, i, 165.

[2] Exodus, xxxiii, 20-23. Ovid, Metam., iii:
"... Corpus mortale tumultus
Non tulit aetherios; donisque jugalibus arsit."

all these are Graeco-Roman features, yet all have their counterpart with nations of the Old Testament.

Public Religion

The deification of natural phenomena, if it has not lain at the root of all cults, must have originated at a very early stage of human mind-development. The savage, or barbarian at one remove from savagery, living in constant, direct contact with nature, warmed or scorched by the sun, cooled or pierced by the wind, refreshed by the rain or drenched by torrential downpour, now revelling in rude health, and then a raving maniac or struck down by mysterious malady,[1] recognizes in the unknown forces which alternately comfort and afflict him a counterpart of the capricious patronage and tyranny which he unquestioningly accepts from his chief, and extends unresisted to his own dependents. He sees in benefits and visitations the works of beings immeasurably more potent than himself, yet not unlike himself, since his feeble imagination cannot grasp, nor his uncouth language express, anything removed from the narrow scope of actual experience. Phenomena, however striking, which do not directly affect his well-being, will excite neither wonder nor inquiry. But all things which visibly influence his life are to him intelligently active, and therefore

[1] It is curious that savages are inclined to regard all illness as the product of malign enchantment. For them, the only "natural" death is the violent one.

alive. The sun, sky, earth, mountain, river, forest, and plants, are either themselves gods or peopled with gods, to whom are attributed every natural disturbance—lightning, a thunderstorm, a deluge, a drought, and all events not of an everyday description, as sickness caused by a poisonous herb, the straying of cattle, or the accidental destruction of chattels by fire. The instinct of the savage moves him to placate by gifts and flattery the mysterious powers, whose constant intervention evidences the interest bestowed upon, and their irresistible sway over, his own destiny and that of his neighbours.[1]

But the sharper-witted barbarian will not remain content with a general propitiation of the gods by offerings and adulation. He will endeavour to enlist their sympathies, and, if possible, elicit from them some expression of opinion as to the result, at all events the wisdom, of any important action which he may contemplate, a hunting expedition, a pitched battle, a foray, a marriage, or the choice of an abode. Strong as this impulse must be, even when living regularly and quiescently amid familiar surroundings, it must have become immeasurably intensified during the wanderings of our Aryan ancestors towards an unknown goal amid the difficulties, the dangers, the terrors of vast unexplored

---

[1] Cf. Gibbon, Decline and Fall, i, 229: "Fear has been the original parent of superstition, and every new calamity urges trembling mortals to deprecate the wrath of their invisible enemies."

regions. Here, if ever, the science of consulting the gods was precious, and would by constant practice develop in time to a remarkable degree of virtuosity. Events following upon certain signs would be narrowly watched, and the tradition of generations would gradually harden into a mass of set rules and formulas, differing, of course, among various tribes in accordance with divergent experiences encountered by each. Where these experiences were communicated among neighbours, certain similarities of ritual naturally resulted, being less marked where, owing to greater distance, inter-communication was infrequent. With some of the Aryan peoples the science of divinity shows a tendency to become hereditary in certain families. Whole tribes or groups of tribes might, indeed, in course of time acquire the reputation of exceptional skill in divination, as was the case with the Etruscans;[1] and we learn from Caesar[2] that Gaulish candidates ambitious for priestly dignities sometimes crossed the sea to study divine lore under the direction of British Druidical hierophants.

Although the ancient Aryans habitually personified natural phenomena familiar to all men, they never clearly grasped and proclaimed the notion of a universal Deity. To them Nature, so far as it was visibly active, was a congeries of animated intelligences; but a central directing Intelligence was as unthinkable in the unseen as in the visible world. Even the

[1] Cicero, De Div., i, 41.   [2] De Bello Gall., vi, 13.

same phenomenon was frequently deified under different names by tribes who failed to recognize that their worship was in substance identical. One of the most ancient deities was Mars. But although he was worshipped under various and sometimes very similar names throughout the Italian peninsula, each city considered its own Mars as distinct from every other. When the inhabitants of the Quirinal Hill federated with the Palatine Romans, their god Quirinus continued to enjoy a separate cult, with its flamen and its priestly college, alongside that of the Palatine Mars, from whom he was otherwise undistinguishable. Yet, especially in very early times, the Roman intellect seems to have dimly apprehended the existence of an all-pervading World-principle. There was a leaning towards monotheism, or rather pantheism, and, unlike the highly individualized and humanized deities of the Greeks, the old-Roman gods, solemn, dignified, and abstract, appear rather as personalized fragments of the universal, intangible Godhead.[1]

The religious history of the heathen Roman State is susceptible of division into four periods. The original Latino-Sabine system of the *first* period combines with the pure and formless Latin nature-worship the ceremonial said to have been introduced by the Sabine Kings, Titus Tatius and Numa Pompilius. Characterized by simplicity, exactness, and

---

[1] See Preller, Römische Mythologie, i, 48, 54, 62 ff.; cf. Cic., De Nat. Deor., ii, 2, 25.

discipline,[1] it supplied the school in which the destiny of the young nation was forged; it infused the qualities and enforced the training which were to carry the victorious eagles through all lands from Scotland to Egypt.

The *second* period roughly represents the space of time from the advent of the Tarquins to the second Punic war. It coincides with extensive political and commercial expansion, and the introduction of important foreign influences. Accordingly, grafted upon the old Latin and Sabine stock, we find Etruscan growths, and Hellenic elements, acquired first through Etruria (always largely receptive of Greek ideas), and later by direct intercourse with Greece and Greekish colonies. Chiefly characteristic of this period we note:

1. The multiplication of gods and cults, the direct or indirect result of conquest. A number of stranger gods are forcibly removed from surrounding cities, to be installed as minor deities at Rome, and new cults are set up by statesmen and generals in gratitude for political and military successes. Imported deities were called Novensiles, the native gods being Indigetes.

2. Increasing tendencies to splendour and display,

---

[1] Preller, Römische Mythologie, i, 21: "Die jungen Jahre Roms wurden in eine Zucht getan, welche auf die Dauer freilich nicht befriedigen und noch weniger den plebejischen Neubürgern gefallen konnte, aber für den Anfang eine ganz vortreffliche Schule jener Gesinnung war, an welche wir bei Rom und den Römern immer zuerst denken."

corresponding with the growing wealth of the Roman nobility, and the gradual promotion of the City to the position of a world-power. Temples and images, almost unknown to Pompilian citizens, now abound. Religious observances become, if less serious, much more spectacular, being usually accompanied by elaborate public games and banquets.

3. To the simple piety of the former age succeeds mysticism and an increasing disposition towards sign-reading and occult learning. Etruscan haruspices reinforce the Roman augurs, and a special college — duoviri sacris faciundis — admittance to which is clamorously demanded by plebeians, guards and on occasion interprets the Sibylline Books.

The *third* period, from the Punic wars to the end of the Republic, witnesses the almost complete disintegration of the ancient Latino-Sabine religion by foreign, now including African and Asiatic, elements. Faith among the educated turns to scepticism,[1] or at best surface-belief; with the vulgar it encourages sloth, and the grosser forms of superstition. Quintus Scaevola (Consul, 659 u.c.) openly asserts the existence of a double religion, the one rational and philosophic for the educated, the other traditional and superstitious for the ignorant. Sacral learning is neglected and largely forgotten; candidates for the priestly offices are elected by popular vote, obtained

---

[1] "Among the educated classes," says Warde Fowler (R. F., 342), "the old beliefs were being eaten away by the acids of a second-hand philosophy."

by sedulous canvassing or lavish bribery; the practices of religion subserve the intrigues of the poli-
tician, the pastimes of the frivolous, and the amours
of the lady of fashion. To the general mob of slaves,
pauperized townsmen, foreign adventurers, idle para-
sites, and crapulous millionaires, with their women-
kind, public devotions are merely pretexts for licence
and brutalities.

In the *fourth* or Imperial period, the centraliza-
tion of political power in the hands of one man
reacts upon the religious system. The City cults are
indeed celebrated more pompously than ever by an
imposing hierarchy, enjoying augmented dignity
and emoluments; but gods and men are alike abased
before Caesar, the focus of all adoration as of all
temporal power, to whom even Jupiter must hence-
forth surrender his title of Optimus Maximus. As
the despotic power of the head of the State gradually
discards its disguises, so the devotion paid to living
and dead princes becomes more exclusive, more
Oriental, and more contemptible. The divorce between religion and ceremonial is now absolute. The
spiritual yearnings of the few must be confined
within doors. The system must run its course until
the ground is cleared for the advent of that old-new
faith, once dimly perceived in Rome, and now announced by a despised handful of Jews, the faith of a
universal morality, enjoined by a universal Godhead.

Of these four periods, only the first two fall within
the limits assigned to this treatise, and in the brief

review we are able to give them, they may be taken together.

The chief public deities of early Rome were the war-god, Mars-Quirinus, and, later, Jupiter (Diespiter),[1] the latter representing the civic rather than the warlike aspect of life. Agreeably with the old-Roman order of ideas, which consistently subordinated force to law and military to civil power, Jupiter and not Mars became the chief god, the Stayer of the State, and its champion against all comers. In accordance with the process of fission common to nearly all important ancient gods, we encounter Jupiter with many suffixes and varied qualities. Roman statecraft was quick to recognize the importance of specially identifying with itself the most esteemed deity of Central Italy. A seeming religious consecration of Rome's hegemony over Latium had been afforded by its presidency (after the overthrow of Alba) over the immemorial cult of Jupiter Latiaris, the common patron of the federated Latin cities. Jupiter in another form soon throned as Optimus Maximus upon the Capitol, his consort, Juno, to the left, his daughter, Minerva, to the right.[2]

---

[1] The old Latin Mars was, however, a god of vegetation, and non-militant. Jupiter (Diespiter) contracted from Jovis (Diovis) and pater. His worship at Rome probably only dates from the absorption of the Esquiline into the Palatine City (Bouché-Leclerq, Manuel, 488).

[2] Images and temples were scarcely known in the earliest age of Rome. Most worships took place in woods and groves, and various trees were dedicated to certain gods, as the oak to Jupiter (Livy, i, 10). The association with Jupiter of Juno and Minerva

Jupiter Stator was installed upon the Palatine. The chief festivals were sacred to him, and he was presumed to preside in the vacant seat of honour beside magistrates and senators over the solemn public feasts. He was the guardian of international law and guest-right. No foreign war could be undertaken which had not been justified to Jupiter by the solemn declaration of the enemy's wrong, and refusal to redress it. When a victorious army returned, its entry was a religious ceremonial in his honour. The general to whom a triumph was accorded by his countrymen borrowed the attributes of Jupiter, not from pride but in token that to the god belonged the victory; and to Jupiter were dedicated the Spolia opima, when a Roman commander had, with his own hand, slain and stripped the hostile leader.

Constantly, though not exclusively, associated with Jupiter, is the notion of Light, allied to the notion of Truth and Rectitude.[1] The days of the full moon were sacred to Jupiter Lucetius. To a people so largely addicted to rustic pursuits, he naturally presented himself as a patron of agriculture, of the crops and vintages, and therefore closely associated with

was borrowed later from Greece through Etruria, where the three deities were known respectively as Tinia, Uni, and Menrfa. Marriage and propagation could hardly be attributed to the early Latin and Roman gods, before the primaeval religion had succumbed to the influence of Greek ideas.

[1] Good and Evil seem with all nations to be bound up with the ideas of Light and Darkness, e.g., the light of Heaven, the Prince of Darkness. Similarly, Right seems always associated with straightness, and Wrong with its opposite.

meteorological manifestations.[1] But as every principle may be viewed under different aspects, the great
god himself had a maleficent side, and the Romans
scrupled not to adore Ve-diovis, the Evil Jove.[2]

Besides their principal deities, the Romans sacrificed to gods of the Tiber, the harbour and sea
(after the possession of the seaport Ostia had opened
the commercial waterway), woods, and springs. The
Dii Termini were gods of the landmarks, which so
many peoples have concurred in regarding as peculiarly sacred.[3] Numberless abstractions derived

[1] The different points of view from which most natural phenomena are capable of being regarded, and the independent ob-
servations of different tribes, or groups of tribes, partly account
for the extraordinary confusion of ideas which strikes us at every
turn in the ancient mythology. The like natural phenomenon or
principle may be worshipped by different peoples under dissimilar
names, and different phenomena or principles are equally susceptible of being worshipped under the same name. Jupiter
Pluvius and Jupiter Tonans might be regarded as one and the
same, and even Jupiter Capitolinus might be imperfectly dissociated from Jupiter Stator (on the Palatine); but there can have
been little, if any, connection, in the minds of the ancients,
beyond the abstraction of the universal Godhead, between the
first pair, originating in the play of natural forces, and the second,
carrying a purely political significance.

[2] Mommsen, Römische Geschichte, i, 163. Preller, Römische
Mythologie, i, 264, recognizes in Ve-diovis merely a youthful
Jupiter, who was likewise regarded as a sun-god, and, in a country
like Latium, not unnaturally associated with epidemics at certain
seasons. His temple, between the two summits of the Capitoline
Hill, was an asylum for outlaws who had fled from justice.

[3] "Cursed be he that removeth his neighbour's land-mark"
(Deut., xxvii, 17).

from everyday pursuits and events were personified
and deified: Satunus represented the seed-time,
Consus and the goddess Ops the harvest, Ceres,
plenty, the Mater matuta, child-bearing. Abstraction
even went the length of imagining a Janus as god
of the Morning and of all Beginning, and dedicating
temples to the Public Conscience (Fides Populi
Romani) and, later, to notions like Fever and Misfortune. Janus (Dianus, masculine of Diana = Luna,
the moon) was originally, like Jupiter, pre-eminently
a light or life-giving god. His temple was closed
in time of peace and open during war, for what
reason is not clear. His double face was retro-
spective of the bygone, and prospective of the com-
ing year. As god of the Beginning, Janus seems to
have been always mentioned first in the invocations
to the deities (Livy, viii, 9), but March, not January,[1]
was for centuries the first month of the Roman year.

As every family had its domestic hearth (vesta),
so was Vesta the hearth of the city, upon which
six[2] chaste virgins maintained the sacred fire. After
thirty years of service they were entitled to retire
into private life and marry; but usually preferred to
retain the amenities of a highly privileged position.
They were exempt from patria potestas and tutelage
(though subject to disciplinary control of the pontifex maximus) and could freely hold property and

[1] It is uncertain whether January was named after Janus (Warde
Fowler, Roman Festivals, 33, 99).

[2] In earliest times, four only.

dispose of it by mancipation or testamentary disposition. They had the privilege of driving within
the City walls, of being preceded by lictors like high
officers of State, and of liberating any condemned
criminal who accidentally crossed their path. Like
the Family, too, the City had its Lares and Penates,
tutelary deities of mysterious powers, whose names
must never be disclosed, lest an enemy, by specious
promises or magic spells and incantations, should
seduce them from the City to its undoing. For, notwithstanding their abstract character, the gods of a
city were susceptible of the temptation of bribes,
the coercion of a magic formula, and, when represented by material images, of bodily capture like
any other citizen. When Rome was sacked by the
Gauls, the Roman gods found hospitality with the
citizens of Caere. Every city of antiquity bore
two names, the one being that known to the world,
whilst the other and true appellation remained a
closely kept secret, lest the city's enemies should
find means to work charms [1] against it. [2] Niebuhr
believed the secret name of Rome to have been
Quirium. The traffickings with the frail gods of
Veii are well known, and many Jupiters and Junos
have been removed from vanquished cities, to be admitted among the inferior deities of Rome, whilst their
whilom votaries swelled the ranks of the Roman plebs.

[1] There is a fundamental difference between the Priest and the
Magician. The former serves his gods, the latter masters them.
[2] Macrobius, Sat., iii, 9.

At the head of the Roman hierarchy stood, in the regal period, the King (Rex). In republican times, the priestly office of rex sacrorum was nominally the most exalted, and actually the least significant. Next in official rank to that shadowy dignitary were the three flamines majores, ministering respectively to Jupiter, Mars, and Quirinus, as did the rex sacrorum to Janus. Chief of the flamines was that of Jupiter, the flamen Dialis, of whom it was required that he must be married in first wedlock, his wife being priestess to Juno, and whom widowerhood disqualified from continuance in office. The priests of the lesser gods were flamines minores, and theirs were the first of the sacred offices to fall to the pretensions of the plebeians. Last in dignity, but politically far the most powerful, was the pontifex maximus. He appointed and exercised disciplinary power alike over rex sacrorum, flamines, and vestals. His decision was invoked in all matters touching public worship, his verdict was decisive of the legitimacy or illegitimacy of marriages, and his political importance may be judged by the obstinacy with which the patricians contrived to retain the office in the hands of their order for many years after the lex Ogulnia had nominally opened it to plebeians. With him was associated a college consisting of four (after 454 U.C. of eight)[1] pontifices ("bridge-builders," or possibly "road-makers"),[2] a

---

[1] Sulla raised the number to fifteen, and there were many later variations.　　　[2] Cf. Clark, Early R. L., 56.

pre-Roman, originally lay institution of engineers, whose avocations encouraged the habit and facility of calculation, draughtsmanship, and writing. Accordingly, the pontiffs, under the direction of their president, regulated the calendar (though with very moderate success), appointed the dates of public feasts, announced the days upon which public business might lawfully be transacted, guarded most of the archives, kept the City annals, and exercised a general supervision over public ritual.

With the flamen Martialis and flamen Quirinalis were associated colleges of twelve under-priests, salii (leapers or dancers).[1] Each curia had its special altar, priesthood, and religious observances under the care of a curio maximus. There were many less important associations or brotherhoods, of immemorial antiquity and obscure origin, as the Luperci, who administered the cult of the Palatine Faunus; the Titii, who celebrated the memory of the king from whom they derived their name; the Fratres Arvales, who sacrificed each year to Dea Dia. Some of these institutions had originally belonged to particular gentes prior to the formation of the City, as the Luperci of the Fabian and the Quinctilian gentes. Trade guilds had their peculiar tutelary gods and festivals, as the smiths, who adored Vulcan and celebrated the volcanalia.

Two priests, duoviri sacris faciundis (increased 387 u.c. to ten, of whom half were required to be

---

[1] Varro, De L. L., v, 85.

plebeians) kept the mystic Sibylline Books, which were consulted in times of crisis when grave danger threatened the State. Generally speaking, the oracle demanded the establishment of some new cult or ceremonial.

The Fetiales, under a chief called pater patratus, were specially associated with the cult of Jupiter, and fulfilled, though in a sacerdotal character, the functions now usually discharged by a Foreign Office. All diplomatic intercourse with foreign governments fell within their department. They protected the interests of nationals who had suffered wrong at the hands of alien States or subjects, bargained for the amount of compensation, or the noxal surrender of the offender, negotiated treaties, and notified declarations of war. The institution was of immemorial age and common to all Italic peoples.

In Rome, the distinction between priestly offices, properly so-called, and divination, or the science of consulting the gods, was always maintained well in view. The augurs and haruspices were, like the pontifices, inferior in rank to the flamines. They were not necessarily inspired by the gods.[1] The auspices constituted an independent administrative department, and, indeed, may have originated in the discharge of purely secular duties during the remote ages of the Aryan migration.[2] The augurs (from avis and garrio) interpreted the flights (or cries) of birds as

---

[1] Cicero, De Div., i, 49.

[2] Ihering (Vorgeschichte) propounds some ingenious theories

D

manifestations of the heavenly will. Etruria was apparently the classical home of the allied science of the haruspices, whose prognostications were founded upon an examination of the entrails of slaughtered animals. Wild birds and sacrifices were not alone in furnishing hints for the guidance of mortals. A Roman army would be accompanied by sacred chickens, whose appetite, or want of it, determined the course of a campaign. The habit, from which Roman soldiers never departed, of intrenching their camp, even though pitched for a single night only, may be ascribed to their fear of being forced to fight at a time when the auspices were unfavourable. The defeat and death of Flaminius was attributed to the neglect of the warnings conveyed by the re- fusal of poultry to eat, and other confirmatory signs. No public business could be transacted without having first consulted the gods,[1] and the high- est offices of State were resigned upon the dis- covery of a defect in the auspices at the time of installation.[2] Dreams were regarded as inspired from above.[3] Lightning would be variously inter- preted according to the direction whence it came.[4] Every momentous event was heralded by prodigies, as when a mule was delivered of a colt,[5] the statues

concerning the non-religious origin of the auspicia. But his ex- planation of the origin of the vestal virgins seems far-fetched.

[1] Cicero, De Div., i, 16; Livy, i, 36.

[2] Livy, iv, 7; v, 17. Cicero, De Nat. Deo., ii, 4.

[3] Cicero, De Div., i, 2, 20, 26. [4] *Ibid.*, ii, 18. [5] *Ibid.*, ii, 22.

of gods were covered with sweat, or there fell a rain of blood.[1] Vergil describes the terrible portents of the night preceding the assassination of Caesar,[2] who, had he lived a few centuries earlier, would assuredly have heeded the premonitions of nature and the adverse auguries, so far as they were not imagined after the event.

In all transactions with the gods scrupulous attention was paid to form, and frequently a ceremony was repeated many times in succession to ensure that nothing was omitted. Conversely, the gods were held to the strict letter of the bargain, however violated in the spirit. In addressing most [3] of the deities the worshipper covered his head. Conversation with the unseen world was only to be entered upon with a calm and serene mind, and a body free of disorder. No person with any physical blemish was eligible for the priesthood. A sore or scab disqualified an augur until healed, and the innumerable disabilities of a flamen Dialis (who was forbidden to touch, among other things, a horse, raw meat or beans, and dared not even name a dog or goat) must have seriously detracted from his enjoyment of office.

Family Religion.

The desire to propagate is, next to hunger, the most active impulse in every department of animal

---

[1] Cicero, De Div., ii, 27.   [2] Georg. I.

[3] Plutarch, Q. R., 10, 11, 13.

life, and only under the influence of a highly artificial civilization are considerations of prudence
occasionally permitted to override it. But the yearn-
ing for offspring was intensified in ancient peoples
by almost equally powerful external pressure.[1] Two
tenets of belief, which the founders of Rome brought
with them, were perhaps as old as human-kind;
firstly, that the spirits of the dead, the Lares and
Penates, could and did direct for good or evil the
fate of the living, and, secondly, that they were largely
subject to the same needs as living mortals, upon
whom they were helplessly dependent for the assuage-
ment of hunger and thirst, and other ministrations
necessary for their happiness in the lower world.

There was no " better land " for the ancients,
unless after death they became gods. The expecta-
tion of the vast majority was to repose in a tomb, to
which they would be committed with due performance
of the rites, their wants being ministered to by periodical sacrifices of survivors. If the latter neglected to
provide for proper interment and for the regular
offerings, sanctified by the practice of ages, the for-
lorn spirit of the dead man was condemned to roam
upon earth, an unhappy and malevolent demon, who
wreaked vengeance upon the living by spreading
disease, by causing cattle to stray and crops to fail.[2]

---

[1] Men would pray and sacrifice for whole days that their
children might survive them (Cic., De Nat. Deor., ii, 28).

[2] More backward peoples (*e.g.*, German tribes) would bury with
a dead man his principal and more necessary movable belongings

To insure against such a calamity was the universal desire, and every man was expected to provide in his lifetime a successor upon whom would unmistakably devolve the duty — enforceable, if necessary, by the central authority—of attending to the sacra. That a father should look to his own children to fulfil the office is what we expect to find. But then it became necessary to be quite certain who were the children. Such certainty could only be secured in ordered married life,[1] the outward sign of which was the nuptial ceremony, whereby the wife became detached from her natural family to enter her husband's. Hence the peculiar sanctity of the marriage tie in early Rome, the reservation of the sacra (and the inheritance) to children born in lawful wedlock, the prohibition of celibacy, and the importance attached to female chastity.

Not all children were equally eligible to perform the sacra to the manes of their ancestors. Daugh-

---

—slaves, weapons, horses, food, etc. But this can only have been usual in the case of wealthy and important men.

[1] The only legitimate conjugal union known to Romans and modern Europeans, though not necessarily non-existent, must have been of rare occurrence—the result of environment, not inclination—among primitive peoples. Monogamy was favoured by patriarchism, as patriarchism was favoured by a pastoral life, tending, where pasture is scanty, to isolate individual families. Ihering (Vorgeschichte, p. 63) holds that matriarchate had disappeared from Aryan institutions before the great westward wandering. Caesar, however (De Bello Gall., v, 14), asserts, though one is reluctant to believe, the existence of polyandry among Ancient Britons.

ters, by marrying, were held to break all sacred connection with their natural family, since to belong to two families was deemed inadmissible. There was probably another reason for placing daughters upon a footing different from that of the sons; it seems to have been the belief of the ancient Aryans that the power of generation was with males exclusively[1]— the female serving merely as a passive instrument or incubator—that the blood of the father, and his alone, rolled in the veins of his child. Thus cognation, or relationship through females (I use the word in its narrower sense), counted for very little. To the sons of the same father (possibly at one time to the eldest son only) fell the duty of performing the sacrifices to him and their remoter ancestors.

Private Religion centred in the Home.[2] The citizen's house was not so much his Castle as his Chapel, which not even the officers of the State, in the execution of their duty, dared to desecrate by violent entry. Probably the deceased members of the family were at first interred in the plot of ground upon which the house stood, and to this circumstance has been ascribed the origin of exclusive ownership of land—with what right I cannot determine. For obvious reasons, the custom cannot have generally prevailed for very long in the growing city, though some of the older families contrived to retain the privilege. The practice of cremation arose at a very

[1] F. de Coulanges, Cité Antique, p. 38.
[2] Cicero, Pro domo sua, 41; Val. Max., iv, 3, 14.

early period; and the XII Tables speak of burying and burning the dead as if both were usual at the time. No creditor could seize his debtor's house to satisfy his claim, and when a criminal paid the extreme penalty, forfeiting life and property, his habitation was not confiscated, but razed to the ground.

Each house contained its hearth or altar (vesta, ara, or focus) upon which the sacred fire was maintained. To have put this fire to any domestic use would have desecrated it; nor was every kind of fuel suitable to feed it. Prayers and devotions were regularly offered before it at least twice in the day. Once a year, on the 1st of March (New Year's Day with the early Romans) the fire was extinguished, and forthwith rekindled with prescribed rites and solemnities, at which the whole family assisted under the presidency of the paterfamilias and his wife. It is extremely probable[1] that there was an intimate connection between the altar rites and the cult of the house Lares, that the adoration of the fire, the emblem of purity as the ancients understood it, was but an adjunct of the worship addressed to the ancestral deities. The altar being the symbol of the domestic Providence, its loss or defilement was the greatest misfortune that could overtake the family, and " pro aris et focis " was the expression used by the Romans to signify that their all was at stake.

It is impossible to estimate at what epoch the

---

[1] F. de Coulanges, Cité Antique, 29. *Contra*, Ihering, Vorge-schichte, 348.

belief in the virtue of the house-altar, the imminence
of the ancestors' presence, the reality of their material
needs, the efficacy of their protection and their power
for mischief, began to decline as living articles of
faith. The ritual itself had hardened into a rule of
life which left its impress upon the legislation of
more advanced ages, and through sheer force of habit
continued to be obeyed even when the strength of
belief had almost entirely spent itself. Enormous
inconvenience must have been entailed by a private
cult demanding the unfailing and unremitting attention of particular persons at one fixed spot. Yet,
long after the substance of faith had disappeared,
its outward forms and trappings commanded the
uncomprehending respect of the successive generations whom they puzzled and plagued.

It must be admitted that the religion professed
and practised by the Romans was not of the highest
order. It was characterized by a formalism pedantic
to the verge of puerility. Founded primarily upon
material considerations, adoration both of nature and
ancestors was largely the outcome of the votary's
fear, rather than the veneration of the humble and
contrite heart seeking spiritual communion with the
Higher Power. Primus in orbe deos fecit timor.
There was no place for the Christian's noblest
ideal—the ideal of an infinitely wise and good All-
Father, to whom all men are equally his children,
and whose solicitude disdains not even the brute

creation.[1] There was no place for the doctrine of after-life reward and retribution; the Hereafter depended not upon a man's own conduct, but upon the diligence of descendants who attended to the sacra. Piety, in Roman eyes the foundation of all moral excellence, meant little more than the respect paid to the memory of the dead. Virtue was synonymous with valour, the quality pre-eminently requisite for the defence of State and house, gods and altar against external enemies. At first sight a low religion indeed; but it was a religion adapted to the times, with some positive and negative advantages of its own which modern Europeans have secured only at the price of centuries of strife and suffering. It permitted as perfect a civil liberty as the ancients could aspire to, and whilst developing the best qualities then attainable to mankind, discountenanced the worst features of the yet older barbarian worship.

1. It left public and private life free from the curse of sacerdotal tyranny. At no time was pagan Rome a priest-ridden community. The civil power was as supreme in Rome as in the most enlightened of modern States. Like the soldier, the priest and the augur were by the Constitution unequivocally

[1] Luke, xiv, 5: "Which of you shall have an ass or an ox fallen into a pit, and will not straightway pull him out on the Sabbath day?" Matthew, x, 29: "Are not two sparrows sold for a farthing? And one of them shall not fall on the ground without your Father." Similarly the Kuran: "Do they look up at the birds flapping their wings? None supporteth them but the Merciful: verily he seeth all."

subordinated to the Magistrate, and indirectly to the People. The sacerdotal order was not a body of fanatics ardent to convert the world with fire and sword, nor a privileged caste cut off from the generality of the nation, and ambitious solely for the aggrandizement of its own estate. Apart from the respect due to their functions, priests and augurs personally claimed no special place in the scheme of government. Nor was the priestly office calculated, in private life, to inspire extravagant awe in the plain paterfamilias who, as the central figure of his own family circle, himself daily discharged quasi-sacerdotal duties. Undistinguished from his fellow citizens when not actually officiating in his sacred capacity, the priest deliberated in the Senate, voted in the comitia, fought in the field, cultivated his property, transacted business, and brought up his family.

2. Proscriptions for heresy are necessarily absent from a community where all religions are considered "by the people as equally true, by the philosopher as equally false, and by the magistrate as equally useful." [1] Each family guarded the ceremonial of its own private cult as an institution independent of the State. Each city, whilst worshipping its own gods, not only recognized those of other cities, but even

[1] Gibbon, Decline and Fall of the Roman Empire, i, c. 2. But such philosophers had scarcely begun to exist in Rome in the epoch under notice, when the families and cities were content to take their own and each other's gods upon trust.

occasionally competed for their favours. A broad
spirit of tolerance characterized the public religion,
and in Imperial times the Roman pro-consul or
legate in the provinces would courteously sacrifice
upon the altar of the local god whose community
the fortunes of war had brought under Roman rule.
Uncompromising Monotheism has, unfortunately,
always tended towards intolerance, and religious
persecution, properly so called, remained unknown
only exactly so long as Rome remained pagan.
Political expediency, indeed, might occasionally
attempt the suppression of, or conveniently divert
public indignation to, a small sect which had osten-
tatiously sundered itself from the rest of mankind;
but the motives which condemned Christians to the
torch or the lions had nothing in common with those
which organized the Inquisition, and lighted the
fires of Smithfield.[1]

3. Whilst the Romans of the regal and Republican ages had not yet entered upon the era of
religious persecutions, they had outgrown those persecutions—no less terrible, though voluntarily suffered—which marked the majority of barbarian, and
disgraced even some of the civilized cults of
antiquity.[2] Animal blood, indeed, flowed at most,
though not at all, rites, but beyond the killing of the
sacrificial victim, wanton suffering to man or beast
was avoided by a people which had not yet learned

---

[1] Cf. Bryce, Studies, i, 53 ff.
[2] *E.g.*, the Moloch-worship of Carthage.

to love cruelty for its own sake. It is probable that among Aryan societies the custom of human sacrifice, infrequent with pastoral and patriarchal groups, developed later with the increasingly militant aspect of life. It is to their credit that the Romans, amid constantly warlike surroundings, contrived to throw off habits which long continued to form an integral part of the rites of other nations. The ver sacrum, or offering of all children and animals to be born in the ensuing spring, or later, still survived as an expedient for averting the wrath or enlisting the sympathy of the deities in times of exceptional trouble and perplexity.[1] But as an alternative to their immolation, the babies were allowed to grow to the age of self-maintenance, and were then sent out of the community to wander whither the gods might direct, and if favoured by them to found new cities. And already in comparatively early times such emergency offerings appear to have been confined exclusively to animal firstlings.[2] Traces of primordial institutions involving human sacrifice are indeed found in the earlier Roman rites. Before Jus had become differentiated from Fas and Crime from Sin, the malefactor was scourged to death, or hurled from the Tarpeian rock, not because he had transgressed against society, but because an offence against the divine law could only be purged by a sacrifice to the out-

[1] Festus, Ver Sacrum; Smith's Dictionary of Antiquities; Ihering, Vorgeschichte, 311 ff.
[2] Livy, xxii, 10.

raged gods. But although in the case of specific iniquities the devotion of the evil-doer himself was regarded as the proper and natural expiation, the wrath of the gods could be appeased, or their active co-operation secured, by the voluntary self-immolation of one or more brave and patriotic citizens. The ill-boding chasm in the heart of the City closed for ever when Curtius leapt into it; and more than once did a Roman leader snatch a doubtful victory by braving not only the ordinary death on the battle-field, but the terrors of an unknown fate beyond the grave.[1] The savage ancient custom survived as a sanction of public morality, or an incentive to the sublimest of human acts. Otherwise, save at one or two supreme crises of public peril and panic,[2] the Roman contrived to reconcile his higher instincts with his respect for tradition by substituting, in his votive offerings, the human image for the human body. The gloomy and forbidding rites of Etruria, the cruelties of Carthage and Britain, and the depravities of Assyria have no place in his uncorrupted ritual.

4. Valuable far and beyond all else was the character-forming influence of a pure and simple worship upon a naturally worthy people. We have already

---

[1] Schjøtt thinks that the conduct of Leonidas and the three hundred Spartans at Thermopylae was a similar act of voluntary self-sacrifice to the gods to ensure ultimate victory. When Rome was attacked by the Gauls, the leading men who remained behind to be unresistingly massacred seem to have similarly "devoted" themselves. Livy, v, 41; Florus, i, 13.

[2] Plutarch, Q. R., 83.

referred to the probably well-founded belief that all
worship was originally inspired by motives no more
respectable than fear and cupidity; but these are
not the predominant notes in early Rome. There
the gods were not contemplated with that abject ser-
vility which a professional clerisy, interposing itself
between Heaven and the laity, has in all ages presumed to exact. Rather did the relation consist in
interchange of mutual benefits, a hearty and business-like reciprocity, and mortals not only drove
hard bargains with their gods, but even occasionally overreached them. The Roman festivals, celebrated with the rough, but simple and decorous
mirth which we associate with village rejoicings,
rather represent the sentiment of gratitude for the
fullness of the earth, a serene reliance upon its continuance, and a cheerful resolve to use to the utmost
the gods' gifts. It was a ritual which, if it did not
consciously inculcate, was certainly reconcilable with
a fairly high standard of ethics.[1]   If our view of its
origin be correct, we must not indeed look upon it
as the fountain of morality. Nor is this necessary.
The fact that a society comprising a considerable
number of individuals has been voluntarily formed,
and continues voluntarily to exist—the mere cohe-
sion without coercion—sufficiently demonstrates a
conscious or intuitive tendency in its members to
conform to certain rules of conduct, without which
all free association is an impossibility. The utmost

[1] Cf. Warde Fowler, Roman Festivals, 344 ff.

that we can expect from a primitive religion, not directly founded upon ethical teaching, is that it shall clarify and not distort, fortify and not corrupt, such primordial social instincts as are already operative. With the Romans religion had struck the deeper note of human life. Under the aegis of the earlier cult grew and thrived the new notion of duty to Country, and where patriotism is conspicuously and universally present, other virtues are seldom wanting. The higher civilization starts at the point where the immortal gods have become more or less identified with moral precepts. Religion so developed will blend with and sanction morality as a superhuman principle commanding what is right, prohibiting what is wrong.[1] But the ancient Roman faith sufficed to inspire filial piety and attachment to the home, pervade family life with an atmosphere of dignity and seriousness, and nourish an ardent loyalty to kin and country. A Curtius, a Regulus, a Decius, these are not freaks, but types. The episodes connected with their names may be largely legendary, but they truthfully illustrate the psyche of the Roman people.

[1] Cf. Cicero, De Leg., ii, 4: Hanc igitur video sapientissimorum fuisse sententiam, legem neque hominum ingeniis excogitatam, neque scitum aliquod esse populorum, sed aeternum quiddam, quod universum mundum regeret, imperandi, prohibendique sapientiâ. Ita principem legem illam, et ultimam mentem esse dicebant, omnia ratione aut cogentis, aut vetantis Dei: ex quâ illa lex, quam Dii humano generi dederunt, rectè est laudata; est enim ratio mensque sapientis, ad jubendum et ad deterrendum idonea.

CHAPTER III

THE GENTES

WHEN a group consists of persons bound together by ties of blood and religion, owing obedience and allegiance to a kinsman, whose direct and personal sway unites them in common dependency, the autonomy of the group, at the least for all purposes of internal government, appears from the archaic standpoint not only appropriate, but dictated by nature no less than by circumstance. Where the instinct of blood-relationship has not yet broadened into the notion of nationality, man's duty will be solely to those among whom he has lived and moved from infancy, whose traditions and observances are interwoven with every action of his life, whose fortunes and adventures involve his own prosperity or ruin, and constitute ordinarily the sole happenings which his narrow purview cares to notice.

Aryan patriarchism was conditioned by nomadic[1] life, and fashioned by the philosophy of a desolate independence. Secure in his solitude at least against

---

[1] It does not of necessity follow that the wandering was continuous.

stranger rivals, the tent-dweller could permit conjugal affection to develop freely, and bestow a
father's care upon children whose legitimacy he was
not concerned to question. His segregation removed
the temptation, by minimizing the facilities, of warlike enterprise, and the practice of bride-stealing
slowly yielded to less violent methods during the
long periods of migration, when peace was the rule
rather than the exception. With the increased esteem which was extended to the wife acquired by
the more tedious process of negotiation and rudi-
mentary courtship, arose the tendency to companionship between the sexes and disrelish for the poly-
gynous life which such companionship negatives.
Already in very remote ages, monogamy (that is,
the union of one man with one woman) was apparently almost universal. The plurality of wives,
which a chief might occasionally permit himself, was
prompted by the respectable motive of maintaining
peace by formal alliance with all those groups which
chance brought into contact with his own.[1] The
position of the Aryan wife and mother—far superior
to that of her sisters of other races boasting a more
elaborate and complex civilization[2]—reacted happily
upon the upbringing of the offspring,[3] and powerfully

[1] Similarly, Tacitus, Germ. xviii, claims that the German chiefs
practised polygyny as a policy, "non libidine."

[2] Ihering, Vorgeschichte, 45; Lecky, Europ. Morals, i, 104.

[3] Ernest Renan, Histoire du Peuple d'Israël, i, 8. Cf. Spencer's
Sociology, i, 667 ff.; Woods Hutchinson's article in "Contemporary Review," September, 1905.

E

strengthened the sentiment of family upon which Aryan morality was based.

Unlike the Israelitish patriarchs, the Aryans, in their westward wandering, were not exposed to the influences of any powerful and centralized civilization. Political relations, peaceful or hostile, could scarcely be said to exist in the limited and intermittent communications between pastoral nomads or semi-nomads, thinly spread over the spacious plains of Eastern Europe. Exchange of commodities could not develop systematically among self-contained groups. If aboriginal inhabitants existed to cross the path of the Aryans, or if strife arose among the Aryan groups themselves, the fighting which ensued must have been a series of mere scuffles for the best grass, the most plentiful water, possibly the most attractive women. Co-operation of groups under a common leader, if it existed at all, must have been infrequent and transitory. But with the occupation of the Italian and Balkan peninsulas came the rise of husbandry, and the marriage of the Group to the Soil. Earth-hunger is a passion with all agriculturists. It proved the solvent of the primordial Aryan societies which had theretofore mostly lived in a state of nature. Territorial jealousy, intensified by the propinquity resulting from narrower boundaries and the filling up of the more favoured lands, now evolved those incipient political consolidations whence ultimately arose the historic commonwealths of Greece and Italy. Societies of peasant-brigands sought aid

and countenance among those nearest allied with them
by marriage or intercourse. United action was, however, only possible where the various group-heads
voluntarily agreed to defer to one chosen chief, and
in the welter of struggling hordes those coalitions
thrived and solidified whose members had best
learned the elementary duty of political and martial discipline. The cardinal principle of patriarchism—the absolute equality of the group-heads *inter
se*, and the absolute subjection of their dependants
—must perforce yield, in all matters of what we
may now call public interest, to the principle
of more or less qualified submission of all to a
central authority, a Prince or King. And since
no lasting association was conceivable without
community of cult, special deities were adopted
or invented as patrons of the new tribal agglomera-
tions.

The gentes which united to found Rome brought
with them the characteristic traits of their earlier
history, though the organization already exhibited
strong marks of decay. The theory of a common
descent of all the gentiles was upheld, however
much the blood-relationship might have become
diluted by the adoption of strangers. Indeed, in
reality it might have been wanting at the very
source in some of the gentes, and the members
might trace an alleged descent from an eponymous
hero-adventurer, whose name had been adopted by
companions-in-arms not connected by blood with

him in any way. The common cult, not common descent, cemented the gentile association.

When Rome was in course of foundation, the gentes still subsisted as autonomous or quasi-autonomous groups, loosely confederated into tribes which periodically celebrated common religious rites, and occasionally took united action for offence or defence under tribal chiefs. The internal economy of the gens was quite without the purview of tribal control, and naturally so. When by accident or design a considerable number of archaic groups, or associations of individuals, coalesce into an embryonic State under a common chieftain, it is to be expected that the latter should in the beginning look for support not to the masses but to a few persons in authority over the groups. He will rely upon their obedience and their fidelity, trusting that the inferiors will blindly follow their own familiar leaders. Commands issued, or laws enacted, by him will be commands addressed to, or laws binding upon, those whom he will hold responsible for the conduct of the different groups making up the nascent body politic. Internal relations, whether personal or proprietary, between the heads of groups and their dependent members will not concern the central government. Such a group will bear outwardly some analogy with a modern protected State, the sovereign of which is supreme in all internal affairs, but must submit to have his "foreign" policy settled for him by his suzerain. A disposition on the part of the central government to interfere in and regulate the internal conduct of the group will mark a distinct advance in the community's history.[1]

It is improbable that the consolidation of the three primitive tribes of Rome was at first more intimate than the previous coalitions of clans into tribes. We have already seen that when once the new City was fairly launched upon its political career, experience demonstrated that a strong central government was the prime condition precedent to the community's combined existence. That it was able to withstand the repeated shocks of external and domestic commotions is due to the thoroughness with which the lesson was mastered. Nevertheless, the State wisely meddled with the existing social fabric only just as much as the public interest demanded and public opinion conceded. The ancient gentile organization was indeed, at the birth of Rome, already moribund, but the narrower family circle which supplanted it long continued to exist for many purposes as a State within the State.

At the moment when the gentile association first emerges from darkness into the twilight of history, it is found to consist in every case of a superior, or

---

[1] Rossbach, Römische Ehe, 34: "Die Familienhäupter und die grösseren Gruppen der Geschlechter standen noch für sich selbstständig da und traten nur dann zu einer Einheit zusammen, erkannten nur dann ein Oberhaupt über sich an, wenn die Noth von aussen her dieses gebot. In allen übrigen Angelegenheiten blieben sie für sich bestehen." Cf. Maine, Ancient Law, c. V. Ihering, Geist d. röm. Rechtes, i, 165 ff.

patron, and a dependent or client class, and, in apparent conformity with the custom of the age, only the former had become invested with civic rights in the newly-founded City. In this the Romans were not singular, since the existence of a semi-servile class appears to have been universal.[1] Those were members of the dominant order whose ancestry, however remote, disclosed no trace of servitude or dependence. Towards each other the patrons and clients of a gens were gentiles and gentilicii, the former assuming a common descent by blood (or adoption) from one ancestor, the latter claiming the same descent derivatively. Although in Rome clients were always accounted freemen, the principal origin of clientage was, doubtless, slavery, and the client usually the descendant of a slave, who had been freed at some more or less remote period by the head of the gens, or a branch of it, for the time being.[2] That the relation between master and slave was not entirely snapped by the enfranchisement was due to the fact that originally even the slave participated in the sacra of his lord; it was not competent to the latter without good cause to expel or release therefrom any human creature once admitted.

It is no longer possible to elucidate whether the headship of the gens may have belonged to the eldest

[1] Caesar, Bel. Gall., vi, 13.
[2] Cf. Mommsen, Römische Forschungen, c. Die Römische Clientel.

male living at the death of the last chief, or the scion of the senior branch of the clan, or what other qualifications may have determined the succession. The Romans always recognized that " with the ancient is wisdom, and in length of days understanding." Seniority in some shape or form had certainly played a leading part long before the Roman era, though possibly not in the very earliest Aryan institutions.[1] We have already seen that by the time the City was founded, the constitution of the gens had undergone important modifications. A gentile head (princeps) now existed, if at all, only in an honorary capacity, as dispensary of the religious rites; matters affecting the internal well-being of the gens as a whole were administered by a council or committee. For all other purposes the authority of the gentile head had been displaced by the power of the paterfamilias, the living male ancestor, over his descendants in direct line.

The dominant members of a gens, if not under

[1] Maine, Early Law and Custom, p. 193, says: "The patriarchal theory is the theory of the origin of society in separate families, held together by the authority and protection of the eldest *valid* male ascendant." The question whether patriarchism represents the very earliest form of primordial society need not detain us. It is dealt with to some extent in Chapter VII of the same work. Ihering (Vorgeschichte, pp. 54, 331) thinks that the ancient Aryans put to death parents grown old and sickly, a custom which may have lost its vogue when agriculture, by increasing the supplies of food, rendered the experience of the old available without the disadvantage of embarrassment to the commissariat. Cf. Maine, Early Law and Custom, 22-23.

the power of a living ancestor, were called with
respect to their sons and descendants by males
patres,[1] with respect to their clients patroni; and in
earliest Roman times the Senate may have been
merely an assembly of the "Elders," or patres.
Descendants of living patres were called patricii, a
term subsequently made to embrace the patres as
well. All patrician members of a gens (gentiles)
were ingenui,[2] that is to say no one of their ancestors,
however far back they traced them, had ever been
a slave or a client. The Fabii, Claudii, Valerii,
Cornelii, Manlii are among the historically famous of
the Roman gentes.

In earliest Rome the gens was still to some extent
a self-contained community, cultivating in common
the land it occupied,[3] and governed by the gentile
council of elders, who administered the joint property, whilst exercising over the members, both patrician and client, a disciplinary control which perhaps
furnished the model for the censura to which the
State subjected all its citizens. The council thus relieved the central government of many duties which

[1] Cicero, De Rep., ii, 12. The word pater, however, did not
exclusively or even primarily denote fatherhood, but rather lord-
ship. The gods and goddesses, even when celibate (as they were
in the primitive Latino-Sabine religious system), were still called
patres and matres.

[2] Ingenuus—born in a gens. In later times the word was
applied to any one born free, irrespective of his ancestry or
legitimacy.

[3] Mommsen, Staatsrecht, iii, 22.

afterwards became part of the public administration. It arbitrated upon disputes between gentiles. Where necessary, it instituted guardians (tutores) over children, and withdrew family property from the hands of a spendthrift parent. It enforced order by admonition and fine. If the former were defied, and payment of the latter refused, a refractory gentilis, whose offence was not cognizable by the State authorities, could be adequately dealt with by temporary or permanent exclusion from the sacra, by expulsion from the gens, and consequent loss of its protection, or by the threat of execrating his memory when dead and prohibiting gentiles from bearing his name. Similar sanctions[1] were no doubt relied upon to enforce awards in civil matters. The duties of the gentile council were not repressive only, and each gentilis expected from his gens succour for his person if a prisoner in the hands of a creditor or foreign enemy, vengeance for his memory (by retaliation or legal process) if slain by a stranger, and protection for his unprovided orphaned children.

Clients were either freed slaves, and their descendants, or families which at one time or other had attached themselves by some species of " commendation " to a gens[2] (adplicatio, susceptio clientis).

---

[1] We are reminded of the excommunication formerly decreed by our ecclesiastical courts. Blackstone, Comm., iii, 101.

[2] Dionys. of Hal., ii, 4. As to the distinction of the two origins, see Ortolan, Instituts de l'Empereur Justinien, i, 27; iii, 33 ff. Mommsen (Römische Forschungen) derives clients without exception from slavery. *Contra*, Soltau, Volksversammlungen, 89 n.

They were not gentiles, but gentilicii, deriving their origin by a kind of artificial lineage from the gens whose name they bore equally with their gentiles. As their connection with the gens was indirect and derivative, so also was their association with the City. The law of earliest Rome took no direct cognizance of the client's existence, or, rather, the means by which the legal machinery could be set in motion were inaccessible to him, save through the intermediary of his patron, whose duty it was to protect him from oppression and maintain him in the enjoyment of such property as he might have in possession.[1]

Material profit was by no means the sole, or even the most important, consideration which determined the patron's attitude. A large clientage was the glory of a patrician family, and the number of adherents in some degree the measure of its eminence; and in the beginning the institution doubtlessly subserved the interest of the State by stimulating among its leading men a healthy and public-spirited emulation. Precisely what services were expected from the client is not clear; but that clientage was

Maine, Early Inst., 145, considers that some of the humbler companions in arms of powerful chieftains may have originally taken service as clients to share with him danger and booty.

[1] Dionys. of Hal., ii, 4. But the entire property of the gens must have originally vested in the hands of the princeps, and the client's monetary obligations which Dionysius mentions can only date from a period when the original gentile organization had already reached an advanced stage of dissolution.

not deemed dishonourable is evidenced by the nature of some of the patron's obligations.[1] It was among the latter's solemn duties to instruct his client in the law, which the latter had no direct means of studying, to defend him when criminally indicted, to inter his remains in the gentile tomb and generally to extend to him the care of a parent. The father's prerogative, the right of life and death, may have likewise belonged to the patron, but abuse was restrained by the religious nature of the bond.[2] There existed between patron and client a general duty of mutual support, which obliged them to refrain from any act of hostility, as by public accusation, giving adverse evidence in court, or (possibly, on the client's part) contrary voting in the comitia. In later times the more idealistic and abstract nature of the association seems to have been partly forgotten, and the client's chief duty to have lain in the direction of occasional money payments, which a wealthy patron would waive, and originally all patrons had been wealthy. The client assisted where necessary to dower the patron's

---

[1] Aul. Gell., v, 13. " In officiis apud majores ita observatum est, primum tutelae, deinde hospiti, deinde clienti, tum cognati, postea affini." Cf. Vergil, Æneid, vi:

Hic quibus invisi fratres, dum vita manebat,
Pulsatusve parens, aut fraus innexa clienti.

Both Ihne and Niebuhr pay too little regard to the ethical element in the relation which subsisted between patron and client, through their association in a common cult.

[2] The human agency of the XII Tables afterwards gave legal sanction to the fas: " Patronus si clienti fraudem faxit, sacer esto."

daughters, ransomed him and his children from cap-
tivity, paid his fines, and contributed to his expenses of
litigation, or the due upkeep of his rank and dignity.

The analogies between clientage and some mediaeval usages are by no means slight. The client's
relation to his patron was indeed personal and religious, rather than territorial, but certainly a number
of them must have tilled the gentile lands[1] under
conditions not dissimilar from early copyhold tenure,
or from villeinage. But we have seen that the
client's status in Rome (whatever the case else-
where) was far superior to serfdom. He followed
the patron to the wars, and the aids which he
owed him resemble those which the mediaeval
vassal rendered to his lord. It must, moreover, be
remembered that the client's civic disabilities, such
as the disqualification from sueing in his own name,
were shared equally by all Roman citizens in potestate, and were the outcome not of his condition but
of the State's policy, which for civil purposes recognized but one responsible head of each of its component groups. The client appears in some respects
to have been less subject to the power of his patron
than the child to his father. He was not in potestate and, it seems, could not be sold, or noxally
surrendered. The duties as between patron and
client were reciprocal, founded, as we have seen,
upon the sacra, and, whilst the institution retained

---

[1] Clients, from colientes, or from cluere, to hear (obey)? Cuq,
Inst. jur. des R., 56; Mommsen, Röm. Forsch., i, 368.

its vigour, conscientiously fulfilled by both parties. Nor were the excesses of tyranny or caprice entirely without temporal check, so long as the gentile council of elders met as a miniature parliament to overlook the internal affairs of the gens.

By analogy with the personal system of clientage, it soon became the practice of conquered populations and colonies to commend themselves to some eminent Roman, and disputes between such communities would frequently be remitted by the Senate to the respective patrons, whose sentence it then ratified.

In the struggle between the orders which convulsed the first centuries of the Republic, clients occupy an intermediate position between patricians and non-attached plebeians. In general, traditional allegiance probably proved stronger than the natural desire for political equality; and the client class, its equivocal attitude derided as sycophancy by the embittered plebeians,[1] at last found itself practically disfranchised by the Publilian plebiscitum excluding it from the popular assemblies. The decay of clientage as an institution was doubtlessly accelerated

---

[1] How exquisitely Macaulay voices the sentiments of the popular party in the throes of a furious class-struggle!

"That brow of hate, that mouth of scorn, marks all the kindred still;
For never was there Claudius yet but wished the Commons ill;
Nor lacks he fit attendance; for close behind his heels,
With outstretched chin and crouching pace, the client Marcus steals,

by this enactment, which rendered clients politically useless to their patrons.[1] But in any case the institution must soon have languished from natural causes. Many of the old gentes had perished in the wars by the time Servius made military service compulsory upon all landholders. The surviving gentes lost their former solid organization after the lands formerly held and administered as impartible common property had been divided up among the component families, and thrown upon the market. On the other hand, the extension of the rights of citizenship to all plebeians, and the growing power of the Tribunes, lessened the client's dependence upon his patron's protection. Many client families and descendants of freedmen, rising to positions of dignity and opulence, and themselves habitually holding and enfranchising slaves, gradually withdrew themselves from the influence of their gentiles. And since new additions to client ranks among Roman citizens became rarer in proportion as the institution lost its vogue, the diminishing client class became con-

His loins girt up to run with speed, be the errand what it may,
And the smile flickering on his cheek, for aught his lord may say.
Such varlets pimp and jest for him among the lying Greeks:
Such varlets still are paid to hoot when brave Licinius speaks.
Where'er ye shed the honey, the buzzing flies will crowd;
Where'er ye fling the carrion, the raven's croak is loud;
Where'er down Tiber garbage floats, the greedy pike ye see;
And wheresoe'er such lord is found, such client still will be."

Virginia.

[1] In the comitia curiata and centuriata the patricians and plebeian Conservatives were of themselves sufficiently powerful.

founded amid the ever-increasing crowds of free plebeians. Apparently by the end of the third century of the City, the death of an intestate propertied client leaving no child or agnate was almost the sole occasion of practical advantage accruing to his patron.

If clients were originally barely "law-worthy," still less so were slaves. But there was no striking distinction, and often no distinction at all, of race, appearance, speech, or manners, no instinctive repulsion between owners and owned, which, in other regions, have supplied some of the most painful chapters in the history of human relations. Chattels at law, ritual included them not only within the pale of humankind, but to a limited extent even of the family, and the simple households of earliest Rome may have witnessed little difference in the treatment of slaves and sons. The slave's grave, like the citizen's, was sacred; the foreigner's was not. Only in later times, when the bond of worship had slackened, and multitudes of war-captives cheapened human flesh and blood, was the law called in to supply a protection no longer accorded by religion and domestic fellowship.

The mere association of kinsmanship and a common cult had proved insufficient to preserve the vigour of gentile institutions. They were displaced by the Roman conception of the Family as an undivided entity, held by tradition and habit in allegiance to the *living* common ancestor. But the whole life of the people remained coloured by the belief that the protection extended by a chief during life-time to his dependent kinsmen, remained operative after his death. The ancestor was still the tutelary divinity of his house; his memory continued to be held in veneration and propitiated by the rites and sacrifices practised by former generations. The gentile cults, and the cults of the narrower family circles, existed side by side. Roughly, it may be said that whilst the latter were addressed to known or ascertained ancestors, the former survived to memorize unknown progenitors, from whom the various branches of the clan professed to derive a common origin. So indispensable was the due performance of the sacra that even the stern Roman military discipline was in some respects subordinated to it. The citizen summoned to join the forces of the State might delay his obedience until he had fulfilled his domestic religious duties, if perchance the day had arrived for their observance, and a Roman might shrink from neglecting the obligatory obsequies even during a national crisis, or under circumstances of extreme danger to life and limb.[1]

The consideration of the Roman Family in the narrower sense, under the regimen of the Patria Potestas, may be fittingly deferred to a later chapter.

[1] Livy, v, 46; xxii, 18.

CHAPTER IV

THE EARLY ROMAN CONSTITUTION

A SCIENCE of constitutional law, or indeed of any " law " in the strict and modern sense of the word, was unknown to the regal period and early Republic; and even the terminology of matured Roman jurisprudence appears to have lacked an expression exactly corresponding with our " Constitution."[1] Yet the relations between private citizen and governing power, like all relations in Rome between dependant and superior, were tolerably well defined with the aid of those customs and conventions which the founders had brought ready-made, and seemed happily calculated to hold the middle way between the arbitrariness of a despotic, and the insecurity of a feeble administration. To these customs and conventions the term Constitution may, without abuse of language, conveniently be applied.

As the internal governing organs of the gens were

---

[1] Cicero could find nothing better than terms such as forma, ratio, genus reipublicae. Ulpian says jus quod ad statum rei Romanae spectat. Instead of developing with the other branches of the law, the doctrine of constitutional checks upon the supreme power fell into neglect with the decay of the popular Assemblies.

the general body of gentiles, the council of elders, and (originally) the princeps, so the Roman State was made up of the citizens in the Assembly of the Curiae (comitia curiata), the Senate, and the King. We are tempted to think of our own Commons, Lords and Crown, but the analogy is misleading, and only useful as an illustration of the fundamentally divergent conceptions of the State in the ancient and the modern polity.

England knows no higher authority than the King in Parliament. Any bill, however far-reaching and revolutionary, having passed both Houses and received the royal assent, becomes part of the law of the land, which it is the legal duty of all subjects to obey, and of every judge to apply, though they and he consider it a monument of folly or turpitude.[1] The ground-law, or if the expression be allowable, the old common law of Rome, was rather assumed to rest upon the Will of the Gods (fas), to whom opportunity was given of manifesting dissatisfaction at any proposed legislative or executive measure by signs and portents, which would be interpreted in the manner described in Chapter II. The Fas represented those elementary social principles which human-made law, or Jus, and Boni Mores, or the

---

[1] Few Englishmen will nowadays care to dispute that misgovernment and mislegislation, by however consecrated an authority, *may* reach a point where open, violent rebellion by every means in his power becomes the subject's right and duty. But the exact limit of endurance is necessarily determined by temperament, and not ascertainable by scientific methods.

practices customary among honest men, might upon occasion be permitted to amplify, but never entirely to abrogate. Normally immutable, it was susceptible of modification in individual cases where divergency involved no desecration. Among such cases were: Adrogation, whereby a paterfamilias divested himself of that quality and became alieni juris, when all the members of his family, if any, were brought equally with him under the power of a stranger; and Testament, or the procedure whereby a man secured beforehand the devolution of his property after his death in a manner not provided by the received rules of succession. The co-operation of the State[1] was invoked to dispense with the application, in a particular instance, of divinely-appointed general regulations,[2] and in all probability this was never done except upon emergencies for which they did not directly provide.

The Roman system, therefore, claimed to rest upon elementary principles of preponderatingly divine origin. Mortal activity, where not purely ad-

---

[1] The function of the curiae on such occasions (in calatis) was passive rather than active; they merely registered the act, and the acquiescence of the gods therein. But it is a likely supposition that the active consent of the community in the form of a pronouncement may at the very outset have been necessary. Cf. F. de Coulanges, Cité Antique, p. 89, so far as concerns Testament.

[2] So, in England, the civil dissolution of a marriage could be effected from the eighteenth century onwards by private Act of Parliament until, in 1857, divorce was made possible by proceedings taken before a lay tribunal.

ministrative, was limited to such supplementary legislation as was not already contained in the framework provided by the higher powers, and, at the most, to the issue by the whole people as a body of particular commands dispensing, by way of exception, with the ordinary rules of Fas. It will at once be seen that the Austinian definitions of Sovereignty, State, and Law cannot possibly be made to square with what, in early Rome, did duty for them; but it is permissible and convenient to employ these expressions whilst bearing in mind the peculiar conditions of the age.

The body having the closest resemblance to a legislative Convention was called comitia curiata,[1] or assembly of all adult male citizens. It was, therefore, even more comprehensive than the body which constitutes the electorate of the United Kingdom since the extensions of the franchise during the nineteenth century. But whereas English constitu-

---

[1] Curia = (1) a house of sacrifice, (2) the sacrificial community. The curia was the political unit, a collection of gentes (or portions of gentes) settled adjacently upon lands. (Soltau, Altrömische Volksversammlungen, i, 1 und 3.) " Curia " (said to be derived from the Sabine town Cures) appears to be the most likely origin of the word " Quirites," frequently translated " Spearmen." The jus Quiritium was the temporal law of the City, in which, originally, only members of a curia had part. Cuq (Institutions juridiques, 21) disputes the derivation of Quirites from *quir*, pointing out that Quirites designated, above all, the body of citizens in their civil, as opposed to their military, capacity. And the usual Roman expressions for spear and spearman were not quir, quiris, but hasta, hastatus.

ehcies return representatives with unlimited power to legislate for them in Parliament, representative Government was unknown in the ancient world.[1] The concurrence of the whole body of Roman citizens was the indispensable preliminary to every act savouring of legislation, and so deeply rooted was this system that it was clung to even in later ages, when the extension of the Roman frontiers rendered the presence of the vast majority of voters a physical impossibility.

The comitia curiata could lawfully only assemble on the summons of the King (or during an interregnum, the interrex) as chief Magistrate, and, as I have said, could only act after the disposition of the gods had been ascertained, by taking the public auspices (auspicia populi Romani), to be favourable, or at least acquiescent. The comitia could not initiate, nor even discuss, measures, but voted Aye or No without debate upon those submitted by the King. It by no means follows that the Roman people had not the right or the opportunity of public discussion. In Republican times, at latest, general meetings of the people (contiones) were frequently convoked by the magistrates for the purpose of making public announcements or eliciting the trend of public opinion. Apparently in furtherance of these ob-

---

[1] That the Roman law of agency never progressed far beyond the embryonic stage, may have underlain the same order of ideas, viz., that no man should be bound politically or civilly, save by his own act.

jects, attendance at a contio, though not compulsory upon any one, was on the other hand allowable even to non-citizens (being freemen) who had no place in the comitia. A meeting of a section of the people to consider and decide upon matters specially affecting itself was called concilium.

Opinions conflict upon the original composition and numerical strength of the Senate, or Elders. Their number was certainly 300 at the time of Tarquin, and for the ensuing centuries. If, as is possible, the gentes, in the earliest times of Rome, still retained each a visible and acknowledged head, it is extremely probable that the Senate would be composed of such heads, nor would this circumstance point to a fluctuating number at a time when the members of a gens were still sufficiently numerous to preclude its extinction. But from a very early period Senators appear to have been appointed for life by the King, each vacancy being filled as it arose, and the dignity was not descendible. The constitutional function of the Senate was originally to act as guardian of the fas. It deliberated whether a proposed measure was reconcilable with general principles, and it is characteristic of Rome that a decision which might seem to fall peculiarly within the province of sacerdotal authority was remitted to all its leading citizens without distinction. The Senate's concurrence (auctoritas) was necessary to every enactment proposed by the King to the comitia curiata and accepted by the latter: Potestas in populo, auctoritas in senatu. In course of time it became the practice, though by no means the duty, of the kings to ask the approval, and thereby ensure the auctoritas, of the Senate before submitting legislation to the people. The Senate thus gradually assumed, side by side with original functions, those of a Council of State, which discussed and influenced all matters affecting the Commonwealth; and this character became accentuated under the Republic by the admission of plebeian members, who, having no knowledge of the patrician sacra, could not concur in conferring the auctoritas. Accordingly, in course of time the Senate, in addition to its original passive function as a mere check or clog upon the legislature, became an active deliberative body.[1]

The regal resembled the senatorial dignity in that it was not hereditary. The magisterial power resided ultimately in the Senate as a whole; its exercise by only one of that body was dictated by political expediency and the sense of what was fitting. The primordial social organization had rested upon the allegiance of the members of certain well defined group-units each to one head. It would have appeared incongruous that the executive power of the Common-

---

[1] Senatus consulit, non jubet. But, in later times again, the Senate usurped legislative power also and exercised it, first subject to the veto of the Emperor, then as the passive instrument of the ruling tyrant for the time being. By the time of Ulpian that jurist was able to state: Non ambigitur senatum jus facere posse. Dig., i, 3, 9. As to the shifting relations between Senate and Magistracy, see Mommsen's Staatsrecht, iii, 1252 ff.

wealth should be exercised jointly by a large number of men ranking equally with each other. Accordingly, the King alone was at one and the same time sole representative of the State in its international relations, civil ruler, military commander-in-chief, and chief priest of the community,[1] but with power of substitution with respect to most of his functions. On his death his delegated powers reverted to the Senate, and, until a successor had been duly installed, there ensued an interregnum, during which individual Senators, designated by lot and termed interreges, successively discharged the regal functions, each for a period not exceeding five days. Each interrex formally nominated his successor, according to a rotation already settled by lot; and the King-elect, when at last the choice had been made by the comitia in the form of a legislative act, was nominated by the interrex for the time being in power.[2] The choice of the comitia, like every other law, required confirmation by the auctoritas of the Senate, after which formal allegiance was declared at a second meeting of the popular Assembly.

Thus the King ruled the State as the father ruled his family, or the gentile chief had originally ruled his clan; the extent and the limitations of the power were correlative. Though supreme in everything

[1] Mommsen, Röm. Staatsrecht, 6.
[2] The first interrex, probably because he had not himself been nominated, could not nominate to the throne.

touching the government of the State, he was in the position of a trustee administering a trust, rather than a despot irresponsibly disposing of the lives and fortunes of his subjects. It is true that his behests, however arbitrary, had to be carried out, and no misconduct disqualified him from further reigning; but though he could violate the law with impunity, we have seen that he could not make it.[1] That he did not rule by divine right is clear from the manner of his appointment, nor did the dignity impart sacredness to his person in the sense claimed for the Stuarts and the Louis. The Roman notion of kingship thus differed radically from that of the seventeenth and eighteenth centuries, or even of important portions of present-day Europe, where royalty existed and exists apart from any question of its inherent usefulness.

The root-notion of Roman political institutions was, therefore, as we were justified in expecting, identical with that upon which the Family System was based. It started by postulating the natural equality of all citizens and citizenesses; but this natural equality the Romans had no hesitation in modifying, or even converting into its antithesis,

[1] It is important to observe that a Roman enactment was essentially an agreement between King and People, and was concluded by question and answer, in form closely resembling the private contract by stipulatio common in later ages. Lex (ligare = to bind, whence also obligatio) meant any kind of obligation voluntarily undertaken, and was applicable to private treaty as well as to enactments by the comitia.

where practical considerations seemed so to require. Women were not less esteemed than men, yet the Romans, realizing that the former, in the then conditions of life, were unable to discharge the chief duties which a State necessarily imposed upon its citizens, hesitated not, in relieving them of responsibility, to deprive them also of the political power and influence which responsibility connoted. So again the Romans, whilst recognizing the equality of all citizens, cheerfully surrendered their fortunes and liberties into the hands of one man in deference to what experience had demonstrated to be, on the whole, the salutary rule of undivided command. But every Senator was eligible for the kingship or consulship, and every citizen, at least from very early times, might aspire to become a Senator.[1] The whole of the political power capable of being wielded by the community was recognized as being in the last resort in the people, who, through the medium of the Senate, transferred the executive part of it to their acclaimed ruler for his life. Accordingly Rome, even under its Kings, was never a true monarchy, but a community of free citizens who, in the interests of the common weal, submitted to be controlled by one of their number. The abolition of kingship, on the deposition of Tarquin the Proud, merely signified that the powers and privileges hitherto irrevocably vested in one person, were now distributed among several, who, in the case of tem-

---

[1] Plebeian citizens, however, as we shall see later, were not admitted to the consulship until the fourth century of the City.

poral offices, held them for one year only. The sovereignty of the people was, as we have already seen, to some extent subjected to restraints which no mundane power could override. In special cases the comitia, in the teeth of fas and custom, would allow the conversion of paterfamilias into filius-familias, change the ordinary course of devolution of property upon death, or pardon an offender whose life was forfeit to the just anger of the gods. But they could not deprive a citizen of his citizenship so long as he remained in the City, or even in Latium; to do so it was necessary to sell him as a slave "beyond Tiber," that is, to the strangers and enemies in the North. Neither, it would appear, could the State at first demand from the citizen any part of his property. Direct taxation, levied in times of stress was, strictly speaking, repayable, and somewhat in the nature of those forced "benevolences" with which our own forefathers were painfully familiar. Service in the field, and labour in times of peace, the King could indeed require, though, as regards the former, again, the people's assent was necessary before an aggressive war could be undertaken; but the State revenue, apart from enforced gratuitous services, was ordinarily supplied chiefly by the income from the State domains, the customs and dues levied at Ostia, fines paid by unsuccessful litigants, and the proceeds of campaigns against neighbouring cities.

Patrician membership of a gens was, in the first centuries of Rome, the indispensable condition of full citizenship. No client, nor person of patrician descent but not belonging to a gens,[1] could have part or lot in the administration or hold public office; and if clients were allowed in the comitia it must certainly have been in the quality of attendants and backers of their patrons, rather than of independent coadjutors. In addition to client freemen having, in strict law, no civic rights, but in practice indirectly exercising them through the gentes to which they were attached, there gradually grew up in and around Rome a free, but non-citizen population without personal attachment. A vanquished town might sometimes make terms with the conquerors, and continue its physical existence, together with the enjoyment of all or part of its lands, at the price of the surrender of its political importance and complete subserviency of its own to the Roman foreign policy. But more frequently the consequence of defeat was unconditional deliverance into the enemy's hand, and total destruction of the city, or at least the expulsion of its inhabitants, whose places were then taken by needy Roman colonists. In the former case the vanquished populations were disarmed,[2] and placed under the protection of Rome as "clients of the King," that is, of the State. In the latter, they were settled in Rome, where their gentes were frequently admitted into the Roman patriciate, whilst the common people became "the crowd" (plebs),

[1] *E.g.*, any one born of patrician parents but not ex justis nuptiis.   [2] Livy, iii, 19.

whose freedom indeed, as Latins, could not be taken from them, but disentitled alike to patrician privilege and the protection extended to clients.[1] The deliberate annihilation of the Alban polity immensely strengthened, materially and morally, the Roman position in Latium. Not only did the survivors reinforce the ranks of the victors, but Rome's ambition to rule Latium now for the first time received religious sanction. For, agreeably with contemporary notions, the Romans could claim to stand towards the other States in the shoes of Alba, whose shadowy presidency over Latium their practical spirit found means to transfer into a substantial political predominance, which soon assumed the form of a suzerainty, and justified in appearance the fate of those cities which were sufficiently impious or ill-advised to rebel.

All accessions, however, were not gained by violent means, for even during the first centuries the commercial position of Rome attracted many strangers, often accompanied by their families, whom a far-seeing Government wisely suffered to abide unmolested. The last-named class would naturally be recruited chiefly from the intelligent and enterprising population of all the middle Italian lands, and no doubt contributed materially to the mental and physical strength of their adopted city. Thus did Rome's growing might and prestige swell the stream of voluntary and involuntary immigrants,

[1] Livy, i, 33.

who, at a comparatively early period, must already have outnumbered the old burgher element.

We are now able to sum up more or less adequately the salient characteristics of the Roman community at the outset of its long struggle for the supremacy of the world. It was first and foremost a community of agriculturists and cattle-farmers, possessed of all the qualities usually associated with a thrifty peasantry, deeply imbued with religious feeling, steeped in superstition, yet preserving withal a shrewd judicial mind, even in its dealings with the gods; very acquisitive and litigious, very full of worldly wisdom and plain common sense. But it was also a community which had become partially industrialized through the influx of enterprising and frequently wealthy immigrants, whom its liberal and stable institutions attracted. Its leading politicians were capitalists[1] as well as soldiers, its aggressive wars were fought for economic benefits as well as glory. Allegiance to the City, the bulwark equally of material and political prosperity, took its place quite naturally beside the habitual allegiance to gens (if any) and family. The first requirement of such a community is public order and equal subordination of all to the law.[2] The harshest sanctions of proprietary and contractual rights merited the approval of a body of men who took themselves and their duties

[1] "Seit Rom stand wa daselbst das Kapital eine politische Macht" (Mommsen, Römische Geschichte, iii, 15).

[2] Cicero, De Rep., i, 45; iv, 2.

seriously. The dread of their enforcement, usually sufficient to secure respect for property and due satisfaction of obligations, went far to supply the want of a regular police, and cure the defects inseparable from a cumbersome administration. Municipal law among most archaic peoples, and again in the commotions of the Middle Ages, somewhat resembled, in its uncertainty and the incompleteness of its sanctions, the Public International "Law" of the present day. The necessities of the Roman community hastened the formation and well-reasoned development of definite judicial norms by the co-operation of men standing in the very centre of public affairs.[1] Such a community allowed small scope for individual idiosyncrasy or vagaries of temperament. It scrutinized with true Republican jealousy both the visible eccentricities of vanity and the outward signs of pre-eminence. Within the City all must go on foot, save the specially privileged vestals and the King, and after the suppression of the latter even the Consuls walked. The dress of magistrates, senators, and private citizens, save for trifling distinctions, was uniform.[2] To wear unpermitted, save on occasions of special rejoicing, the

---

[1] Cf. Cic., De Orat., i, 44.

[2] The toga (tegere = to cover, perhaps allied with the Anglo-Saxon teog, and the German zeug = stuff, material) was the characteristic dress of Romans in times of peace. "Romanos, rerum dominos, gentemque togatam" (Verg., Aen., i, 282). The Gauls were called " breeched " (braccati).

garland reserved for distinguished warriors on the days of their triumph was accounted akin to treason.[1] Even the ancestral cult might not be pushed to capricious extremes, and only eminent families might retain the waxen masks of departed forefathers, and display their features in the funereal processions of prominent members. The citizen must be frugal of living,[2] dignified of bearing,[3] moderate of speech. Above all, he must be sober of thought. The Roman never snatched at the unattainable, and never cried for the moon. Although he imported into his own legal system whatever appeared practical and useful of the known Hellenic institutions, he never, even in later ages, really assimilated the philosophical and idealistic products of the exuberant Greek imagination.

[1] Pliny, Hist. Nat., xxi, 6. Caesar was grateful to the Senate for allowing him habitually to cover his baldness with a chaplet.

[2] See Cato's recipes, De Re Rustica, lxxvi ff. Among the earliest Romans a thick kind of gruel (puls) was the commonest food. Meat was comparatively seldom eaten; bread or cake was used only at sacrifices.

[3] The citizen walked with stately gait; slaves bustled.

CHAPTER V

THE REFORMED CONSTITUTION OF SERVIUS TULLIUS

ROME'S elevation to the metropolis of Latium brought with it the usual economic concomitants: mercantile expansion, increase of wealth, and a large accretion of strangers. The policy followed respecting the last-named was, upon the whole, not unworthy a State which aspired to a spacious and splendid future, and Rome soon circumvented the rule (natural enough to the ancients) that men who had no part in the City cult could not invoke the City law.[1] To Latins and aliens (peregrini) was extended, in fact, if not in law, the commercium; they were suffered not only to reside, but unmolested to carry on business in Roman territory, and enjoyed at the hands of a liberal administration that protection of person, property, and contractual rights which the law itself as yet denied to non-citizens. Even the virtual ownership of Roman soil was permitted to Latins, though probably not to peregrini. Religious, as well as political, scruples may have prompted this last restriction, as

---

[1] Die alte Zeit ruht auf dem Gegensatz einander ausschliessender Gemeinden und Staaten. Sohm, Inst. d. Röm. Rechts., 80.

they certainly dictated the limited application of the jus connubii. The desire to safeguard the sacra had formerly prompted a jealous supervision of matrimonial alliances which might endanger them, and marriage between members of different groups was still hampered by the ideas of more ancient ages. A Roman citizen could not contract justae nuptiae with an alien unless a special treaty authorized "just marriage" between the nationals of the two States. Even unions between Romans and Latins belonging to one of the anciently federated cities were similarly treated, for since Rome had become arbiter of Latium, connubium was only granted as a favour. Within Rome the conditions were still less satisfactory. No international treaty could be concluded between the State and a portion of its own citizens; hence inter-marriage of a Roman patrician with a plebeian, although socially recognized, failed to establish manus to the husband, or patria potestas over his issue, and disqualified him for the higher priestly dignities. Until the nettle was firmly grasped three centuries after the City's birth, the anomalous position endured that a Roman citizen might contract with a foreigner a marriage of full legality, which was under no circumstances possible with a large portion of his countrywomen.

At some uncertain epoch of the regal period the patriciate became alive to the necessity of modifying the policy hitherto observed towards the

" Uitlander " element. Deprived of the privileges of citizenship, some of which were formal only, stranger denizens also escaped its burdens, which were very real. Enjoying all the material advantages of residence in a well ordered and commercially progressive community, they were exempt from military service, the corvées, and the compulsory loans which then took the place of direct taxation. The patriciate, with such assistance as they could claim from their clients, furnished the labour for the public works, and assisted the Government in its financial straits. And upon the patriciate, as the Populus or people,[1] devolved the heavy strain of maintaining by force of arms the political supremacy which plebeian and stranger joined them in exploiting. With the march of events the position had become untenable. Constant wars, waged partly from necessity and partly from ambition, drained the patrician element of its best blood, and threatened it with an ultimate extermination, only temporarily retarded by occasional admissions of new gentes into the Roman patriciate from vanquished neighbouring cities, or as voluntary recruits.

[1] Populus, allied with populari (to ravage or devastate), signified as much Army as People, and under the earliest constitution could only apply to the patriciate. After the recognition of the centuriae as a legislative body, populus would include both patricians and plebeians. It is only in much later times that populus could be used, as "people" is often colloquially used in English, to mean the commonalty, and sometimes the poorer commonalty, only.

To meet these dangers was the avowed purpose of the various reformatory measures, probably inaugurated on the model of the Grecian colonies of southern Italy, in the reign of the sixth King of Rome, Servius Tullius, and named after him. The Servian reforms may have been merely what on their face they appeared to be—a makeshift dictated by political exigences—or a scheme designed by far-sighted statesmen, compelled to study, whilst disdaining, the narrow prejudices of the patricians, and leaving to the logic of events the full fruition of their plans.[1] Their immediate effect, however, was to cause the stranger population to share the burdens of the burgher class without corresponding increase of rights. The first act was probably to subject all residents, whether citizens or non-citizens, and whether occupying land or not, to the impositions decreed by the King in the public interest. This was succeeded by the step — vastly more important in its ultimate consequences—of transforming military service from a personal obligation of the citizen into an incident of land tenure, irrespective of the holder. All landowners (assidui), whether patrons, clients, or plebeians, together with all adult males in their power, now alike served in the ranks.[2] The older division of the population

[1] Cf. the various authors cited by Soltau in his Altröm. Volksvers., p. 231 ff.

[2] Landowners, whom sex or youth disqualified from military service, supplied horses for the cavalry, and their fodder.

into patricians and clients was superseded, for the purpose of the new reforms, by the division into landholding burghers and their clients, landholding Latins (foreigners other than members of the federated Latin cities being probably barred from acquiring land interests), all of whom were now liable to taxation and military service, and non-landholding citizens and denizens, liable to taxation only. Probably military service was graduated so as to call the poorer classes, who could not leave their farms without loss and suffering, less frequently to the standards than the more fortunate of the population, a relief which was held to justify the preponderance of voting power accorded to the latter in the later comitia centuriata. Yet plebeians became either at once or very soon eligible for military command, and what we know of the usual order of battle-array certainly acquits the patricians of any tendency to spare themselves.

Incidental to this reform was the institution, or, at all events, the more regular practice of a system of land registration, and the periodical enrolment of citizens. It had become a matter of public importance that there should be an authentic record of all freeholders, and this was only possible by the establishment of a register, somewhat on the principle of our Domesday Book, which was subjected to periodical revision in order to record changes of interest. Similarly, it became necessary that conveyances of land should take place with publicity, and by certain unmistakable tokens. Hence the important part played by Mancipation in the law of property during the ensuing centuries. And it is probable that the system of collective landowner-ship, now almost the last mainstay of the gentile organization, received its death blow from the Ser-vian reforms.

Whether or not it had been intended that the centuries, into which was divided the reinforced Roman army, now increased to some 20,000 men, should develop into a regular political assembly and have a voice in affairs of State, such was the inevitable outcome. The age-limits for military ser-vice were from the seventeenth to the sixtieth (for service in the field only to the forty-sixth) year; but older men of course voted in the century in which they had served when the citizens assembled centuriatim as a political body. The Assembly of the Centuries being, in theory, the mobilized army, always met outside the City wall, whilst the curiae or Assembly of Burghers in their civil capacity, in-variably met within.[1] That the comitia centuriata, the People in Warlike Array, should decide, in pre-ference to the comitia curiata, upon the question of

---

[1] More precisely, within the Pomerium. The exact meaning of Pomerium has no bearing upon our subject; it is discussed in the chapter, Der Begriff des Pomerium, in Mommsen's Röm. Forsch-ungen, ii. The above rules were invariably followed by the older Assemblies of the Curiae and Centuries. The later Comitia Tri-buta and plebeian Concilia were less regular in their practice. Mommsen, Staatsrecht, iii, 378 ff.

Peace or War, was the first and most obvious step towards legislative power; and this was succeeded by gradual further encroachments. The comitia centuriata comprised all the members of the older body (save in those rare instances where a citizen possessed no land), as well as the newly admitted elements, containing many men equal in intelligence and wealth with their patrician comrades; they therefore assumed from the first a character more representative of the community at large. Nor was the innovation of a nature to greatly alarm the patricians. The artificial organization of the centuries, and their cunningly manipulated relative voting power, conferred upon the wealthier classes an overwhelming predominance; at the same time the presence of plebeians in those classes, whilst tending (for the present) to strengthen the position of the governing order, deprived in appearance the new assembly of the invidious exclusiveness which characterized the old. To the Assembly of the curiae, when once the new order of things had become established, remained, besides formal State functions, for instance, the declaration of allegiance on the appointment of a new King (under the early Republic, Consul or Dictator), only its legislative competency in curial, gentile, family matters, such as Arrogation and testamentary declarations. Upon the establishment of the Republic its degradation was strikingly exposed, and its ancient significance for ever destroyed, by extending the suffrage even to plebeians who had

not availed themselves of the newly acquired right
to form plebeian gentes.

NOTE TO CHAPTER V

In his learned but highly controversial treatise Ueber die
Entstehung und Zusammensetzung der altrömischen Volksversammlungen, Dr. W. Soltau seeks to show that from the beginning
non-patricians formed part of, and voted in, the comitia curiata.
The intimacy of the religious bond uniting patrons and clients
might tend to support the proposition, so far as it relates to the
latter, but for the sharp distinction which we should expect the
earliest Romans to have drawn, and which apparently they did
draw, between public and private relations.   One may admit (as
do Niebuhr and others) the participation of clients with the
patricians in the curial sacra, and even their presence in the
comitia curiata calata, and the contiones, but scarcely the active
influence over public policy which the suffrage in the comitia
implies.   And it appears incredible that this latter right should
have been exercised by non-client plebeians in regal times, at
least in the more strictly constitutional period before Servius
Tullius.   It is true that Soltau is careful to exclude from the
plebeian voters (1) residents enjoying only commercium and
connubium without political rights; (2) Forctes and Sanates, or
Latins forcibly converted into Roman subjects; and (3) the
majority of Roman freedmen (libertini).   After making these de-
ductions, it is not clear what important class of plebeians, other
than clients, would remain to assist and vote in the assembly of
the curiae, but the acknowledgement of any non-client plebeian
element in the comitia curiata at so early a period involves
consequences, which the majority of modern Romanists concur
in rejecting; and although Soltau anticipates and ably deals with
the obvious objections to his theory, I cannot think that he con-
vincingly disposes of them.

1. The participation of non-client plebeians is opposed by religious obstacles which Soltau appears to insufficiently appreciate,

if we bear in mind the characteristics of the period under review. For instance, one of the chief functions of the comitia was to supervise and control the individual gentes in vital matters like Testament, Adrogation, and detestatio sacrorum. It is impossible to suppose that the concurrence of plebeians, having no gens and no recognized religion, could have been tolerated in such functions. Soltau accordingly assumes (p. 89) that even non-client plebeians may from time immemorial have had gentes of their own. I can neither find sufficient support for the theory nor approve his interpretation of Cicero's definition: "Gentiles sunt, qui inter se eodem nomine sunt; non est satis: qui ab ingenuis oriundi sunt; ne id quidem satis est: quorum majorum nemo servitutem servivit: abest etiam nunc: qui capite non sunt deminuti." On this head I must refer generally to subsequent chapters.

2. It is highly improbable that any unattached plebeian element existed in Rome till commerce and the fortune of war brought it thither. Trading strangers, intent only upon their traffic, and contingents from vanquished populations, ruined and rendered homeless, godless and destitute of every tie which bound men together, cannot have been admitted to the franchise to vote on equal terms (viritim) with their conquerors upon internal and external affairs of vital importance to the State, such as peace or war, and the election of Kings. We know that the Romans wisely encouraged immigration, but no polity is sufficiently stable to endure the presence in its sovereign body of masses of men entirely out of sympathy with it. Therefore it would have been necessary, as Soltau foreshadows, to sharply distinguish between various classes of plebeians in order to eliminate the naturally disaffected; and the absence of all allusion to so important an item in the scheme of government is stranger than the failure of ancient historians to deal with the admission of plebeians to the curiae in the post-regal period with the clearness and prominence due to so important an event (p. 80).

3. To grant the above proposition involves an entire revision of our view relating to the institution of the order of the Centuries, as an enlightened measure tending to a juster distribution of political power and responsibility, whilst materially strengthening

the Commonwealth. But the supersession of patricio-plebeian comitia curiata, with equal voting power, by the oligarchically ordered centuries would represent the most retrograde and reactionary step known to history, a deliberate transition from advanced democracy, tempered by kingship, to the unbridled rule of a wealthy monopolizing minority. The political acumen displayed by the Commons, and the steady progress of the popular power during the first three centuries of the Republic, are in strange contrast with so sinister a process. It is preferable to believe that the admission of plebeians to the comitia curiata was only achieved when that body had already been replaced for most purposes of practical politics by the comitia of the centuries, in which the plebeians were already, albeit inadequately, represented. It was a further concession to the plebs, which they had earned by their co-operation against the common tyrant, and which, in the altered position of the assembly, no longer appeared dangerous to the patriciate.

4. If the Constitution had permitted the presence of independent plebeians in the comitia, the Kings, whom the plebs would always support as its natural protectors, would have habitually utilized the popular body as a convenient counterpoise to the Senate. There is no indication that any such policy was consistently followed.

5. To mitigate the above and other considerations, Soltau finds himself impelled to a course of reasoning which ends in denying all political significance to the comitia curiata from the outset, places all practical sovereignty entirely in the hands of King and Senate, and degrades the Roman to the level of the Zulu polity in the days of Tshaka. A lex curiata is no longer a pact or treaty between King and People, binding both, but something imposed by the mere will of the former upon the latter. Lex is derived not from ligare but from legere. Yet we find this abject and powerless body of citizens claiming to elect a king (Livy, i, 17), and electing Tullus Hostilius (*ibid.*, i, 22), Ancus Martius (*ibid.*, i, 32), Tarquinius Priscus (*ibid.*, i, 35), before their accession. Servius Tullius, who first ascends the throne without the people's order (injussu populi), but with their goodwill and consent (Cicero, De Rep., ii, 21), as well as that of the Senate (Livy, i, 41), never-

theless, after many years of a successful and popular reign, "regularizes" his position by soliciting election at the hands of the people (*ibid.*, i, 46). Tarquin the Proud alone, in an age of growing disorder, though he condescends to canvass for popularity (*ibid.*, i, 47), affects to reign without the people's consent, and is deposed for this and other violations of the Constitution. See also the corresponding accounts of Dionysius, ii, 15; iii, 1, 12, 15; iv, 1, 10.

CHAPTER VI

THE REVOLT OF THE ARISTOCRACY (CIRCA 243 URBIS, 510 B.C.)[1]

ORIGINALLY operating largely as an instrument of class selfishness, the Servian Constitution really represents the first step towards the ultimate overthrow of patrician supremacy. The abolition of the kingship, by accentuating the disparities, precipitated the struggle between the privileged and the non-privileged classes: the Servian reforms supplied the vantage-ground from which the latter conducted their fight for political equality. The old simple division into citizens with equal political rights, and a class with neither rights nor liabilities, save such as were incidental to public order and decorum, had yielded to an arbitrary system which cast upon all men the burden, and withheld from most the advantages, of civic life. The most "democratic" (in the modern sense) of societies, considered apart from the rest of man-

---

[1] The date is open to doubt, as is the entire chronology of the regal period. It seems improbable that only seven kings, three at least of whom are said to have been removed by violent means, should have reigned during nearly two centuries and a half, a period not reached by any seven consecutive Roman emperors or English monarchs.

kind, the patriciate, through the effects of warlike
conquests and organic changes in the body politic,
had developed, as against the generality of the inhabitants, into an aristocracy, with all an aristocracy's
usual virtues and failings—the latter as yet unchecked by the criticism and the example of a powerful
middle class. The bulk of the non-patrician orders
resented their poverty, and all of them the degradation of their political and religious disabilities, the
more keenly as their own prowess contributed to
win for the City the glory and material advantages
of successful warfare, which the patricians then contrived nearly to monopolize. But so long as the
regal power overawed alike gentes and plebs, the
oppression of the latter was mitigated or disguised.
The hand of the King lay heavy upon all, but
heaviest upon those whom wealth and position
marked out as specially fit to bear the burdens
inseparable from a policy of foreign expansion;
whilst proximity to the throne exposed them to the
malice, caprice, and arrogance of a haughty despot,
whose growing sense of irresponsible power was
uncurbed by the conventions of former ages.

It has been urged with some plausibility that
Rome itself had fallen under the dominion of alien
invaders; that the conquests of the later reigns
had been achieved under foreign leadership, as
Saxon England, after having succumbed to the
Normans, itself subjugated Normandy and Ireland
under the first two Henrys; and that the aboli-

tion of kingship was the consequence of successful armed revolt resulting in the expulsion of a
foreign tyrant. Colour is lent to this theory by the
fact that the last three Roman Kings were almost
certainly of non-Roman extraction, that Etruscan
chiefs had succeeded in establishing their rule in
parts of Italy farther south than Latium, and by the
peculiar hatred of the mere name of king (as applied
to a temporal ruler) which later Romans consistently manifested. Yet the revolution which cul-
minated in the expulsion of Tarquin the Proud, and
his gens, is also explainable by normal domestic
developments. Rome had become a ruling city, but
its empire was maintained by grievous imposts
upon the population, whilst the privileged class,
which alone derived countervailing benefit from the
political situation, was indignant and alarmed at the
lawless encroachments of the executive. The accounts of Livy and others seem to demonstrate that
the reigns of the last three Kings were periods of
growing internal disorder. Warlike triumphs had
inflated their pride, developing an inclination for
pomp and sumptuousness, as well as contempt of
traditional usage and a dangerous disregard of constitutional forms.

The legal machinery for dethroning a King, or
otherwise punishing his misrule, was wanting in
Rome as completely as it is wanting in England,
and the Romans had not invented those ingenious
checks which now guard our English liberties.

Finally, the arbitrariness of the second Tarquin brought about a compact between the patrician aristocracy and the better-class plebeians, as the pretensions of the second James produced the temporary alliance between the parties afterwards known as Tories and Whigs, which resulted in the English Revolution, the Bill of Rights and the Act of Settlement. The spirit in which the change was effected eloquently testifies the sobriety and political maturity of the Roman people. The conservative character of the English Revolution is rightly insisted upon by Lord Macaulay. That of the Roman was more so.[1] Disguise it as they might, the English gentlemen in Convention assembled were not a legally constituted body, and the dynastic change they effected was grounded upon a palpable subterfuge. Less formidable difficulties confronted L. Junius Brutus and his colleagues. No kingly family had had time to establish a line of dynastic descent, and the sovereign power residing in the people, which they had theretofore transferred irrevocably to one man for life, could, without undue straining of the Constitution, be conferred for a limited period, and upon two or more persons. Sacral law, indeed, it was deemed dangerous to interfere with openly, and its requirements were thought to be satisfied (or possibly the gods hoodwinked) by allocating the title of King (rex sacrorum) to the least powerful official of the new government,

[1] Cf. Bryce, Studies, i, 169.

who was invested for life with certain of the religious duties formerly discharged by the head of the State. All executive functions, that is to say all political powers capable of being abused, were henceforward vested for the period of one year jointly in two officers of State, called in the beginning Praetores, Judices, or Consules, the last of which titles soon prevailed.[1]

The Consuls were elected by the comitia centuriata, and nominated by their predecessors, the function of interrex being now exercised only in cases where such nomination had for any reason been omitted; and from this time probably dates the definite recognition of the Assembly of Centuries as the regular law-giving body. The command of either Consul was equally efficacious without the assent of his colleague, but was annulled by the latter's active dissent.[2] In the field, the command of the troops alternated between the Consuls daily, unless operating at a distance from each other when, as frequently happened, hostilities were proceeding in more than one theatre of war. Each Consul appointed half the officers of the army. As in the case of the King, no Consul was responsible for his acts so long as he retained the imperium. At the end of his term he became again a private

[1] Consules may mean "those who leap or dance in company," alluding to the rites to be performed by both the magistrates. More probably the expression implied co-deliberation, whence consilium, "a sitting together," as distinguished from concilium, "a calling together."

[2] Mommsen, Röm. Staatsrecht, 28 ff.

citizen, amenable to the law, and answerable for any misdeeds committed during his tenure of office.

Apart from the check to tyranny which the restricted term of the office afforded, some important limitations of the consular power were devised by the leading politicians :

1. Although the Consuls, and not the Rex Sacrorum, offered up prayers and sacrifices, and consulted the auguries on behalf of the community, they had not, like the King, the nomination to the priesthood. Vacancies in the priestly and augural colleges were filled by coöptation. Non-collegiate priests, and vestals, were appointed by the College of Pontiffs under the presidency of its Pontifex Maximus.

2. Crimes being deemed to be committed against the gods, even the King had had no prerogative of pardon. On appeal by the criminal to the people (provocatio), however, the latter might, in the exercise of their supreme power, and provided the auspices permitted, decide that the offence should go unpunished. But if the King refused to permit the appeal to be made, the people could not prevent the sentence from taking effect. By the lex Valeria 245 urbis, it was taken out of the Consul's power to refuse to allow such an appeal where the offence was not military, and the decreed penalty was death, exile, or stripes. The provision was extended by a later enactment to the infliction of heavy fines; and these legal safeguards of the citizen's person [1] and pocket were subsequently re-enacted by the XII Tables.

[1] Acts, xxii, 25 ff.

H

3. The King, as the person in whom the sum total of the executive power resided, had been able to exercise it personally or to delegate it at will. This discretion was now limited in important particulars. Already in the early years of the Republic, civil suits were decided by inferior magistrates or private citizens appointed for the purpose (in judicio), the Consul taking an active part only in the interlocutory stages (in jure). Two Quaestors exercised ordinary criminal jurisdiction as delegates of the people, rather than of the Consuls. Treason was dealt with by two extraordinary functionaries called duoviri perduellionis. The Quaestors also acted as guardians of the Exchequer, assuming a supervision and an indirect control in matters of supply.

4. A natural consequence of the revision of the Constitution was the abolition of the oppressive privilege formerly enjoyed by the Kings of having their land cultivated by the community free of charge to themselves.

The comitia curiata, whose dwindling significance is referred to in the foregoing chapter, had been now superseded for most purposes as the chief legislative body of the State by the Assembly of Centuries, and citizenship had become the birthright of every inhabitant of Rome, except slaves, and aliens enjoying only hospitium (guest-right), or commercium.

Notwithstanding general advantages, the new constitutional changes brought detriment to important sections of the population. The King had stood in the position of overlord *de jure* to the State clients, and *de facto* to all other plebeians, who had expected and received from him that protection which the secular law generally refused them. Such a position was clearly incongruous where the magistrates were private citizens invested temporarily with limited executive power, and with the kingship fell the chief bulwark behind which the more helpless of the plebs sheltered from the oppression of the favoured caste.

Whilst in the City the Consuls were far less despotic and awe-inspiring than their regal predecessors, the community still recognized the danger of dividing or curtailing the authority of the general in the field. A Consul was freed from the new constitutional checks whilst directing military operations. He had, moreover, the right of nominating an " Army-Master " (magister populi) or Dictator,[1] in whom were temporarily revived all the powers of the former Kings, including even that of disallowing the provocation, and who was not accountable for his official acts when retiring into private life. But the Dictator's term of office came to an end with that of his appointer, and in any case after six months, the period of a normal campaign. On the analogy of Consul and Quaestor, the Dictator was bound to appoint as subordinate coadjutor a Master of the Horse, magister equitum.

[1] Cicero, De Republica, i, 40. Though the occasion of a Dictator's appointment was nearly always a warlike emergency, his authority was not confined to the camp.

CHAPTER VII

THE STRUGGLE OF THE ORDERS BEGINS

FROM their own point of view the patriciate, and, to a lesser extent, their wealthy plebeian allies also, had successfully solved the constitutional problem. Arbitrary government had been confined to a point sufficiently guaranteeing the liberty of the subject, whilst provision had been made for emergencies where wide discretionary power could not safely be dispensed with. The revolution made the chief magistrates largely amenable to the Senate, whose members alone in time became eligible for the consulship. The Senate comprised since the overthrow of the kingly power, and probably as the reward, stipulated beforehand, of plebeian assistance, a large number, perhaps a majority, of the lower order, who, however, whilst entitled to vote on a division, could not take part in the deliberations (concilia), and being by reason of their religious disabilities debarred from concurring in the auctoritas,[1] naturally as yet only indirectly influenced the course of government.

[1] Plebeian Senators were called conscripti, the full Senate was usually designated by the term patres (et) conscripti—"Lords and Associates."

Through their formal admission into the State, the general body of the plebeians had acquired the citizen privileges of jus Quiritium, patria potestas, Testament, curial and gentile organization. The differentiation between civil and martial law had substantially progressed; and both were becoming disentangled from ritual. The inclusion of all citizens under the law of the City now sharply distinguished Romans from Latins and foreigners, and further accentuated the national and patriotic sentiment which in Rome, even whilst internal discord raged, dominated patrician and plebeian alike.

But the rigid gentile system, by prohibiting the connubium, perpetuated the unnatural separation of the two orders. A patrician woman intermarrying with a plebeian lost the gentilitas, and a plebeian woman intermarrying with a patrician did not gain it. Such unions entailed important legal disadvantages and were moreover decried as incomplete and irregular by the more straight-laced of the patricians. The only remedy would have been to override gentile custom in one of its most sacred phases by a purely secular enactment, and for this public opinion was not yet ripe.

Not only were even the most eligible plebeians practically debarred from intermarriage with patrician families; religion stood in their way in every department of civil life. Although the secularization of the law was proceeding apace, no plebeian could yet take any leading part in the rites which dominated every public act; and the privileged class alone knew the formulae for determining those days upon which public, particularly judicial, business might or might not be lawfully transacted [1] (dies fasti, comitiales, nefasti). Offices of the State therefore devolved as of course upon patricians exclusively: the appointment of a plebeian Pontiff or Consul would, in early republican days, have appeared sacrilege, and scarcely less so the admission of the plebs to the minor magisterial offices.

This inequality had always existed, and since, at all events, the Servian reforms it had existed as a genuine grievance. But the full pitch of its odiousness now for the first time appeared. Strained relations between the Kings and the Senate had driven the former to look for a measure of moral support to the plebeians, whom in return they protected from the grosser forms of oppression. The revolution had thrown all the power of the State into the hands of the Senate and Magistrates, with unlimited opportunities to abuse it. The Consuls, themselves members of the patriciate, and raised above their fellows only for a brief space of time,

[1] Ille nefastus erit per quem tria verba silentur; Fastus erit, per quem lege licebit agi. Ovid, F., i, 47. The three words (do, dico, addico) represent the solemn form which preceded judgement. Days nefasti (religiosi, vitiosi) were times of purification or festival, or the anniversaries of some great disaster. And see Varro, De L. L., vi, 29 ff. A secretary's indiscretion, in 450, put the public in possession of most of the pontifical secret formulas.

had neither sympathy with the non-privileged classes nor power to protect them.

Most serious of all, in a community largely dependent upon husbandry and cattle farming, was the agrarian question, which thenceforward preoccupied successive generations of politicians and, unsolved, finally wrought ruin to the Commonwealth. The land of the small freeholders was becoming exhausted through intensive cultivation,[1] and barely sufficed for their needs. Yet the situation was aggravated by the gradual monopolization of the common grazing lands and other State domains, which plebeians had helped to conquer, and the enjoyment of which they had formerly shared, by patrician and a few wealthy plebeian families. These lands remained, indeed, State property, but although the favoured occupants were nominally bound to pay rent, their friends and relatives in office were studiously careless in collecting it. The loss of public revenue may not have been serious; but the abuse, by contracting the scope of subsistence of the poorer classes, accelerated the impoverishment of a peasantry already threatened by frequent and not always fortunate wars.

The cup was made to overflow by the immoderation with which many plutocrats exploited their position. The creditor upheld his rights with a rigour all the more hateful because the legal process which enforced them was administered by patrician judges, and regulated by secret forms removed from

[1] Ferrero, Greatness and Decline of R., i, 4.

the scrutiny of the defendant. Defaulting debtors (whether by misfortune or other cause) became, either under the original contract (nexum), or by judicial award (addictio), the bondmen of their creditors; and the insolence of wealth too frequently vented itself in private imprisonment and personal outrage. So long as a nexus abode in Rome he could not indeed be deprived of his citizen rights; but it was in his creditor's power, subject to certain restrictions, to sell him as a slave beyond Tiber.

The chief remedy for which the poorer plebeians clamoured was a juster participation in the enjoyment of the lands at the Government's disposal; but this the patricians persistently evaded, and the plebs, whose wealthier members were themselves interested in the continuance of the abuses, were not strong enough to enforce. From time to time, when the political co-operation of the plebs was urgently required, or when discontent approached the point of open revolt, the Senate decreed heroic palliatives, as an extinction of existing debts and the liberation of bondmen debtors. Such measures of course only afforded temporary relief, leaving the root evil untouched, and, by the action of economic laws (which hold good at all times and everywhere), in the end added to the depression of the debtor classes.

About the year of the City 260 (493 B.C.) plebeian soldiers, returning from a successful campaign to their poverty, and many to their prisons, and finding the Senate again obdurate to their demands, marched under their plebeian officers to a hill between the Tiber and the Anio, with the real or professed intention of founding a new city. The accomplishment of the project, which might have given a widely different course to European history, was frustrated by prompt surrender of the governing classes. The two parties agreed upon a compromise, in which, inasmuch as the old abuses were not materially checked, nor the law of debt modified, the advantage must be said to have lain chiefly on the side of the more business-like patricians. Nevertheless the compact was hailed by the plebs as a great political victory; the law ratifying it was called the Sacred Law,[1] the place temporarily occupied by the seceders the Sacred Mount. Provision was made by this legislation for the settlement of the poorest families upon public lands; debts were remitted, imprisoned debtors liberated, and immunity was secured to the seceders for their sedition and desertion under arms. The only permanent reform was an important political measure whereby the institution of Tribunes of the People (tribuni plebis) was either inaugurated or definitely recognized. The two[2] Tribunes, with whom were associated two Ædiles with similar but inferior powers, were only eligible by and from the plebs,

[1] All solemn compacts between the orders resembled international treaties, and were called leges sacratae.

[2] Mommsen, Staatsrecht, ii, 274. Their number was increased to four or five in A.U.C. 283 and to ten in A.U.C. 297. The original number was doubtlessly adopted in analogy with the Consuls. Soltau, Volksversammlungen, 494.

and not having the auspicia were not, legally, State ·
officials. They had no faculty to initiate or control
legislation. Their political significance lay in their
power (jus auxilii, intercessio) to hamper the executive, by forbidding any particular administrative act
about to be performed by a State officer. This power
was only exercisable within the City walls; in the
field it would have been obviously subversive of all
discipline. It was preventive only. At a word from
the Tribune, the unwilling recruit, so long as he
remained within the City, escaped punishment for
his desertion, proceedings against the debtor or
criminal were suspended, and the public officer was
rendered powerless to discharge his duties; but the
intercession must take place before the realization of
the act objected to, and at the request of the person
against whom it was directed. For this reason a
Tribune was required during his term of office never
to pass a night without the City, and never to close
the door of his house. The person of every Tribune
and Ædile was declared inviolable.[1] Capital punishment was threatened to any citizen offering him violence or resistance, and all officers of State were
included in the ban, contrary to the hitherto recognized maxim that no magistrate, so long as he re-

---

[1] Contact with a Tribune's or Ædile's person may have been
unlawful because he was an object either of special reverence as
the creation of a sacred law, or of peculiar abhorrence as a monster,
whose quasi-magisterial authority desecrated the sacra. Probably
each order held its own view and both sensibly agreed to differ.

mained in office, could lawfully be called to account for his acts.

We are compelled to believe that the power exercised by the Tribune developed very gradually to the proportions we find it to have assumed later. Originally, no doubt, his privilege was merely to succour an individual plebeian in danger of oppression by a magistrate. This jus auxilii was necessarily exercised by the Tribune on the instant, without pausing to weigh the merits of the case, since he had no power to remedy the alleged oppressive act once performed. Even the concession of so much shows the desperate straits in which the patricians and wealthy plebeians found themselves as a result of the threatened secession. The development of the jus intercedendi, and the monstrous power of interference with the procedure of Legislature and Senate, cannot possibly have been contemplated by the governing classes at the outset.[1]

The plebs now emerged as a disciplined political organization. Conventions (concilia plebis) were habitually convoked by the Tribunes (under the lex Icilia of 262)[2] to discuss affairs relating to their order. Their resolutions (plebi scita) had not yet indeed the force of law, for the Constitution, in theory at least, still refused legislative functions to bodies not comprising the whole of the

[1] Cf. Soltau, Volksversammlungen, 522 ff.
[2] Another measure of the same name, in 298, appropriated the unoccupied land on the Aventine for artizans' dwellings.

citizens,[1] but undoubtedly the plebeians treated their own decrees as binding upon themselves, and they soon, under the guidance of their Tribunes, assumed an informal criminal jurisdiction over all citizens without distinction, where offences against their own order were in question, as, among others, Cnaeus Marcius (Coriolanus) found to his cost.[2]

At first the plebeians voted curiatim in their concilia; that is, they assembled at the summons of their Tribunes in the same order as if the comitia curiata had been convoked by the Magistrate, the essential difference being of course the absence of patrician citizens. But such an assembly would still include clients and freedmen, whose traditional attachment to their patrons was distasteful to the more radical party. In 283 a measure, carried at the instance of the Tribune, Publilius Volero, inaugurated the system of voting by tribes, which confined the suffrage to landowners, and political preponderance

---

[1] "Es giebt nach römischen Staatsrecht keine Gemeindeversammlung ohne wenigstens theoretisch allgemeines Stimmrecht." Mommsen's Römische Forschungen, chapter on Die Patricisch-plebejischen Comitien, at p. 154. (The centuries did not at first include non-freeholders, cf. p. 87 supra, p. 138 infra.) Mommsen characterizes the usurpation by the plebs of a criminal quasi-jurisdiction as "Lynch-justiz" (Forschungen, i, 179), which, however, political necessity excused.

[2] That famous prosecution, however, certainly took place later than the date (263) assigned to it by Livy, ii, 35. Mommsen, Römische Forschungen, ii, Die Erzählung von Cnaeus Marcius Coriolanus.

to the independent plebeian peasantry.[1] At the same
time the Senate confirmed the legality of the concilia plebis, and the Tribunes' right to propose and
carry resolutions in them (jus agendi cum plebe).[2]

[1] Mommsen, Staatsrecht, iii, 152.

[2] Prior to 283 U.C. it is possible that tribunes may only have
been appointed by co-optation. Soltau, Volksversammlungen,
502 ff.

CHAPTER VIII

THE DECEMVIRATE AND THE DAWN OF WRITTEN LAW [1]

CONCEIVABLY the simple plebeian peasant-soldiery, whose secession to the Sacred Mount threw the Government into such consternation, may themselves have felt considerably embarrassed to formulate their desiderations to the best advantage. The evils from which they suffered demanded (in the order of their importance) firstly, administrative reform (regarding the State lands); secondly, reform of the law of debt; thirdly, constitutional reform. Neither the first nor the second object was permanently achieved. The Constitution indeed, though it remained in theory unchanged, had in practice been subverted by the formation of a new State within the State, the introduction of a co-ordinate system of plebeian governance with an underlying tendency to tyranny and the avowed purpose of hampering the regular authorities. But whatever

[1] " Written law " is, of course, not here used as the equivalent of statute law. The commands of the old comitia curiata, and afterwards of the Centuries, in substance no doubt represented activity which would now be left to the Executive, but were certainly statutes.

satisfaction plebeians derived from obstructing the executive and prosecuting persons in high places, they soon realized that so long as the principles upon which the law was administered remained a sealed book to them, so long would they continue, notwithstanding their organization, in hopeless inferiority to their patrician adversaries.

Whereas custom which rests upon religion is in its essence all but immutable, the wisdom of secular institutions is uniformly subject to challenge and review, and among a litigious people the science of jurisprudence emerges whenever reverence or superstition has ceased to stifle criticism. More than the correction of definite political abuses, therefore, the preoccupation of the plebs was now to laicize the law to the extent of bringing it within the intellectual ambit of the meanest citizen. To this end political agitation now became directed.

Weary of constant obstruction, and dreading the further undermining of fundamental institutions, the patricians, after eight years of stubborn resistance, in 300 urbis, purchased the abolition of the hated Tribunate by the promise of a written and published Code. A mission was dispatched to the Grecian colonies of Italy with the object of studying Hellenic institutions. Two years later, upon the return of the mission, the comitia centuriata, by a remarkable enactment, temporarily transferred the whole of the executive power to a college of ten persons (decem viri consulari imperio legibus scribundis) who were to prepare and publish the Code. That plebeians were declared eligible for the Decemvirate indicates the wane of ancient traditional influences, which however were, in the first instance, still sufficiently powerful to secure the selection of all the decemvirs from the patriciate. In 303, a Code of Ten Tables had been elaborated, which, engraved upon wood, were displayed in the Forum. Supplementary provisions being then found desirable, a new Decemvirate was appointed in 304, this time comprising members (according to Niebuhr in equal number) of both orders, and two new Tables were added.

Unfortunately, only fragments industriously gleaned from later writers remain to us of the XII Tables. So much is clear, that they did not profess to be a complete statement of the law, and dealt only incidentally with fundamental institutions which, like patria potestas and patronage, were ingrained in the social system, and called neither for express confirmation nor detailed exposition. The XII Tables were, in general, declaratory rather than remedial; where remedial they restrained more than enlarged; and what innovations there were seem to have been made in what we should call the adjective, rather than the substantive law.

1. Procedure naturally occupies a prominent place in all archaic legal systems where, in the absence of an efficient police, the fiat of a court may be often

successfully defied, and a right is scarcely considered in the abstract, as a thing apart from its actual enforceability. The XII Tables commence by regulating the various stages of an action at law with a minuteness strangely in contrast with the later detached references to the most important branches of substantive law. Special attention is directed to hampering the process of the recovery of debts, and the judgment creditor seeking to enforce his right is hedged around with conditions, restrictions, and delays. But when these had been observed, the law took its course, and bondage at home or slavery abroad awaited, as hitherto, the debtor who, after all the statutory respites, could neither himself discharge his obligation nor find a sympathiser to do so. It is even said to have been declared law or enacted by the XII Tables, that an unsatisfied judgment creditor might kill his defaulting debtor. Although supported by weighty authority,[1] we cannot think this interpretation correct. At some very early epoch, indeed, death may have been the lot of a defaulting promissor, for inasmuch as every solemn bargain was originally held to be witnessed by the gods, its breach would be an affront to the latter, and might be thought to demand the sacrifice of the delinquent. Between nations recognizing no common gods, treaties were, for this reason, strictly speaking, impossible. The international practice (which I have already men-

---

[1] See Ortolan, Instituts, i, 106, 126. Also Mommsen, Römische Geschichte, i, 152. Contra, Muirhead, Roman Law, sect. 36.

tioned) of surrendering to the disappointed State
the author of a repudiated treaty probably also had
a religious origin. But what we know of the nexum,
as entered into between private parties at Rome,
certainly suggests no specially sacred character, and
the secularization, which was the life-blood of the
decemviral Code, would not countenance under
colour of religion a judicial award which amounted
to a death decree. There is no reason to suppose
that the nexus or addictus lost his patria potestas,
his capacity to make a will, or any other of his citizen
rights. His creditor, although enabled to detain
and turn his person to profit, had no dominion
over him, as over a child, slave, or noxally surrendered tortfeasor. The debtor's status, therefore, remained a part of the public law of Rome. Putting
him to death was contrary to public policy as well as
against the good order of the City, and cannot have
been lawful in the then state of the community.
The passage imputed to the XII Tables, so far
as it is held to establish the creditor's power of life
and death, becomes entirely discredited by the
grotesque atrocity of the alleged provision immediately following. The law bore heavily indeed upon
the defaulting debtor, but the meaningless brutality
of a direction to partition his corpse among his
unsatisfied creditors, if several, is alien to the spirit of
Roman law, and irreconcilable with Roman common
sense. Nor could we account for the presence of
such a provision in a Code so obviously inspired by

a very general desire to advantage the humbler population.[1]

Without, I think, unduly straining what we are told of the text of the Code, we may assume the judgment debtor's position to have been substantially as follows: He either paid with his head (*i.e.*, person, capite poenas dabat), that is he became a quasi-slave of his creditor until he had worked off his debt, or he could be sold as a true slave trans Tiberim. In neither event could his property (if any) be attached. His familia was in any case inalienable, and at that time no means existed of sequestrating his pecunia.[2] If he died in bondage, however, his debt, so far as it was still undischarged, would devolve, with his assets, upon his heirs. Selling him into slavery created a different situation. His debt was cancelled by the capitis deminutio maxima, and the creditor could pursue the claim no further. But neither could any one, as the law then apparently stood, inherit of him either ex testamento or ab intestato. Therefore, as the State did not yet succeed to persons dying heirless, his property was, strictly speaking, res nullius and might be seized by the first comer. But even if those who would have been sui heredes could have been legally deprived of the familia, the religious sanctity of the house and land pertaining to it precluded any violent entry by a stranger, and the

---

[1] The Tables attempted (of course, unsuccessfully) to limit the rate of interest to ten per cent. per annum.

[2] As to familia and pecunia, see pp. 206 and 260 ff.

small pecunia would be promptly appropriated by next of kin. The creditor's claim, so far as it remained unsatisfied, was thus defeated, and it is therefore highly probable that an insolvent debtor was scarcely ever sold as a slave, except when the purchase price covered the whole of the debt, or a plurality of judgment creditors complicated the process of recovering through the debtor's personal services. Where there were several creditors, probably selling into slavery was the only practicable course; and the words: partis secanto . . . si plus minusve secuerunt ne fraude esto, may refer to the case where several creditors, or several co-heirs of a deceased creditor, had proved their claims.[1]

2. The institution of the Agnatic Family was one of the cardinal principles of religion as professed by the Romans of the age. The power of the paterfamilias over descendants was now incorporated in the avowedly human-made law, with the proviso that it should cease over a son who had been thrice sold by his father. Similarly, although a simple device enabled the wife to defeat the husband's acquisition of manus over her by prescription, the principle of male control was affirmed alike over maid, wife, and widow. While the ancestor lived, the unmarried daughter, and the married daughter

---

[1] The subject is dealt with by Muirhead, Roman Law, ss. 31, 36, and more fully by Kleineidam (Personalexecution der XII Tafeln, notably p. 224 ff.) and Bachofen (das Nexum), though some of the conclusions differ from those above.

not in manu, remained under his power. Upon his
death they became subject to the tutelage of the
nearest agnate, as did also the widow who had been
in manu of her husband or his ancestor. Only vestals
were freed, in honorem sacerdotii, alike from the
father's power and the tutor's control.[1]

3. The decemviral legislators, far from legalizing
the probably increasing practice of intermarriage between patricians and plebeians, expressly denied the
jus connubii between the two orders. So reactionary
a measure in an otherwise democratic Code must
have been indicated by strong reasons. Probably
the legists (who included plebeians, for this particular
provision was the work of the later decemvirs) fore-
saw that wedlock generally must tend to lose its
character of permanency in proportion as the looser
plebeian notions invaded the patrician circles which
set the fashion to Latium. If these misgivings were
really entertained they were only too well justified,
as we shall see later.

4. The law of intestate succession was clearly
established for patricians, clients, and plebeians; and
every citizen was declared entitled to dispose of his
property by testamentary disposition, though not
yet, apparently, at his absolute discretion.

5. A further stage in the dissolution of the gens
is indicated by the insertion in a civil Code of the
religious sanction which protected a client from his
patron's oppression, and by assigning to the next of

[1] Gaius, i, 145.

kin functions theretofore exercisable by the gens under its separate jurisdiction, such as the curatorship over lunatics and spendthrifts.

6. The XII Tables also dealt with the law of contract, torts (including theft), property, and crime, by provisions with which we are not here directly concerned.

7. Some provisions, such as those regarding funeral customs, the destruction of deformed or monstrous offspring (portenta, monstra),[1] and punishments allocated to certain offences savour unmistakably of the sacral law, and represent further encroachments of Jus upon Fas, or the blending of the latter with the former.

8. With the following important exceptions, the Code dealt on the whole but slightly with constitutional questions and public law generally. The criminal offender, being deemed an enemy of the gods, and consequently of the State, fell to be judged by those whose duty it was to fight the State's battles, and capital punishment,[2] which the concilia plebis had theretofore presumed to inflict, was declared to be the exclusive prerogative of the comitia centuriata. The provocatio was confirmed. To the conquered populations[3] the Tables brought, or confirmed, at

[1] Voigt, XII Tafeln, i, 250 ff.

[2] That is to say, any punishment depriving a citizen of life, liberty, or citizenship. Until late Republican times a citizen, whose life was forfeit, was usually allowed to evade the extreme penalty by voluntary exile, which was equivalent to civil death.

[3] Called Forctes and Sanates (Festus, s. v. Sanates). The former were those "firm" and upright communities who had not

least elementary civic rights by the grant of the commercium, that is, the right to use Roman forms of contract and conveyance, and (probably) Roman actions to enforce them. To the plebeians generally they promisèd freedom of association (sodalitas), whilst sternly repressing seditious combinations; and the death penalty awaited alike the traitor to his countrymen, the corrupt judge, and the false witness.

The great achievement of the XII Tables, was to have laid down a set of rules knowable to every man and binding upon the Magistrates. The divorce of Religion, with its unknown and uncertain application, from Law was complete, at least so far as concerned that law with which the plain citizen was brought into everyday contact. The value of such a concession was enormous, and it was not at the moment considered too dearly purchased by the abolition of the Tribunate, and of the criminal jurisdiction which the plebeian concilia had usurped.

Internal commotion was not, however, at once appeased by the promulgation of the XII Tables. By surrendering the Tribunate, the plebs had thrown down a bulwark of tremendous resisting power, in exchange for paper (or rather, wooden) guarantees, of which the value had yet to be worked out in practice.

revolted against their conquerors; the latter were subject peoples who, having thrown off their allegiance in a fit of temporary derangement, had returned to sanity and obedience, and were now placed on the same footing as the faithful. The nomenclature proves that Roman patriotism was capable of the same naïve egoism which foreigners affect to find in Englishmen.

On the other hand, the patricians had assisted to transfer all the power of the State into the hands of a small patricio-plebeian junta, without providing constitutional means to dislodge and dissolve it when the scope of its usefulness was exhausted. The Decemvirs, apprehending the strength of their position, seemed determined by subterfuge and excuse to indefinitely delay the surrender of the power with which they had been invested. Such procrastination, if persisted in, would have tended ultimately to establish some prescriptive rights exceedingly dangerous to public liberty, and a fresh political deadlock now arose.

Obscurity shrouds the events leading up to the revolution which swept away the Decemvirate,[1] but the revolt would seem to have proceeded more naturally from the patriciate than from the plebs, who temporarily enjoyed, through their comrades among the Decemvirs, a share of magisterial power, the retention of which, on the resumption of the regular consulate, traditions of centuries would be invoked to defeat. Be this as it may, the abortive attempt to perpetuate decemviral rule synchronizes with a renewal of the dissensions, culminating in a

---

[1] Revolutions may arise from small occasions but not from small causes; and we cannot place reliance in the Virginian legend, which, like the Lucretian, ascribes a general political upheaval to a single outrage. These stories are, however, of value as illustrating the esteem in which the early Romans held female honour. It is regrettable that the most beautiful of Macaulay's Lays should lack historical authentication.

second secession of the plebs to the Sacred Mount (about 305), and the re-establishment of the consular dispensation (L. Valerius and M. Horatius being nominated Consuls by an interrex) with some modifications, nearly all favourable to the people, by the legislation known as the leges Valeriae Horatiae. The substance of these measures appears to have been as follows :

1. The Decemvirate was abolished and the former Constitution restored.

2. The right of the plebs to elect Tribunes was revived and solemnly guaranteed. In addition to their former powers, Tribunes were now entitled to watch from the door the senatorial debates and prevent by their intercessio the passing of any obnoxious resolution.[1] The presence of the Tribunes ensured that senatusconsulta were correctly promulgated and duly acted upon. Similar power to impede the passing of measures in the Centuries and Tribes (I shall deal with the latter assembly presently) had either already been usurped by, or were now extended to, the Tribunes.

3. It was enacted that ten plebeians, who, like Tribunes and Ædiles, were declared inviolable as to their persons, should arbitrate upon disputes between parties of their own order upon remit from a Tribune. Such a separate informal or quasi-judicial system the plebs had probably already en-

[1] *I.e.*, Senatusconsultum; the auctoritas to be given to laws by the patrician Senate was removed from the Tribunes' cognizance.

joyed. As they operated without the mysterious forms by which procedure was bound in the State Courts, these tribunals no doubt at first commanded the sympathies of plebeian litigants, though their decrees must have been difficult to enforce against an unwilling and shifty loser. The plebeian judges of course claimed no jurisdiction when one of the parties was a patrician, and with the fusing of the two orders the separate plebeian judiciary seems to have disappeared.

4. The usurped criminal jurisdiction of the plebeian concilia had been abolished by the XII Tables, at least in capital cases. But the Tribunes were enabled to bring capital accusations before the comitia centuriata, and they could still, with the concurrence of the Assembly of Tribes, fine any citizen to his utter ruin. Thus any Tribune, though standing constitutionally outside the hierarchy of regular State officials, divested of all constitutional responsibility and deprived of the most modest share in constructive government, was nevertheless furnished with enormous powers to work mischief, the sole check to which was the intercessio of his own fellows. In a State where either Consul could at all times veto any act of his colleague, where all State officials were subjected to the veto of any Tribune, the Tribunes themselves could veto each other, and even proceedings in the Senate were liable to similar constant interruption, we might well marvel how government could have been carried on at all. That on

the whole the administration was nevertheless fairly efficient, and the law not only carried out, but even progressively developed, is due partly indeed to the comparative simplicity of public affairs in those early times, but, above all, to common sense and moderation, coupled with an ardent patriotism, ever maintained at the highest pitch by the pressure of surrounding foreign enemies.

5. When face to face with the foe the Romans never hesitated to suspend constitutional safeguards, and in the field the Dictator retained undisputed sway over the citizens under arms. His orders no Tribune can stay. From his death sentence, and his alone, there is no appeal;[1] under all other circumstances the citizen capitally condemned has the privilege of the provocatio.

6. Most important of all was the provision that plebiscita, which by virtue of the lex Publilia (283 urbis) were already binding upon the whole body of citizens without any reservation, where they concerned individual plebeians or the internal administration of the plebs only, should, even if they impinged upon the province of the regular legislature, nevertheless have the force of law, provided they had been approved by senatusconsultum[2] before

---

[1] This has been doubted, see Ihne, Röm. Verfassungsgeschichte, 65 n.

[2] A senatusconsultum or resolution of the whole (patricio-plebeian) Senate, differed entirely from the auctoritas, which was given on the passing of a lex by the comitia, as a guarantee that the measure was not contrary to the fas, and accordingly could be

the concilium plebis had actually voted upon them. In the then state of party feeling the restriction might have rendered the enactment nugatory but for the growing force of public opinion and the moderating influence of many patricians. Measures demanded by the unanimous voice of the Commons could usually no longer be safely rejected by the Senate, which henceforward sought rather to evade by dilatoriness and distractions whatever it dared not expressly disallow. This provision of the leges Valeriae Horatiae, therefore, effected an important devolution of powers from the comitia centuriata to the concilium plebis, as when a modern legislature confers upon an inferior body authority to frame by-laws, with the limitation that such by-laws, so far as they concern the general public, shall be submitted to, and approved beforehand by, a Government department.

The promulgation of a written code of law, the resuscitation of the tribunate with increased powers, and the recognition of the plebeian concilia had now secured for the commonalty a formidable position in the State. The "trimmers" of the plebs, the scions of the plebeian plutocracy, whose inclinations had hitherto leaned towards the patriciate, now threw

pronounced by the patrician Senators only. The larger body decided upon purely temporal, the smaller (professedly) upon religious considerations, the sincerity of which the Commons would have doubted when applied to plebiscita. For upwards of a century and a half longer (until the lex Hortensia 467) the distinction between lex and plebiscitum was carefully observed.

themselves into the popular movement, and adroitly turned it to their own advantage. Already about 309 urbis their influence in Senate and forum wrung from the reluctant patriciate their consent to the famous plebiscitum of Caius Canuleius, which, by establishing the jus connubii between the two orders, repealed the one anti-popular measure of the XII Tables. Henceforward marriage between a patrician and a plebeian could be justum matrimonium; the offspring was legitimatized, and the most invidious of all class distinctions removed. We shall see later how this measure profoundly modified the law of husband and wife and influenced the whole of society.

Affairs having come to this pass, it is matter for wonderment that the governing classes did not, as a preferable alternative to the unnatural and hybrid position created for them, circumvent the religious difficulties which still separated the orders by a statutory enactment admitting plebeians en masse into the patriciate. In regal times the admission of gentes from outside into the Roman patriciate had been not infrequent. A thoroughly broad-minded policy would have similarly enrolled born citizens of Rome the more readily as the plebs included men who, notwithstanding all disadvantages, had risen to affluence and eminence, men deemed worthy to hold military commands, and even to sit in the Senate. There are various explanations which, combined, probably furnish the answer: The liability of all freeholders to military service had stopped the drain upon the blood of the patriciate, removing the pressing necessity and the habit of new initiations. Moreover, the position of a highly privileged minority in a rising and powerful commonwealth had blunted the ancient ideas of equality, and many patricians who would not start at the notion of acknowledging as equals strangers already holding patrician rank abroad, might hesitate to exalt countrymen of their own, whom constant intercourse had accustomed them to treat as inferiors. And finally, there was the technical difficulty that since the establishment of the Republic, or very soon thereafter, there was no body legally competent to legislate for the patriciate alone,[1] as the plebeian concilia, under the law of 283 U.C., and possibly earlier, could legislate for the plebs.

About or shortly after the period of the XII Tables and the Valerio-Horatian legislation, dates the rise of a new legislative body in Rome, the comitia tributa.[2] In imitation of the system adopted since 283 in the plebeian concilia, the new body consisted of freeholders only, with this difference, that it included, whilst the plebeian assembly excluded, patricians. To it was at first referred the

[1] Mommsen, Forschungen, i. Nichtexistenz patricischer Sonderversammlungen in republikanischer Zeit.

[2] Tribus = districts, or, as we might call them, " constituencies." Their number was increased from time to time, and they had of course lost all connection with the ancient tribal distinctions of Ramnians, Titians, and Luceres.

election of (urban) Quaestors, hitherto nominated by the Consuls, and of the military Quaestors, or officials, created about this time, charged specially with the administration of the war chest. In accordance with the original design, the Tribal Assembly always bore the outward marks of a subordinate legislative body (comitia leviora), and although during the fourth century of the City we find it gradually electing all the minor magistrates, its legislative activity, properly so called, and its limited criminal jurisdiction, do not appear to have been habitually exercised until some time after the institution, in 387, of the Praetor, who convoked and presided over the Tribal Assemblies.[1] No laws are extant creative of the comitia tributa or defining their powers, but apparently their purely legislative competency was limited by law or custom to occasional general legislation on matters of private law.[2] It was a large step in the direction of enlightened democracy. The system of voting in the tribes was viritim,[3] and it appealed to freeholders of moderate fortune (whose influence, by the voting procedure in the centuries, had been too frequently swamped through the artificial preponderance of the wealthy), whilst the exclusion of non-freeholders from the tribes still kept at bay the riff-raff of the town, the

[1] The oldest known lex tributa dates from 422; Mommsen, Römische Forschungen, i, 160.

[2] Muirhead, Roman Law, sec. 17.

[3] That is, the freeholders of each district (tribus) voted equally, and the vote of the majority was then the vote of the district. In early Rome all voting was open.

enfranchised slaves and improvident proletariat. Like those of the centuries, the tribal enactments were leges, binding the whole people, subject to the auctoritas of the patrician Senate.

NOTE TO CHAPTER VIII

The rise and progress of the comitia tributa and concilia plebis have occasioned more controversy than any other of the Roman institutions. Far from laying themselves open to the reproach, sometimes addressed to writers on International Law, of "following each other like sheep," it may almost be said of the modern Romanists on this head, that tot homines quot sententiae. Most of them defend their views with German thoroughness and German disputatiousness, and he who has essayed to explore the chaos of conflicting opinion may be pardoned if he find his task more irksome than edifying. Regarding the gradual assumption of legislative functions by the (patricio-plebeian) comitia tributa and plebeian concilia respectively, and their relations *inter se* and towards the State, I have ventured to prefer, on the whole, the view elaborated by Soltau in his Gueltigkeit der Plebiscita, which, though drawing somewhat upon the imagination to amplify, does not go the length of arbitrarily altering the Livian text. We find three separate enactments of the comitia centuriata, each using almost identical language regarding plebiscita:

1. That introduced by the Consuls L. Valerius and M. Horatius about 305 : ut quod tributim plebs jussisset, populum teneret. (Livy, iii, 55, 67; Dionysius, xi, 8, gives a similar account.)

2. That introduced by Q. Publilius Philo, whilst Dictator in 415, of whom Livy says (viii, 12): "tres leges secundissimas plebei, adversas nobilitati tulit : unam, ut plebiscita omnes Quirites tenerent; alteram, ut legum, quae comitiis centuriatis ferrentur, ante initium suffragium Patres auctores fierent: tertiam, ut alter utique ex plebe, cùm eò ventum sit ut utrumque plebeium consulem fieri liceret, censor crearetur."

3. The lex Hortensia de plebiscitis in 467 to the effect, ut quod plebs jussisset omnes Quirites teneret. (Livy, xi, 26; Pliny, N. H., xvi, 15.)

Mommsen appeals to the dicta of the Roman jurists on the subject of the Hortensian law (Römische Forschungen, i, 200), and points out (*ibid.*, Die patricisch-plebejischen Comitien) the absence of all trace of the rise and gradual growth of the (patricio-plebeian) comitia tributa as a legislative body, unless the Valerian and Publilian laws are referable thereto. Concluding that they are so referable, he would have the Valerian enactment read: "ut quod populus tributim jussisset populum teneret" (a most awkward phrase), and considers the rendering of the Publilian measure to have been mutilated (entstellt). It seems impossible to disregard Soltau's misgivings (Gült. d. Pleb., pp. 8, 113 ff.) at reconstructions of ancient texts by which their apparent meaning is vitally changed without obvious necessity. Soltau plausibly explains the non-existence of any special enactment creative of the patricio-plebeian Tribal Assembly, by pointing (pp. 82 ff., 114 ff.) to the probably accidental origin of that body, which, the precedent once established for the elections of minor magistrates, it was afterwards found convenient and (from a popular point of view) advantageous to suffer to develop into a subordinate legislative assembly (comitia leviora). Its enactments in all matters within its limited competency were leges, like those of the centuriae, and therefore distinct from plebiscita (Römische Forschungen, i, 155). The effect of these several statutes, so far as they refer to the validity of plebiscita, appears to have been as follows: By the leges Valeriae-Horatiae a plebiscitum, which (by virtue of the lex Publilia Voleronis, 283) already bound the plebs, but not the patriciate where the rights of the latter body would have been affected, was now made generally binding upon the whole Commonwealth, provided the bill (rogatio) had been sanctioned by senatus-consult before the concilium voted upon it. But as there were no means of forcing the Senate to declare itself for or against any rogatio, popular demands could be and frequently were evaded for years by procrastination, and probably the lex Publilia Philonis of 415 (not to be confounded with the earlier lex Publilia) sought to supply legal machinery for forcing the Senate to show its hand

K

(Soltau, Gült. d. Pleb., 148 ff.). At the same time it required that the patrum auctoritas, which the Senate had theretofore been accustomed to confer upon each lex after it had passed the comitia curiata, centuriata, or tributa (as to the last, Soltau *contra*), should be pronounced, or declared to be withheld, beforehand. A later lex Maenia applied the same provision to the elections of magistrates. But the ingenuity of the Senate still contrived to evade the law (Livy, xi, 26), and after a third secession of the plebs (this time to the Janiculum) the lex Hortensia at last placed plebiscita upon the same footing as leges (Aul. Gellius, N. A., xv, 27; Gaius, i, 3; Just., Inst., i, 2, 4). The consequence was that a senatus-consult, which had never been necessary to validate a lex, was now equally unnecessary to validate a plebiscitum; and consequently we find the plebeian scita, after 467, correctly called leges. As, moreover, the patrum auctoritas had sunk to a mere formality through the operation of the statute of 415, nothing seemed now to stand between the popular Assemblies and supreme power. We shall see that, in reality, the result was far different.

CHAPTER IX

FURTHER CONSTITUTIONAL DEVELOPMENTS TO THE
BEGINNING OF THE PUNIC WARS

DOMESTIC affairs during the first centuries
of the Republic pivot upon an incessant three-
cornered struggle. We find the patriciate, formerly
omnipotent in the nation, nay, the nation itself,
gradually pressed back from its vantage-ground by
sheer weight of numbers; and unlike the English,
the Roman plebs is enabled to maintain with scarcely
any vicissitudes a continuous though deliberate progress in one direction. The masses, mainly swayed
by economic preoccupations, clamour for land, and
"novas tabulas," which mean partial repudiation of
their debts. The "nobility" of the plebs, like our
early Whigs, combine with jealousy for the rights of
property, and too great tolerance of jobbery, a robust
patriotism and sound though narrow political intelligence. Those marked out by birth, wealth, or talent
for the leadership of the plebs, boldly aspire to the
reins of government, though in so doing they must
ride rough-shod over time-honoured considerations
of State and gentile religion. They would have
derided the modesty or caution of the mediaeval

English Commons who deprecated advising upon questions of State policy,[1] as they would have contemned the poor spirit of the sleek bourgeois in Faust, who was not ashamed to say:

> Dankt Gott mit jedem Morgen
> Dass ihr nicht braucht für's Röm'sche Reich zu sorgen,
> Ich halt' es wenigstens für reichlichen Gewinn,
> Dass ich nicht Kaiser oder Kanzler bin.

But as the domestic cult belonged exclusively to the family, so, in the estimation of the patriciate, the cult of the City belonged exclusively to those families who had originally founded it. A magistrate who neglected the sacred rites prescribed by ancient form was unthinkable. Yet their performance by a plebeian was accounted impious, and amid the wreck of prerogative the patriciate still preserved its exclusive privilege of magisterial office. Against this palladium of the superior order ambitious plebeians now levelled attacks which for many years convulsed the Commonwealth. Most of the patricians professed, sincerely or otherwise, to defend the State's sacred institutions, whilst their opponents claimed that personal merit must not be eclipsed by antiquated questions of form, and that, rightly considered, every part of the public cult was the birthright of the Roman citizen.

It seemed at first impossible that common ground could ever be reached, and the consulate remained patrician for further eighty years after the Valerio-

---

[1] Hallam, Europe during the Middle Ages, p. 486.

Horatian Reform. As a kind of compromise, the annual practice of electing Consuls was occasionally departed from, and a number of war tribunes,[1] who might be patricians or plebeians, with consular powers, were now annually chosen by the comitia centuriata, on the plausible pretence that two generals were insufficient to direct military operations simultaneously in several theatres of war.

The uniform successes of the popular party should have demonstrated to the patriciate their powerlessness when confronted by the united forces of the plebs, yet they persisted by manifold devices in fighting a losing battle. Foreseeing the inevitable conquest of the consulate by the Commons, they contrived betimes to temporarily snatch an important part of its power by creating the censorship[2] (312 urbis), to which were transferred the administration of the Exchequer, and the right and duty of periodically revising the lists of senators and citizens. Compensation was found by the plebs when, in 333, the comitia tributa successfully insisted upon the admissibility of plebeians to the quaestorship.

But the desiderated reforms were economic as well as political. The wealthy plebeians, indeed, though they aspired to complete equality with patri-

---

[1] The number might vary as circumstances required, Livy, iv, 16. The tribuni militum consulari potestate must not be confused with the older military tribunes, who were mere army officers, and not magisterial officials.

[2] The censors' term of office was originally five years, afterwards reduced to eighteen months. Livy, iv, 24.

cians, had no incentive, beyond the public spirit and probity of the more enlightened among them, to reform administrative abuses which redounded to their own increasing advantage. To the poorer classes of the plebs, on the other hand, the right of lawful intermarriage with the patriciate, or eligibility for high office of State, seemed of small import when measured with the demand for juster distribution of public lands and mitigation of the debtor's burden.

The two currents clearly appear in the legislation of the period, and particularly in the Licinian Rogations, which, after years of obstinate opposition, the united plebeian order ultimately (387 urbis) imposed as laws upon the patriciate. They were: (1) Discontinuance of the consulary tribunate; (2) Resumption of the consular regimen with the proviso that henceforward at least one Consul should always be a plebeian; (3) Admission of plebeians to the priestly college having charge of the Sibylline books, the number of members being increased from two to ten (decemviri sacris faciundis), a demand probably prompted by suspicion of the sincerity of patrician priests; (4) Prohibition that any single citizen should graze more than 100 head of cattle and 500 sheep upon the State domains, or possess more than 500 jugera (about 330 English acres) of land; (5) Obligation upon landholders to employ a minimum number of free labourers proportioned to the number of slaves; and (6) Relief to debtors by deducting from the unpaid principal of outstanding debts all interest theretofore paid, and by extending the time for repayment of the balance. Even now the law itself, as between creditor and debtor, was not changed. It was many years later (in 428 or 462) that the lex Poetilia effected the release of all nexi, and, though not abolishing nexal contract as between creditor and debtor altogether, deprived it of most of its advantages from the former's point of view, whilst modifying in favour of the latter the process of law whereby he could become addictus.[1]

Already in 312 the patriciate had sought to break the fall by detaching censorial from consular powers. With the like end in view, and with equal inefficacy, the judicial functions of the Consul now (387) became attributed to the praetorship, and curule[2] Ædiles were created to discharge the duties of police and municipal administration over the heads of their plebeian namesakes. From both these offices commoners were disqualified for a time—but only for a time—on religious considerations of more or less cogency. These and other manœuvres prolonged, without modifying, the issue of the long class-struggle, and it is tedious, and, for present purposes, unnecessary to follow in detail the events whereby every politic-

---

[1] Muirhead, Roman Law, sect. 31. The cessio bonorum, which discharged the debtor entirely on his surrendering the whole of his estate to his creditors, was only introduced towards the end of the Republic, or later.

[2] Only the superior magistrates could sit in the sella curulis, or chair of high office, which was originally emblematic of the kingly power.

ally important office of State was in turn rendered accessible to the masses.[1]

Futile to effect the purpose aimed at, the successive segregations of special functions from the consular office nevertheless bore important constitutional consequences. Under the oldest Constitution the executive power, or imperium, was undivided and indivisible; and the King who entrusted the discharge of part of his duties to a deputy, could revoke his commission

[1] Following are the chief magisterial and sacral offices of political importance, in the order in which they successively became opened to plebeian candidates:

OFFICES.		INSTITUTED IN		PLEBEIANS MADE ELIGIBLE IN	
		A.U.C.	B.C.	A.U.C.	B.C.
Military tribunes with Consular power . .		309	445	309	445
Quaestor . . . *circa*		252	501		
		(as a permanent office)		333	421
Military quaestor . .		307	447		
Magister equitum *circa*		252	501	386	368
Consul . . . . *circa*		243	510	387	366
Curule aedile		387	366	387	366
				(patricians and plebeians to be elected in alternate years)	
Dictator . . . *circa*		252 *	501	398	356
Censor		312	442	403	351
Praetor		387	366	417	337
Augur		immemorial		454	300
Pontifex				(first pleb. pontifex maximus actually elected in 502)	
Pontifex maximus *circa*		243	510		
Interrex		immemorial		Never	
Flamines majores . .					
Rex sacrorum . . .					

* Doubtful, see Livy, ii, 18.

at pleasure. Even under the earlier consulate this indivisibility was clung to in theory, each Consul being invested with the full imperium without any attempted apportionment, although the appointment of Quaestors suggested that the old rule now stood less firmly. But the deliberate creation of offices having separate competencies of their own, and ranking co-ordinately with the consulship, entirely disposed of the old idea of undivided imperium, and by weakening the magistracy, further confirmed and amplified the influence of the Senate, which laws like the Publilian and Hortensian had been deliberately designed to undermine.

Under the regal and the earliest republican Constitutions, the chief Magistrates had largely dominated the people, whilst themselves subjected in an increasing degree to the influence of the Senate. The course of ages had transformed them to little more than adjuncts of that body. The old notion of single, undivided mastery, had given place to a system of officialism in which duties and responsibilities were departmentally apportioned in a manner not unlike the practice of modern nations. Although the principal Magistrates were chosen by the people, they remained for the most part amenable to the Senate, which could always checkmate a refractory Consul by the exercise of its power to appoint a Dictator. The tribunate lost its former special significance when the political conditions which prompted its creation no longer existed; and the Tribunes, once

the champions of the radical party, and constitutionally outside the magistracy, gradually assumed the
character of ordinary State officials, being recruited
almost exclusively from the plebeian aristocracy.

The State still consisted, as from the beginning,
of the National Assembly, the Senate and the Magistracy, but their relative positions and influence had
shifted considerably. The oldest national assembly,
the comitia curiata, had practically passed out of
public life as a law-giving body, and was represented
at its formal sittings by a handful of lictors. The
comitia centuriata exercised supreme criminal jurisdiction, elected the chief Magistrates, and still fulfilled their most ancient function of sanctioning
declarations of war. Since, probably, the lex Hortensia, they also voted upon treaties of peace and
alliance. Nearly all other legislative power was
nominally exercised either by the patricio-plebeian
comitia tributa or the plebeian concilium, the distinction between the two bodies being wellnigh
effaced owing to the reforms of the last two centuries and the enormous numerical preponderance.
of the lower order. Originally the assemblies had
excluded from membership citizens not holding land.
These latter, who had meanwhile been made liable
to military service, in course of time were, after
some hesitation, admitted to Centuries and Tribes,
in such manner as to diminish, without however
quite destroying, the ancient predominance of wealth
in the former, and of the responsible middle classes

in the latter. Yet it is curious to observe how the nominally supreme popular bodies defeated their own object by striving for more authority than they could wisely administer. The fickle and superficial Commons too palpably required the corrective of superior foresight and expert knowledge, and the Senate, besides absorbing in great part the powers of the magistracy, even succeeded, by the middle of the fifth century, in increasing its former formidable influence over the Legislature, despite all previous efforts to reduce it. We have already alluded to the complete failure of the Roman mind to evolve a method of government by popularly elected representatives. The system by which all Roman burghers assembled, when duly summoned, to vote negatively or affirmatively upon any project of law by the Magistrate submitted, had worked well enough in a territorially and numerically diminutive community of primitive habits and with an archaic administration. The growing complexity of political life demanded intelligent interest, consistent attention, and constant intercommunication, if private citizens were to make their influence felt in the State. This was only possible when storm and stress supplied the driving-power. After its victorious struggles, the popular party was content to enjoy the comparative prosperity afforded by internal reforms and expansion abroad. The extension of the Roman territory alone sufficed to hinder political organization by permanently ensuring the absence of large numbers of citizens from the comitia. It likewise relieved the pressure of population and drew off the more restless elements. Under these circumstances, and with rules of procedure which placed the assembly nearly at the mercy of an energetic presiding magistrate, the comitia lost both the prestige and the ability to deal satisfactorily with any but the simplest questions, unless with the guidance of officials, who were themselves virtually nominees of the Senate, and in case of need could, by a Tribune's intercessio or the discovery of an unfavourable augury, defeat any proposed independent action of the citizens.

The Senate was itself subjected to the influence of the Censor, in whose discretion it lay, when periodically revising the lists of Senators and citizens, to exclude unworthy and obnoxious persons. This discretion, however, appears at the period which we have now reached to have been exercised judicially, and not independently of the Senate itself, and it was further curtailed by the Ovinian law, which enacted that no person having occupied at any time the position of Consul, Praetor, or Curule Ædile, should be so excluded, unless for good reason assigned. Moreover, annulling the old rule that patricians only might take part in the senatorial debates, it was laid down that this right should now belong, without distinction, to all higher ex-officials. As the latter had been at one or other time elected (at all events nominally) by the people, the Senate might not unjustly regard itself as a quasi-representative body, which by reason of superior knowledge and matured experience was certainly more fitted than the comitia for responsible rule. Notwithstanding some corruption and nepotism, the Senate of the fifth century stands out as one of the most efficient governments the world had, or has, seen. The fact that the more influential members had themselves held high office, and might expect to do so again, secured a fairly harmonious co-operation with the acting magistrates, which ordinarily removed complex questions of policy from the ken of a public unable to appreciate their intricacies.

The legislation, of which the Licinian reforms are the type, shows clearly the nature of the compromise effected between the privileged patriciate, the rich plebeians, and the masses. Social dignity and politically innocuous religious functions the patriciate still affect to regard as their peculiar patrimony, whilst sharing the substance and emoluments of office with their plebeian rivals. The wealthy classes generally, to secure quiet enjoyment of their privileges, consent to a certain amount of undisguised confiscation, and to mitigate, though not entirely to remove, the misuse of State property, by allowing to their humbler fellow citizens a somewhat inadequate participation.

Whilst approving the overthrow of an antiquated system based upon decayed prejudices, it is idle to deny that political contests, then as now, were seldom conducted with wholly clean weapons. Whether the Licinian provision, ne quis amplius quam quingenta agri jugera possideret, referred only to realty in private ownership, or to State land as well, the object of the restriction was to artificially depreciate by compulsory sales the property of those who were unfortunate enough to have invested capital in land interests beyond the new statutory limit.[1] Even less defensible was the treatment meted out to creditors. In this respect, not only the Licinian, but all the popular legislation was frankly dishonest. The generous, but mischievous, tendency of ill-balanced minds is to ignore the standpoint of the oppressor, whilst extolling his victims as models of all the virtues, and grave political errors have been committed by assuming a capacity for just and efficient self-government in backward communities, merely because they had been governed unjustly and inefficiently by an autocracy. With the Roman capitalist, hauteur frequently turned to insolence, and severity to outrage; yet the so-called popular legislation, whilst powerless to prevent either, actually entrenched his monopoly by depressing the middle class; since men of moderate fortune dared not to

[1] Ortolan, p. 181. One can scarcely refrain from sympathizing with the words put by Livy (vi, 41) into the mouth of Appius Claudius: "quia pecunias alienas, quia agros dono dant: tanta dulcedo est ex alienis fortunis praedandi," referring to Sextius and Licinius. But possideret might after all only apply to possessores (precarious holders of State domains) not freeholders. Even so, it was a great hardship to bonâ fide holders.

engage in business with the knowledge that contract and property were the football of politicians.
Failure to redeem a promise was considered dis-
graceful as between honourable men, and unde-
serving of sympathy. On the default of a debtor,
the first impulse would not be one of compassion,
and a creditor seeking to enforce his bond could only
proceed against the *person* of his debtor, who, if
fraudulently inclined, could not be compelled by any
process of law to surrender his property in satisfaction;[1] neither did execution involve any loss of
civic rights to the debtor, or bring his family within
the power of the creditor.[2] The latter's remedy was
to obtain what he could by personal coercion, and,
in a hard age, duress would readily take the form
of physical mal-treatment. For the Legislature to
condone default, and declare that interest paid should
count as repayment of capital, was spoliation. To
prohibit interest altogether was folly. It is not
astonishing that the creditor's terms, and his conduct on their non-fulfilment, became harsher in
proportion to the risk he ran of seeing his rights
arbitrarily overridden for reasons of mere political
expediency. Finally, the popular movement, however justifiable in itself, was not conducted by its
leaders with that sincerity which inspires respect, even
where agreement is withheld. That it was largely

[1] F. de Coulanges, Cité Antique, 75, writes in the same sense,
though apparently he is thinking of landed property only.
[2] Livy, ii, 24.

in the hands of well-to-do plebeian politicians, who exploited the misery of the masses to further their own political advancement, explains the obstinacy with which the patriciate continued to hold aloof as a privileged class long after the substance of privilege had been destroyed.[1] The author of the famous Licinian Rogations was himself the first offender against his own measure, for the dishonest evasion of which he was heavily fined.[2]

The era of triangular class struggle practically closed with the passing of the Licinian laws, and it may be said that in the ensuing century Rome's polity, though unsound at the base, for the time approached nearer to the Republican ideal than any other community of classical or mediaeval times. The age of elegant literature had scarcely dawned; and that wonderful system of law which still sways the legists of Continental Europe as yet awaited its evolution under Praetorian Equity. But all the essentials of a high civilization were present, if some of its elegancies were lacking. It was a period of solid, but not flamboyant, prosperity, a prosperity which, albeit largely built upon the ruin of other communities, yet tended to the ultimate good of mankind. Old social barriers were removed, and

---

[1] Mommsen is exceedingly severe upon the old aristocracy, but one cannot help suspecting some of his strictures to have been coloured for the benefit of his own Prussian Junker, a term he constantly applies to the Roman patriciate.

[2] Livy, vii, 16.

the later class distinctions were as yet unobtrusive, though present in embryo. The equestrian order did not, until after the Punic Wars, emerge as a separate, privileged ring of usurers, forestallers, and tax-farmers. The families which swayed the Commonwealth had not unlearned the lessons of moderation, and the assertiveness of a superior class is pardoned if equipoised by self-restraint. Although we need not literally accept the accounts of Senators leaving the plough to assume the command of armies, and subsequently returning to it,[1] still the Roman gentry lived for the most part upon their estates as simple country squires, who wisely refrained from marking disparities of fortune by vulgar ostentation of living. To battle they led forth troops of hardy peasants, whose service in the field was now[2] requited by the State with money payments, strong in the conviction of inner worth, fortified by the knowledge of former triumphs, and their discipline as yet unspoilt by the lavishness of the war-god's favours. Not the adventitious genius of individual leaders but the disciplined valour of the people as a whole successively overthrew Latin and Volsce, Tuscan and Gaul, Samnite and Greek and Tarentine.[3] Upon the nations of Italy, as upon a whetstone, the

[1] Cf. Val. Max., iv, 4, 5.

[2] Since the siege of Veii (captured 358 urbis) when for the first time the Roman army kept the field for several years without disbanding for the winter.

[3] Cf. Bryce, Studies, i, 59.

Romans sharpened not only their swords but their wits. A wise diplomacy sought to perpetuate the fruits of martial success by conferring upon vanquished cities, and newly-established Roman Colonies, a judiciously graduated scale of civic rights. Above all, the unique juridical genius of the Romans tended to fortify their dominion over peoples who reluctantly admired the strength and symmetry of the new dispensation. Only the prestige of acknowledged moral superiority could have withstood the terrible strain to which Hannibal was shortly to subject the fidelity of the socii. It is significant that when, towards the end of the Republic, the allied and vassal nations revolted from Rome, they could devise no political institutions which were not slavishly copied from the conquerors.

Although earlier premonitory symptoms were not wanting, the decadence of the old-Roman system of politics and morals first gathered its momentum in the reaction which succeeded the tremendous tension of the first two Punic wars. If, at this turning-point, Roman ambition could have confined itself within the limits of Europe, had Roman statesmanship at this stage exerted its peculiar virtues to consolidate its conquests rather than to extend them, had Carthage [1] been left to work out its own destiny, and the two leading civilizations—the European and the Semitic—to develop on natural lines, the corruption of Western blood and culture could have

[1] Cicero, De Rep., i, 48.

been arrested, and a free, national Italy might have found time to reclaim barbarian Europe before yielding up the sceptre of empire. It was not to be. The Punic wars displayed at its apogee the high standard of citizenship which had erected Rome's greatness. The Romans had owed their conquests to their virtues; they were now to owe their vices to their conquests. With the ensuing subjugation of Africa and Greece and Egypt began freedom's long drawn-out agony. Worse than the luxury which the plunder of Empires supplied, worse even than the strange depravities introduced from East and South, was the destruction of mental balance in a ruling coterie called suddenly to wield an all-wide and irresponsible power at a moment when the old morality was nearly dead, and the new as yet un-born. Worst of all was the progressive demoralization of a denationalized metropolitan populace, which had forgotten how to work, think, or fight, and in the end existed only to decide by its venal vote which group of politicians, by maintaining it in pauperized indolence, had purchased the privilege of exploiting a subject world.

CHAPTER X

MARRIAGE

MARRIAGE (even if the term be restricted to unions intended to be durable) is older than any definite system of religion,[1] and with the most primitive, as with the most modern, of mankind, was probably a matter only of sentiment, business, or convenience. Ancestor-worship placed marriage upon a higher, or at least a different plane when it taught that the repose and well-being of the dead depended upon the ministrations of the living, demanding the maintenance of the sacred fire, and faithful performance of regular sacrifices, by a never-ending line of legitimate descendants. The old-Aryan conception of wedlock, as an incident of the ancestral cult, was exclusively religious. The ancestor-worshipper entered upon matrimony in fulfilment of a sacred duty to raise up offspring having both the right and the obligation to continue the family. And this was the central idea which coloured and pervaded the earlier Roman marriage-practice.

Before the Italiot hordes had crystallized into

[1] Cf. Westermarck, Human Marriage, 50.

cities and polities, the ceremonial constituting recognized marriage would be the concern of the gens, or at most, the two gentes, within which it took place. Excepting unions by confarreatio, which we shall specially consider later, marriage in Rome was a private act, solemnized without any intervention of the State, although the pontifical college had doubtless, in very early times, already laid down certain ceremonies as the minimum necessary to establish justae nuptiae[1] in Rome. In every case the essence of legitimate union was the consent and approbation of the gods, to obtaining and witnessing which nearly the whole of the prescribed ceremonial was directed. In this it must be taken that all Roman citizens—patrician, client, and plebeian—stood alike. It is unthinkable that such a community as archaic Rome ever tolerated conditions under which irregular unions were the sole sexual relations possible to the majority. It is, to my mind, equally inadmissible, having regard to what has been said in former chapters, that any purely civil form of marriage can have been recognized or widely practised in the early days of the State. It was not until the importance of the religious aspect had weakened in the popular imagination before the encroachments

[1] Originally nuptiae meant strictly the ceremonies attending the formation of the marriage-tie; matrimonium, the tie itself. The latter expression was at first employed to denote unions not religiously consecrated (or at least which did not rely for their validity upon ritual), which stricter patricians were inclined to regard as a lower form of marriage.

of a self-reliant, mundane jurisprudence, that certain
civil attributes came in course of time to be held
necessary and sufficient to "just" marriage, without
inquiry whether divine approval had or had not been
sought and obtained. The later law ignored the
religious element, and prescribed as the sole essentials of marriage: Connubium, Marriageable age,
Consent of the parties (usually manifested by the
domum deductio), and Consent of the eldest living
male ancestor where a contracting party was alieni
juris. The bridegroom, if more than one of his male
ancestors were alive, required the consent of all of
them. Although traceable in part to the jus sacrum
and the jus divinum, these essentials represent the
formalization of legists who apparently never attempted to comprehend their history. Yet through
long ages of unbelief and materialism, ancient religious forms continued to be observed to an extent
which depended mainly upon public opinion and
individual predilection.

The luckiest time for weddings was considered to
be the second half of June, May being unsuitable
because of various solemn festivals, during some
of which sexual intercourse was forbidden. The
Roman wedding, like every important enterprise,
was preceded by taking the auspices,[1] and the first

[1] Cicero, De Div., i, 46. Plebeians had originally no right of
active participation in the *public* auspices, and remained to the
last ineligible for the higher priestly offices, but there was nothing
to prevent their taking auspices on private occasions, or, if

act of the marriage ceremony was the sacrifice.
Every form of life, animal and vegetable, was held
to be equally the gift of the gods, and procreation
being avowedly the exclusive object of the marriage,
the appeal on such occasions was directed chiefly to
the fertilizing and vitalizing divinities of husbandry.
Flowers decorated the house, and garlands were
worn by bridegroom and bride, kinsfolk and guests.
Great care was bestowed upon the preparation of
the bride. The day preceding the wedding she had
gone through the ceremony of solemnly discarding
the toga praetexta, worn by maidens and boys, which,
with her dolls and toys, were devoted to the gods as
a formal leave-taking of childhood. Invested in her
bridal raiment, the all-white[1] toga pura and tunica
recta woven in the ancient fashion, girdled with the
woollen belt with the knot of Hercules—probably
the precursor of our "lover's knot"—her hair parted
into six locks with the hasta caelibaris,[2] and ar-

ignorant of the formulae, employing an augur to do so. The
divinities consulted were the old Latin and Sabine gods, who,
though in many cases identical at bottom with the more specifi-
cally national deities, were on domestic occasions regarded more
in a homelike and familiar aspect. Thus, the chief patroness of
the nuptial festival was Juno pronuba.

[1] White, the colour most agreeable to the gods (Cic., De Leg., ii,
18), was the usual wear in the early ages. Black was always
mourning wear until the Empire, when vivid hues had become so
fashionable that plain white was considered sufficiently funereal.

[2] Plutarch, Q. Rom., 87. In earliest ages it may have been
customary to cut off the bride's hair with the hasta caelibaris, and
probably a feint was always made of doing so. That ancient

ranged with woollen bands (vittae), her head covered[1] by the flammeum or red veil, symbolizing the sacred fire of the new home at which henceforward she was to worship, and surmounted by a wreath of flowers of her own gathering, she was led into the circle of expectant guests by her pronuba, a married friend who had assumed responsibility for her due preparation. Upon joining of hands by bride and bridegroom—dextrarum junctio[2]—the sacrificial victim, a swine or sheep, was forthwith immolated; but the ceremony would be interrupted, and the projected union postponed or abandoned, upon the detection of any adverse sign during the sacrifice, or any natural disturbance, as a thunderstorm. If nothing of bad omen occurred, the bride would thereupon pace with the bridegroom around the house-altar, preceded by a boy with the hymeneal torch of white-thorn, and followed by other youths who had not yet

instrument was retained as a part of the time-honoured ceremonial, but if, in historical times, a single tress was still severed, it would be with a more modern and convenient appliance. The hasta caelibaris, unlike the ordinary weapon of offence, was curved in shape and did not symbolize the husband's proprietary right. Rossbach, Römische Ehe, 286, 290 ff.

[1] The act of covering the head (nubere, obnubere) gave its distinctive name to the religious marriage ceremonial. But it was always usual to cover the head during worship.

[2] Ad. Pictet, Origines Indo-Europ., ii, 336: "Le contact des mains a été de tout temps le symbole naturel d'une promesse donnée, surtout en ce qui concerne le mariage. . . . La dextrarum junctio faisait partie, chez les Romains, de la cérémonie des noces." Cf. Pliny, H. N., xi, 45.

doffed the toga praetexta. Towards evening, after a solemn repast, came the domum deductio, simulating the ravishment of the bride from the parental abode, undoubtedly a survival of bygone ages, when nomad Aryan braves had been accustomed by force and stealth to win their partners from neighbouring camps. Fashion ordained that the bride should display reluctance and offer resistance. With mock violence, amid tears and reproaches, she was torn from her mother's arms, dragged from the house, and led through the streets, between two of the youths who had already officiated. Spindle and distaff, symbols of her housewifely duties, were carried after her, relatives and guests, and probably an uninvited crowd, followed in a kind of triumphal procession. The bridegroom, going before, scattered nuts to the children in token that he had put away childish things, the wedding fescennines[1] were chanted and shouts of Talasse![2] rent the air. At

[1] The name was said to be derived from the Etruscan town Fescennium. Sometimes the opportunity would be seized to grossly vilipend unpopular personages by singing libellous verses, a practice against which one of the enactments of the XII Tables is supposed to have been specially directed. But usually the fescennini were merely rough popular doggerel, perhaps largely improvised, in which the occasion was improved with bucolic coarseness and plain speaking: "procax fescennina locutio," Catullus, Carm., 61; "joci veteres obscoenaque dicta," Ovid, Fast., iii. In this form they may have somewhat resembled the Schnadahüpfeln of the Tyrolese and Bavarian peasants. Fastidious ears would probably prefer the latter.

[2] The Romans continued to repeat formulas and invocations long after their significance had been forgotten, and no classical

the entrance of her new home the husband advanced
to meet her, and upon his asking who she was, she
pronounced the solemn formula, Ubi tu Gaius, ego
Gaia.[1] She bound the doorposts with wool to symbolize her wifely duties in the household, and anointed
them, in sign of fertility, with wolf's or swine's fat.
She was then lifted over the threshold,[2] fire and
water were offered to mark her introduction into the

writer has satisfactorily explained the meaning of Talasse. Probably Talassus was an ancient Sabine god, whom Rossbach believes
to have been identical with Consus. (Römische Ehe, 347.) Livy's
explanation is, of course, as mythical as the remainder of the
episode he describes.

[1] Possibly this pronouncement may have been made a second
time when the marriage was coemptione. Perhaps the formula
denoted that the bride had now adopted her husband's name.
Mommsen, R. F., i, 11; Karlowa, R. Rechtsg., ii, 156. A more
likely explanation, to my mind, is given by Rossbach (Röm.
Ehe, 355) following Plutarch. Gaius (oldest form Gavius) is connected with a word signifying "cattle," which in primitive society
stood for wealth in general. The sentiment expressed is, therefore, "Where thou art Lord (the owner of cattle) there am I
Mistress." Rossbach mentions, only to reject, a less delicate interpretation. Possibly, however, nothing more was meant than that
a man had found his complement. Gaius was a common name,
and the formula might have the homely meaning: Wherever
thou, Jack, art, there will I, Gill, be.

[2] This is by some supposed to have been part of the mock
violence used towards the bride. But if the order of the events
is correctly given above, she had before entry already evidenced
by word and deed her acceptance of the situation, and further
force was meaningless. Perhaps she was lifted over to avoid an
omen; an unfortunate stumble upon the threshold would have
condemned the marriage as unhappy; cf. Catullus, Carm. 61,
"transfer omine cum bono limen aureolos pedes."

new cult, a coin was handed to the husband to represent her dowry, and another presented as an
offering to the house Lares, a third having been
previously dropped in the street to propitiate the
spirits of the crossways—Lares compitales. She
then retired with the pronuba, who prepared the
nuptial bed, which the husband was not permitted
to approach until night had set in. On the following
morning, the guests having reassembled, the young
wife took her place beside her husband and performed
her first sacrifice at his ancestral altar.

The picturesque and impressive ceremony, of
which only the salient features have been handed
down to us, continued, though not without modification, to form part of the nuptials of most Roman
maids throughout the pagan period. But in historical
times it was, except in confarreate marriages, without
influence upon the legal status of the spouses *inter
se*, and the secular law, which overlay sacral custom,
left auspices and ritual to be observed or neglected
at the caprice of the individual, demanding only
Connubium, Marriageable Age, or Puberty, and
Consent. We have now to inquire how far these
requirements were themselves the products of considerations which had their root in prehistoric
conditions.

Connubium.—Connubium was uxoris jus ducendae
facultas, the right of contracting a valid ("just")
marriage according to the civil law of Rome, and
founded upon sanctified custom (fas), statutory enact-

ment, or international treaty. Originally designed to prevent intermarriage between persons too closely related by blood, or strangers who were not associated in cult, the rules of connubium were both exogamous and endogamous. The table of prohibited degrees was widely drawn, extending originally, it is believed, so as to include second cousins, and in this respect it was immaterial whether the relationship was agnatic or cognatic, and of the full or half blood. It may have been that the ancient Aryans understood the dangers arising from marriages between persons very closely related by blood; or that the precaution arose from sound primordial instinct.[1] But it seems equally easy to assume that the true motive lay in moral, rather than physiological considerations. The intimate association which continued to exist among gentiles and familiares in the early days of Rome admitted and compelled, among closely related persons of opposite sexes, a degree of familiarity which was considered innocuous only so long as the mind was habituated to regard them in the light of brothers and sisters, repelling as incestuous any suggestion of sexual intercourse.[2] Accordingly, we are prepared to find, and do find, the restrictions upon connubium due to

---

[1] Cf. Westermarck, History of Human Marriage, cc. 14, 15.

[2] Following this order of ideas, it seems reasonable to suppose that the prohibited degrees were co-extensive with the circle of the jus osculi. Cf. Plutarch, Q. R., 6; Muirhead, R. L., 26; Smith, Dictionary, ii, 139; Bryce, Studies, ii, 411. But contra Rossbach, R. Ehe, 434.

relationship relaxed in later ages,[1] when the gentile bond no longer involved habitual physical propinquity; a relaxation in no way connected with the slackening of the moral sense among society at large.

Persons who, though strangers in blood, had become agnatically related at law by adrogation or adoption, were under the like disability, which, however, ceased when the artificial agnatic tie was severed by emancipation, except in regard to those who had stood closest in the adoptive relationship.[2] Parents could not marry their children's widows or widowers, nor step-parents their step-children.[3]

Perhaps the intimacy produced, if not by habitual domestic fellowship, at least by frequent personal intercourse, may have originally prompted the withholding of connubium between gentilis and gentilicia (or gentilicius), as it would also explain why there could be no just marriage between patron (or patrona) and liberta (or libertus); notwithstanding that in each case there was to some extent community of cult. But in the historical period the bar to intermarriage was undoubtedly the servile descent, or the quasi-servile position of one of the parties. The old form of clientage was already obsolescent in the

---

[1] The prohibited degrees were first narrowed in the sixth century urbis, after the first Punic War. Subsequently, marriage between first cousins was permitted. Later still, for the convenience of the Emperor Claudius, intermarriage with a brother's daughter was legalized, but scarcely any one availed himself of the permission (Suetonius on Claudius), and it was again prohibited by Constantine.

[2] Gaius, i, 59, 61.   [3] *Ibid.*, i, 63.

early Republic, and the lex Canuleia did not exclude clients from its benefits. But the taint of servile birth forbade just marriages of freed with freeborn persons generally, and they were not expressly legalized until the early Principate.[1]

Whilst the Roman citizen was denied the right to wed his near relatives, the policy of the older society had been, nevertheless, to confine the scope of alliances; and marriage outside the gens—gentis ecnuptio —when allowed, was originally subjected to special supervision. Probably a client was at one time unable to look beyond his gens at all for a yokemate. A gentilis could contract just marriage with the member of another gens; and so could a citizen with the citizen of a foreign State, if connubium with its nationals had been established by immemorial custom or special treaty between the cities.[2] The jus connubii had perhaps always existed between Rome and most of the Latin cities, perhaps also with some cities of Etruria. We have seen that all or nearly all Latium was to some extent united in a common cult, and that a large proportion of the divine lore of Rome undoubtedly originated from beyond Tiber. Originally, as has already been pointed out, the unattached Roman plebs had neither the sacral community, which was the normal postulate

---

[1] Dig., xxiii, 2, 23. Mommsen, Staatsrecht, iii, 429-30. Senators and their descendants were still excepted.

[2] Intermarriage with barbarians always remained in bad odour. Milesne Crassi conjuge barbara turpis maritus vixit? Horace, Odes, iii, 5.

of intermarriage, with patricians, nor the faculty extended to recognized political bodies, of concluding solemn compacts in their corporate capacity. But the Leges Sacratae, which were in form and substance analagous with treaties between independent nations, advantageously altered the status of the plebs, and the lex Canuleia in 307 urbis removed the unnatural barrier.

It seems difficult to escape the conclusion that what is called confarreatio, which, according to the Roman legists of a later age, was the distinguishing characteristic of patrician marriage, was originally the ceremony peculiarly applicable to inter-gentile alliances only. The old Roman marriage service must have been substantially as we have already described it, for marriages of all kinds. The alleged distinguishing incidents of confarreatio are the use of the far, or sacred cake, the seating of the nubentes upon a sheepskin, certain spoken formulas (certa et solemnia verba),[1] particulars of which have not been transmitted to us, the assistance of the principal State priests, and the presence of a prescribed fixed number of ten witnesses. But it is exceedingly doubtful whether the cake of far, or spelt, though it gave its name to the ceremony, was peculiar to confarreate marriage; nor is it easy to assign to the sheepskin its special significance, assuming it to have played a part in the confarreate ceremony only. On the other hand, the presence of representatives of the

---

[1] Gaius, i, 112.

State is, without special exigency, inexplicable. If anywhere, Government concurrence was superfluous in ordinary marriages between patricians. Marriage was entirely a domestic matter of the gens, and later of the family; the gentile sacra, far from requiring external assistance, had laid down the ceremony in its essentials long before Rome had existed as a political entity, and the whole trend of the gentile tradition was antagonistic to the intrusion of the State. I cannot help thinking Professor Cuq[1] correct in his conjecture that the presence of State priests and the ceremony known as confarreation were usual only with intermarriages between persons of different gentes. On such occasions the presence both of high priests and witnesses is useful and natural. A gentilis was about to renounce her sacra, and deprive her kinsmen of tutelage and other rights *in posse*. The rule (which afterwards passed into law) that flamines

---

[1] Cuq, Institutions juridiques, p. 208. " Le mariage est resté un acte d'ordre purement privé, qui n'est soumis pour sa formation à d'autres règles que celles qui résultent des usages domestiques et de la religion." The absence of a minister of religion from a marriage ceremony need not denote that a slighter degree of sanctity attached to it. Even under the Christian Emperors no ecclesiastical benediction was required before the ninth century A.D., and then only in the East Roman Empire. In Western Europe, privately celebrated marriages were recognized until a Decree of the Council of Trent (A.D. 1563) expressly demanded the presence of a priest and witnesses (Pothier, Traité du Mariage, in vol. iii, 284-291; Blackstone, Comm., i, c. xv, says: " The intervention of a priest to solemnize this contract (*i.e.* marriage) is merely juris positivi, not juris naturalis aut divini").

majores and reges sacrorum must have been born of
confarreate marriage, perhaps sprang from jealous
precaution against the gradual monopolization of the
principal sacral offices by one or a few gentes, a
rivalry for which seems indicated by the retention of
separate colleges for the cults of Mars and Quirinus,
and of obsolete tribal distinctions. The number of
ten witnesses has so far baffled conjecture. They may
have represented the ten gentes comprised or represented in the bride's curia, or the number may have
been arrived at by doubling the minimum number of
witnesses required to validate an ordinary conveyance.[1] The certa et solemnia verba, in so far as they
may have differed from the received formulas of the
ordinary marriage-service, probably had reference to
the detestatio sacrorum, by which the bride solemnly
dissociated herself from sacral community with her
own gens before entering her husband's.

Unions between persons lacking the jus connubii
with one another thus, in the eye of the public and
of the law, fell into two very distinct classes. Conjugal associations seriously entered into where connubium, though wanting, was not expressly withheld by morality—for instance, the union of a
patrician with a plebeian before the Canuleian Law,
or of a Roman citizen with a peregrina, with whose
State no connubial treaty existed—were readily dis-

---

[1] Marriage was sacred to the benign (as opposed to the
destructive) deities, and even numbers were more agreeable to
the former.

tinguished by society from mere adventitious or promiscuous intercourse, and soon attained to some recognition by the State as matrimonia juris gentium, though they could not confer either manus or patria potestas. But unions of closely-related persons were reputed incestuous: they were not only of no effect civilly, but, whether existing under the form of marriage or otherwise, involved the heaviest penal consequences upon the parties. Children born of such unhallowed loves were deemed accursed and devoted as monsters to the gods. The Decemvirs, by their express prohibition of marriages between patricians and plebeians, which was the proximate cause of the lex Canuleia, maladroitly gave themselves the appearance of branding them as contrary to public decency, and by affecting to cast opprobrium upon a number of existing honourable unions, aroused a righteous and intense indignation at a disability which only now became intolerable.[1]

Marriageable Age. — In the prehistoric period the age-limit, if fixed at all, would be established by the custom of the gens. More probably no such limit existed, and the sole test of nubility was actual puberty in the boy, and viripotency in the girl, determined by physical examination. In course of time the marriageable age became arbitrarily fixed at fourteen for males and twelve[2] for females, limits

[1] Cicero, De Rep., ii, 37.
[2] The earlier age for girls propter votorum festinationem, says Macrobius, Som. Scip., i, 6.

which remained in force throughout the Empire, and still hold good for some countries, including England and Scotland, notwithstanding physical differences induced by race, climate, and civilization. Even marriage between impuberes, though null at the time, became validated by cohabitation of the parties with the intention of entering into marital relations upon puberty. No doubt marriages were usually contracted at what would now be considered a very early age. At seventeen the youth assumed, with the toga virilis,[1] the responsibilities of a full citizen, and probably little time elapsed between that event and taking a mate, for in ancient Rome the right was practically synonymous with the obligation to marry.[2] Economic objections did not, as now, exist against early unions. A son's marriage did not generally change his position in the father's household, where married sons and grandsons with their families continued, during the simpler ages, to reside under one roof.[3] Remaining under the patria potestas, his personal services continued at the disposal of his ancestor, and his very disability to hold property independently strengthened his title to joint enjoyment of the family possessions.

[1] Aul. Gellius, Noct. Att., x, 28.

[2] Cic., De Leg., iii, 3. Cf. Friedländer, Röm. Sittengeschichte, i, 248 ff.

[3] Valerius Maximus, iv, 4, 8, mentions the Aelii, who lived in this manner at a period subsequent to the Punic Wars. It seems that a similar custom has not yet died out in Eastern and South-Eastern Europe; Maine, Early Law and Custom, 239 ff.

As the advent of procreative power produced a right and obligation to exercise it for the propagation of legitimate offspring, liberorum quaerendorum causa, so the converse resulted from its decay; marriage at an advanced age was reprobated by society, and at one period forbidden by law.

Consent.—A man or woman under the power of any person could not marry without that person's consent. Apparently the rigidity of family discipline at first admitted no exception, and children of an imbecile or a madman, who was incapable of consenting, remained in enforced celibacy, pending his decease or return to sanity.[1] Moreover, a grandson in potestate required the consent, not only of his grandfather, but of his father, upon the principle that no man should have an heir forced upon him against his will, as might be the case were the father's consent dispensed with, a precaution unnecessary with women, who married out of their family altogether.

---

[1] Later this was doubted, and the view became general, in the case of daughters at least, that the absence of the father's dissent implied his consent. A constitution of Marcus Aurelius expressly released children of imbeciles from the restriction, but it was reserved to Justinian to finally settle the law in favour of the madman's son, besides effectually providing for the coercion of an unreasonably recalcitrant parent of sound mind. Cod., v, 4, 25. Children of an absent father might validly marry without his consent if the absence lasted longer than three years, or even before the expiry of the three years if the match were a suitable one. Dig., xxiii, 2, 10-11.

Consent of the parties themselves, even though alieni juris, was in historical times certainly equally necessary to a valid marriage. But it has been doubted whether in the earlier period the parent had not the right of giving away his child in marriage even without the child's consent. The more reasonable view seems to be that upon this point the later and the earlier law of Rome coincide. It is true that duty and interest urged the ageing ancestor to make timely provision for the continuance of the family, and an unwilling adolescent was liable to sacerdotal or censorial penalties for neglect of a sacred duty. But there is a wide difference between a general obligation to marry, and forced marriage with an unfavoured partner. The ancient principle expressed by the later maxim, Nemo invitus haeredes suos habere potest, is not, however, of itself sufficient to disprove the theory of compulsory marriage, since the man might deprive himself of heirs by refusal to perform the marital act, and the woman, who for obvious reasons was not equally at liberty to do so, could not originally have heirs at all. In practice, recalcitrancy was probably as rare as it still is among nations where parental authority assumes a quasi-sacred character. Nor need we assume any pronounced inclination for or against a given person among the majority of youthful Romans, whose opportunity of frequent intercourse with the opposite sex was confined to relatives within the prohibited degrees. But although consent might have been

occasionally extorted by pressure, I cannot think
that the ancients would usually conceive a marriage
ceremony performed by compulsion as other than
a desecration of the gods whom it professed to
honour.[1]

MANUS

What was the effect of the marriage act upon the
woman? It is undoubted that in the early ages of
Rome just marriage involved the submission of the
woman to her husband or his ascendant. At civil
law, a wife having passed under the Hand was in
respect of the husband loco filiaefamilias, co-ordinate
with her own daughters, and when a widow, the
ward of her nearest agnates, who would probably be
her own sons. Her subjection to the private jurisdiction of the family-head followed as a matter of
course, and even death was accounted not too grave
a penalty for an injured husband to mete out to the
unchaste or unduteous wife. Except the relationship
of gentilitas, which she retained when married within
her own gens, her civil relationship with her natural
family was snapped. She could no longer inherit ab
intestato of her father, but only, in equal shares with
her own children, of her husband. Property of course,
if alieni juris, she could not have held during her
spinsterhood, but if sui juris at the time of the
marriage cum manu, what property she might have

---

[1] Cf. F. de Coulanges, Cité Antique, p. 429.

possessed passed to the husband, or, if himself in potestate, to his ascendant. Property acquired by her during coverture became the property of the person in whose power she was; but neither she nor her husband could be sued in respect of ante-nuptial debts contracted by herself, until the equitable jurisdiction of the Praetor came to the aid of the creditor.[1]

Would a purely religious marriage, but without confarreation, suffice to bring about this result? We think there can be no doubt that membership of a cult involved a subjection to its Head, only qualified by the rules of the gens and the precepts of the fas; and as no person could simultaneously belong to the cults of two families or gentes, it follows that the marriage of a girl according to rite, and her sacrifice at the husband's house-altar, operated in the earlier ages to separate her from the control of her natural father, and to create over her a new power strictly analogous to, though not at first necessarily identical in every effect with the manus produced by confarreation, coemption or usus.

I have already endeavoured to show that the religious rite by which just matrimony was contracted did not originally involve the presence of State priests, or the other distinguishing characteristics (if any) of the so-called confarreate ceremonial, except in the case of an inter-gentile marriage. Before we consider the incidents of inter-gentile

[1] Gaius, iii, 84; iv, 38, 80.

alliances, it is desirable to study a little closer the nature of manus at civil law.

Nothing is known to us in the nature of manus which would of itself indicate a connection with the ancient law founded upon and derived from religion. The civil law, so far as it concerned itself with the private relations of persons, recognized, as a general rule, exclusively the Heads of Families, a principle which, as we have already seen, had its foundation in the process of the formation of the political community. Where, therefore, a person in potestate was obtruded upon the notice of the law, there was no alternative but to deal with him not directly, as an individual, but relatively, as an integral part of his family, and to throw upon the recognized head of the latter all civil responsibility for his good behaviour, whilst on the other hand admitting an absolute right, equivalent to proprietorship, in the head over his dependant. The same form of action at law enabled the paterfamilias to recover a child, slave, or beast which had been wrongfully withdrawn from his possession, and the law condemned him to make reparation for any damage wrongfully caused by his child, slave, or beast. Manus was originally the general term expressive of the property-owner's dominion, and when human relations began to be regulated by civil law, it was applied to the man's right over his chiefest and most important belonging—his wife. The theory of the law of course in no way corresponded with the relations which existed in

practice between paterfamilias and his dependants.
The corrective of his dominion was left to be supplied
by the sacral law, which recognized and protected
wife, children, and even slaves, as individual partici-
pants of a family cult. Nor did the civil law remain
consistent with its own fiction. Affecting to acknow-
ledge no distinction between a wife or son and a
slave, in reality it distinguished very clearly between
all three. It had consciously attempted to graft a
relatively modern and purely secular law of Property
upon a more ancient religious law of Persons. A
law of property can only have begun to emerge with
any distinctness when the system of gentile common enjoyment was in its decadence, whereas the
authority of the Ancestor reached back into the
ages beyond the great Migration. Accordingly, the
application of proprietary to authoritative rules is
admittedly forced; and the position of the wife—
and to a somewhat lesser degree of the children
—towards the paterfamilias unmistakably discloses
the double set of principles derived from these two
widely separated sources. Thus by analogy with,
but notionally different from Dominium, Usucapio,
Mancipium, we have Manus and Potestas, Usus, Coemptio. The legal status of the wife is still further
discriminated, even at civil law, not only from the
position of a chattel, but from that of a child. Manus
and patria potestas, though constantly brought into
line, are readily distinguishable. Roman jurists
habitually used the words loco esse, to indicate not

an exact but a qualified similarity, and the term,
loco filiaefamilias,[1] no more assigns to the wife for
all purposes the position of her husband's daughter,
than loco servorum is intended to allot to free
persons in mancipio the precise condition of slaves.
Thus, whilst the property of a person in potestate
was at civil law unreservedly at the disposal of the
Head, the property which the wife might bring into
marriage, res uxoria, either in her own right or as
the gift of her relatives, was not necessarily lost to
her for all time. In case of dissolution of the marriage, she had a prima facie right to the return of
part or all. It is true that if the dissolution had been
induced by her own fault, the husband, in the exercise
of the judicium domesticum, might decree its for-
feiture, and the limits assigned by the sacerdocy to
his discretion are not ascertainable; but the distinction clearly marks the wife's status as a thing
apart. It is also doubtful whether manus included,
even at civil law, the right of sale, mancipation, or
noxal surrender of a wife.[2] Again, the husband,
though entitled to appoint by will a tutor to his wife,
might also by will leave the choice of a tutor to

[1] The wife in manu, although loco filiaefamilias, was nevertheless called materfamilias, a phrase which, though it correctly
denotes her position in fact, is in entire disagreement with that
which legal fiction affected to create for her. Aul. Gell., Noct.
Att., xviii, 6.
[2] Karlowa, II, i, p. 153. The mancipation of the woman in coemption, particularly fiduciary coemption, was a clumsy contriv-
ance ad hoc.

herself (tutoris optio),[1] a discretion not conferrable
by testament upon a person in potestate.[2]

The custom of acquiring manus by civil act may
have been introduced into Rome from neighbouring
cities, or have become gradually legalized by the
practice of the Roman plebs. Conveyance of property by mancipation was in all probability well
known in Italy, and there is no adequate reason to
doubt that Roman plebeians, certainly from the time
of Servius Tullius, and probably before, enjoyed
rights of commercium, and could validly acquire and
vest property. But the status of plebeians during the
regal and early Republican periods was precarious,
and in matters touching sacra and auspices they were
generally helpless when the validity of any ceremony
was challenged. Moreover, clients who chafed at
the restriction obliging them to marriage within the
gens would welcome the establishment of a civil
practice which overrode it. Distrust of the sacerdocy, and the desire for family relations of unassailable legitimacy, would suffice to suggest the practice
of blending with the religious ceremony a civil
procedure (coemptio) founded upon that by which
the transfer of the higher class of property was usually
effected. Defects in taking the auspices, or in the
later rites, were now cured when the woman had
passed into the hand of her husband by the known
formalities of the law.

The precise form in which coemption took place

---

[1] Gaius, i, 150.   [2] Karlowa, II, i, 154.

has not been preserved to us, but it may have been somewhat as follows: The man asked the woman, in the presence of at least five Roman citizens of the age of puberty, besides a balance-holder, whether she would be to him materfamilias, to which she responded affirmatively, and in her turn asked whether he would be to her paterfamilias, receiving also an affirmative reply. This marked the consent of both to contract the marriage, and, on the part of the woman, to so contract cum manu. The act of mancipation then followed, the formula being perhaps to the following effect: Te ego ex jure Quiritium in manu mancipioque meo esse aio, tuque mihi coempta esto, etc.; her answer being: Ubi tu Gaius, ego Gaia. The ceremony was not complete without the auctoritas of the father, or tutor if the bride were sui juris.[1] Already prior to the XII Tables, coemptive marriages between patricians and plebeians (incidentally a strong indication of wealth among the latter) appear sometimes to have taken place.[2] Had

[1] Karlowa, II, i, 158. The fact that even the father is only mentioned as auctor is considered by Karlowa to show that the woman acted as a principal, and that there was not even a pretence of her being sold by him.

[2] The act of coemption, of course, placed the woman in the man's power (mancipium), but as, where connubium was wanting, marriage was at most juris gentium, manus cannot have been created, and the above formula would not be strictly appropriate. Karlowa, II, i, 167, thinks that such marriages were " just " even before the lex Canuleia, and conferred potestas upon the father over the issue, though not gentilitas upon the latter, nor upon the wife if she were

the law remained neutral, connubium between the orders would in course of time have grown up by custom. The decemviral blunder, to which we have already referred, violently precipitated the consummation which it sought to check. The effect of the lex Canuleia was to validate all marriages which were non-just by reason only that the parties belonged to different orders, so that a plebeian wife entered her patrician husband's gens, and became patrician, as did also the issue of the marriage. The inability of plebeians to take part in the ceremony of confarreation was unaffected, for it involved public sacrifice to the State gods, which plebeians were only as yet entitled to perform in privacy.[1] When the City magistracies had, one by one, been opened to the plebs by statute, this point was no longer important. The sole remaining disadvantage was the disqualification for the higher priestly offices[2] of persons not being the issue of confarreate marriage, and not being themselves so married; and as these offices carried no great political power, the exclusion was not resented by the plebeians.

We have now to consider the second means of creating manus over the wife, which the secular law, as declared in the XII Tables, afforded. If the

the plebeian. This seems to be allowing too little time for custom to pass into law.

[1] Karlowa, Röm. Rechtsges., II, i, 165.

[2] The offices of flamen of Jove, Mars, Quirinus, and of rex sacrorum. Gaius, i, 112.

application of Mancipation to marriage was artificial, still more so was that of Usucapion. Transfer of persons in potestate by the copper and the scales was a well-known process, and however essentially coemption may have differed from mancipation, the outward analogy was sufficiently discernible. The analogy of usucapion with usus was much slenderer. As a rule, usucapion gave quiritary dominion over property, not originally taken violently or theftuously, which the present possessor had received in good faith and held under some just title for a full year, in the case of movables, or for two years in the case of immovables. It was a principle limited to Things: there is no instance of the usucaptibility of free persons in the law of Rome. Yet in the end plebeian ingenuity created and established the Usus, whereby a woman, after a full year's cohabitation with her husband, was held, by analogy with usucapion, to have passed under the Hand.

We now turn to the power originally conferred by Confarreation. We are given to understand by the Roman jurists that this power was manus, and in all respects equivalent to that created by coemption or usus. But there seems reason to suspect some confusion of thought if the statement is to hold good for the most ancient times. The language of the jurists was the language of the Roman civil law. Marital relations similar to those expressed by manus are much older than the Roman or any law, nor are they confined to the Aryan race. The power of the

Roman husband was merely an incident of the supreme authority which vested in him as chief priest of the family, so much so indeed that so long as an ascendant was alive, the latter, and not the husband, wielded it.[1] When the young girl had formally dissociated herself from her natural ascendant's cult with his concurrence, and had been admitted to the cult of the husband, by marriage solemnized conformably with the gentile family sacra, the union by virtue of the sacra alone was what lawyers afterwards called " just," and the issue, if approved by the head of the cult, came, as members of it, under what the law knew as the patria potestas. Indeed, so long as the patriarchal integrity of the gens was kept nearly intact, a girl wedded within the gentile circle remained under the authority of the gentile head, and only changed her allegiance by marrying into a strange gens. All this was older than Rome, older perhaps than the Aryan race. The marital and parental authority derived from the religious rite was curbed by the rules of the gens, and by the precepts of the fas as declared from time to time by the sacerdocy—restrictions which were afterwards ascribed to individual law-givers by the naïveness of historians, trained like Dionysius, to seek the source

---

[1] If a woman married cum manu a filiumfamilias, whose father subsequently emancipated or gave him in adoption, the woman remained in the power of her father-in-law, and upon his death became sui juris. She could not fall again under the manus of the husband, since he no longer belonged to his natural father's family.

of all law in the manifested will of an omnipotent autocracy. These restrictions of authoritative power came in part to be incorporated with the civil law of Rome.

In the regal period plebeians had no gentes, or had sprung from broken and ruined families, whose sacra had been lost or partially forgotten. Most of them were ignorant of divinity and incapable of detecting the hidden sacral flaw which would render their marriages unjust, degrade their wives to concubines, and stamp their children as bastards incapable of succeeding to the father's heritage. Not inclination but bitter economic necessity directed the struggle of the plebs to secularize the law, including the law of marriage. Coemption must have become common when the received religious dispensation of the community had suffered its first great wrench in the abolition of kingship, and plebeians had begun to miss the aegis of the royal patronage. The Kings had in part anticipated, the early Consuls wholly disdained, the functions which a later age entrusted to a praetor peregrinus. Instinctively, plebeians set about to supply secular safeguards, and when once sufficiently established, coemption and usus rendered unassailable the hitherto precarious justness of their marriages.

Where manus was habitually acquired by a purely civil act, the religious side of the marriage service continued to be celebrated with a degree of con-

scientiousness which depended upon the individual,
and, among plebeians, became to some extent merely
decorative. Honour was still paid to the gods, and
the marriage was desisted from if the auspices were
palpably unfavourable; for the rest the plebeian,
whilst enjoying the beauty, was freed from the anxious
meticulosity of the patrician marriage service. The
more straight-laced patricians, though unable to gain-
say the legality, were reluctant to admit the equality of
the plebeian civil matrimonia with their own religious
nuptiae. Nevertheless, they could not fail to perceive the convenience of a public ceremony which,
whatever defects might in other respects occur,
placed the lawfulness of the union beyond doubt,
legitimatized the expected offspring and conferred
marital power upon the husband. Moreover, the
desire was strong to differentiate their own from
plebeian unions by some striking feature. The instrument for achieving such a result lay close at
hand, and confarreation gradually became adopted
as the normal and distinguishing mark of all patrician
weddings.

Much speculation has been expended upon the
relative age of the various modes of creating marital
power. The above theory, if correct, supplies the
answer. The ancient religious marriage, according
to the rites of the gens, reaches far back into pre-
Italiot ages; but confarreation can hardly be more
than coeval with the settlement of the Tribes and
the growth of some regular system of international,

N

or extra-gentile, relations. The practice of celebrating
intra-gentile, as well as inter-gentile, marriages by
confarreation was, probably, firmly established in the
infancy of the Republic, and is more recent than the
rise of coemption. Coemption, as we have seen, was
a plebeian device for avoiding the danger of defeat to
the intention of entering upon a just marriage, owing
to some flaw in the ceremony. It is impossible to
attribute to it extreme antiquity. Coemption, it is
true, has been held to have been the original form
of Roman marriage. I have already submitted that,
to my mind, the non-religious element of the marriage
service represented at first merely a supplementary
and precautionary measure, until its proved suffici-
ency dwarfed the importance of the religious rites.
But the connection of coemption with mancipation
equally negatives the antiquity of the former. If
coemption had always been practised by the plebeians, we must imagine them an order of men with
great laxity of religion and, comparatively, a highly
developed jurisprudence. Neither is characteristic
of the early Latins, and we should be thrown back
upon the theory—now rejected by overwhelming
authority—of an original non-Latin, probably non-
Aryan, conquered population—a population, moreover, which although more civilized than the Romans, has, nevertheless, left no authentic trace of
its existence. Coemption most likely obtained recognition soon after the Servian reforms had invested
plebeians with a status in the community which

the State could not, and the King from motives of interest would not, ignore. When coemption was recognized side by side with mancipation, usus took its place side by side with usucapion.

It is relevant to enquire whether any real connection existed between coemption and the custom of bride-purchase, which complemented and then superseded that of bride-stealing. Both practices had no doubt once counted among the normal institutions of old-Aryan society; and although neither can have survived the establishment of settled and ordered political communities, the mimic ravishment of the woman portrayed in the domum deductio may, with tolerable certainty, be considered a remnant of the ancient usage of bride-stealing. A similar claim, which has been set up in favour of coemptio as a survival of bride-purchase, rests upon less trustworthy foundation. Bride-purchase was a very ancient practice, and coemption, relatively, a new one. Generally speaking, however numerous the exceptions, women and, still more, children, during the migratory period, must necessarily have constituted a constant source of danger by embarrassing the movements of the camp, besides increasing the difficulties of food supply. Consequently, the woman was of account only as the indispensable wife and mother. The boys were tolerated in anticipation of their future importance, but girls under the nubile age were mere useless encumbrances. There was accordingly a natural tendency to abandon girl babies, and import one's wives ready grown, if necessary by violence, from weaker or more timorous neighbours. But such an usage, if universally followed, would have speedily ended in the complete extirpation of females, and consequently of the whole race, since to bring up one's girls was to invite constant and disastrous attentions from outside. A counter inducement was found in the practice of infant betrothals—the forerunner of the Latin sponsalia;[1] and peaceful courtships ended in a suitable gift to the father, compensating him for the danger and expense of rearing his child. Thus the instinct of racial preservation evolved bride-purchase, and saved the girl babe's life by investing her from birth with a future or prospective value. Of the two methods, peaceful and violent acquisition, the more forcible was probably the less usual, and the first to disappear. The abduction of a stranger life-partner, and her violent installation at the family shrine, could not fail to shock all but the rudest spirits among a religiously-inclined and ancestor-worshipping race. A mere captive could not often aspire to the dignity of an Aryan wife, and female spoils would be usually relegated to the position of slaves, whilst their descendants might rise to that of clients. When the tribes became territorial, international comity must

---

[1] The formula of the sponsalia was: Spondesne Seiam filiam tuam Lucio filio meo uxorem dari? Dii bene vortant! Spondeo. Originally it gave a right of action in Latium, but soon lost its binding character in Rome, when marriage itself became easily dissoluble.

have put an end to the ravishment of stranger women for the purpose of making them wives.[1] Regular warfare between the cities took the place of former raids and forays, and the consequences were far more serious, involving, as they usually did, the complete political destruction and social enslavement of one of the belligerents. The conditions which had evoked bride-purchase entirely passed away when a stable political State guaranteed to each citizen his belongings.[2] Women became plentiful as female infanticide tended to disappear; and budding civilization recognized that the maintenance of a wife in due comfort and dignity involved moral and intellectual gain, indeed, but also material expenditure, towards which the father—in lieu of receiving compensation—was now expected to contribute.[3] The transition from the old order to the new is probably represented by the practice which gradually grew up for the father, instead of allocating his daughter's purchase-price to his own advantage, to bestow all or part upon her as a wedding gift. But when the wife came under the marital power, as at first she invariably did, the gift passed absolutely to the husband or his

[1] As Rossbach points out, the legendary rape of the Sabine maidens is founded upon the domum deductio, instead of vice versa.

[2] Cf. Westermarck, History of Human Marriage, 222.

[3] Evidently this stage had not yet been reached by the Teutonic tribes in the first century of our era, of whom Tacitus says: "Dotem non uxor mariti sed maritus uxori confert."

ascendant; and it therefore became usual to stipulate[1] beforehand that the fund, instead of falling into the husband's family property, should be administered by him as a thing apart, and revert to the donor on the death either of husband or wife, or be forfeited by the husband in certain contingencies, for instance, unjust repudiation. With this stage the era of regular marriage settlements was practically reached, and the Dos, or dowry, which figures so prominently in the later law of marriage, took its place as a recognized legal institution. Later jurisprudence not only made the promise to provide a dos, promissio dotis, enforceable by action at law, but acknowledged the woman's right to be dowered by her father or ascendant if he could afford it. The Roman wife doubtless owed not a little of her dignity to the economic independence which her marriage portion guaranteed.

We are therefore driven to suspect a hiatus between the disappearance of bride-purchase and the rise of coemption. Coemption is admitted on all hands to have been grafted upon mancipium or nexum, but this was only possible with the aid of a legal fiction as alien to the untaught Italiot intelligence as barring the entail would have appeared to early English feudal tenants. But even nexum itself bears the stamp of a fairly developed mer-

---

[1] Agreements of this kind could be made binding in law when the XII Tables had authoritatively laid down: Cum nexum faciet mancipiumque, uti lingua nuncupassit, ita jus esto.

cantilism, and, although possibly older than Rome, seems necessarily to belong to a social stage in which wife purchasing had become an anachronism.

Consensual Marriage (matrimonium consensu, sine manu)

From time immemorial marital power—exercised however by the husband's ascendant if living—had constituted the most important incident to the ancient religious marriage-tie, whether contracted with or without confarreation. A condition of just marriage was now capable of arising by the purely civil ceremony of coemptio, or the operation of usus, each of which was creative of manus. In the earlier Roman conception, therefore, marital power was inseparable from just marriage of any kind. The power had, however, originated not as an essential of marriage itself but solely as a consequence of the bride's initiation into her husband's family cult, and this initiation was no longer indispensable to just marriage when coemption and usus had become firmly established. Many circumstances were concurring to relax, especially in the plebs, the strictness of ancient customs, and particularly the notions bound up in domestic worship. With the increasing authority and importance of the State the temples of the City gods had begun to overshadow the house-altars. Prestige and conquest had swelled the population with involuntary recruits—some, men of broken fortune, of wrecked homes, adventurers of all kinds, free-thinkers by force of circumstance, whose looser habits condoned a partial or total neglect of sacred ritual. Religious consecration sank to a perfunctory and increasingly disregarded office when the civil law expressly made just marriage possible without it. Nor could it long escape notice that if just marriage could be contracted at all without religious rites, it could be equally well contracted without manus. And here at last we join hands with the classical jurists, who laid down connubium, marriageable age, and consent[1] as the sole indispensables of just marriage.

Incidentally, as the civil gradually bore down the sacral aspect of wedlock, and manus became inseparably associated with one of three possible modes of acquisition—confarreation, coemption, or usus—a new order of ideas arose which withheld the woman from the manus of the husband, even though she had consented to sacrifice at his house-altar. A marriage only religiously solemnized, if without confarreation, which was possible to patricians only, became of itself no longer creative of manus. The wife, although she might nominally sacrifice to her husband's ancestors, did not enter his agnatic circle, but retained unimpaired her agnatic connection with

---

[1] Ulpian, v, 2: Justum matrimonium est, si inter eos, qui nuptias contrahunt, connubium sit, et tam masculus pubes quam foemina (viri)potens sit, et utrique consentiant, si sui juris sint, aut etiam parentes eorúm, si in potestate sint. Dig., xxxv, 1, 15: Nuptias non concubitus sed consensus facit.

her natural family. A wife married sine manu, therefore, remained under her natural father's potestas,
so much so, that he could at any time recall her from
the husband's custody,[1] and even surrender her noxally to a third party—abuses of authority which were
no doubt forbidden by custom and sacerdocy, though
they remained unchecked by the civil law until far
into Imperial times.[2]

Speculation has been aroused by the fact that the
marital power, which anciently undoubtedly accompanied every just marriage, should so soon have
become neither essential nor usual, and have ultimately disappeared without a struggle. A solution
has been sought in the theory of an express enactment elevating unions sine manu from marriages
juris gentium to the dignity of just marriages.[3] Such
a statute would merit to stand beside the lex Canuleia
for importance, but without disputing the possibility
of its one-time existence and subsequent vestigeless
disappearance, the gradual and spontaneous evolution of society, such as we know to have taken
place, seems to furnish a less far-fetched though
equally sufficient explanation.

The XII Tables afforded the first statutory confirmation of the definite breach with the ancient
order of ideas. The analogy of usus with usucapion
was pursued to its logical conclusion by the enactment that a wife not already under Hand could pre-

---

[1] Cuq, Just. jur. des Rom., 111.   [2] Cod., v, 17, 5.
[3] Karlowa, ii, 168; contra Sohm, § 79.

vent manus arising through usus by absenting herself for three consecutive nights (usurpatio trinoctii)
from her husband's abode before the completion of
an unbroken year of cohabitation,[1] provided such
absence took place usurpandi causa, with the deliberate intention of breaking the use. Henceforward
manus gradually fell with women into a disfavour
proportioned to the ease with which it was defeated.
Coemption, having sunk into disrepute, was retained
only to further designs entirely foreign to its original
purposes. The vogue of free and just marriages
soon found its way into the charmed circle of the
patriciate. Confarreation, once the distinguishing feature of inter-gentile, and, later, of patrician marriages
generally, was increasingly rejected by Roman
ladies. The result was a scarcity of eligible candidates for the higher priestly offices, which were only
open to those born in confarreate wedlock, and
themselves so married.[2] Finally, in the early Principate, statutory enactments were made to limit the
effect of confarreation.[3] Henceforward a woman
married farreo changed her family and came under

---

[1] A father could not force his married daughter to break the
use, except indirectly by reclaiming her from her husband before
manus had arisen. The provision of the XII Tables seems to me
to dispose of any doubt as to the justness of marriages sine manu
at that period. To facilitate the perpetuation of non-just marriages would have been not only contrary to public policy, but
apt to defeat one of the chief purposes which the plebs strove to
effect.
[2] Gaius, i, 112.   [3] Tacitus, iv, 16.

the marital power only " sacrorum causa." Her civil status remained unaltered, and she neither lost her ties of agnation in her father's family, nor acquired any in her husband's.

Although marriage by mere consent of both parties, and lasting only as long as such consent endured, arose at a comparatively early period, some ages must have elapsed before the full effect of the modernized union had been translated from legal theory into the received practice of society. During the period now under review, the stringency of the ancient conception of the family still remained strong enough to hold in check that deplorable licence which found free vent in the corrupt luxury of a later civilization. It is therefore not within our present purpose to investigate in how far the legal instability of the marriage-tie was responsible for those social phenomena which ultimately wrought ruin to the classical world, and the process by which that instability arose is only very briefly indicated in the following section.

DISSOLUTION OF MARRIAGE

Originally there may have been no complete dissolution of marriage possible during the lifetime of the parties.[1] A wife had no remedy against the

---

[1] In later times the indissolubility of marriage still held good with regard to flamens. Festus: "flaminis uxor, cui non licebat facere divortium."

misconduct of her lord. A paterfamilias[1] had the alternatives of putting an erring wife to death or excluding her from the domestic sacra. Such a sentence, which far transcended the bounds of moderate correction, was not pronounced arbitrarily, but deliberately, with due regard to the fas and the rules of the gens, in his capacity of priest-judge presiding over the domestic tribunal.[2] The judicium domesticum ordinarily consisted of all the male adults of the family, but where a materfamilias stood arraigned for a serious offence, natural relationship was admitted to its rights, and humane custom demanded the concurrence of all the accused's cognatic kinsmen.

Divortium under the civil law was dissolution of marriage by mutual consent of the parties. Being possible only when the wife was not in manu, it was of more recent date than Repudium, where the husband put away his wife for some grievous fault. Repudiation, when it became established, lay within the domestic imperium of the paterfamilias. But confarreate marriages, which had been celebrated with the concurrence of the State priests, were dissolved (also with their concurrence) by a prescribed ritual styled the diffareatio, which

[1] It must be constantly borne in mind that the paterfamilias need not be the husband of the offending woman; he might be the husband's ascendant.

[2] Gide, Etude, 104: Les anciens Romains considéraient les devoirs de famille comme d'une nature trop noble et trop délicate pour les livrer au contrôle indiscret des tribunaux et aux débats d'une procédure publique.

contemporaneously destroyed the marriage-state and the manus.[1] The dissolution of a coemptive marriage did not of itself break the manus, and the wife was entitled to a remancipation.[2] Repudiation was allowable broadly upon any act by the wife which struck at the root idea of conjugal association. Unchastity threatened to introduce into the family under false pretences spurious issue, whose offerings at the house-altar would have outraged the Lares and Penates. Such conduct was necessarily ground for repudiation,[3] but equally so was the fathering upon a paterfamilias of a stranger child, or the taking of magic potions with the object of procuring offspring, since so to violate the course of nature was a grave affront to the gods.[4] But repudiation might also follow upon far lesser lapses, such as immodesty of bearing or indulgence in fermented

---

[1] The rites were of a frightful and odious nature (Plut., Q. R., 50) and evidently designed to discourage frequent repetition.

[2] Gaius, i, 137.

[3] Sterility has been mentioned as a ground for repudiation, seeing that it defeated the object of the marriage (Coulanges, Cité Antique, 52). But a remedy lay to hand in Adoption, a course which imposed itself when the sterility lay with the husband. The cited case of Carvilius Ruga belongs to an age when the restrictions of the fas had weakened, and only custom continued to hold the husband, and the wife not in manu. It is impossible to suppose that divorce, however seldom, had previously been unknown.

[4] The incident of the female "poisoners," narrated by Livy, viii, 18, is probably such a case. At all events the facts are incredible as described, cf. Ihering, Vorgeschichte, 422.

liquors. No more heinous crimes were possible to the Roman materfamilias than incontinence [1] and drunkenness [2]; and so great was the horror they excited that a woman was expected by her conduct and demeanour to avoid the suspicion, or even the suggestion, of guilt. A woman, apprehended in the act of adultery, might, together with her paramour, be forthwith slain by the wronged husband.[3] In all other circumstances the faithless or intemperate wife was put upon her trial before the domestic tribunal, and only upon due conviction suffered the extreme penalty.

The new institution of consensual marriage worked a slow and silent revolution in the law of divorce. If we may consider consensual marriage in the light of a contract at all,[4] at the period when it first emerged into recognition, it was a contract between the man and woman to live as spouses so long as both concurred in the desire to continue the cohabita-

[1] Cicero, De Rep., iv, 6. Men refused to salute a female relative of bad character.

[2] But we cannot accept Cato's suggestion that the purpose of the jus osculi was to detect by the smell any recent indulgence in strong liquor (cf. Aul. Gell., x, 23).

[3] Horace, Sat., ii, 7, 61. Cato, apud Gell., x, 23. The first breach in the privilege was not made until the early Principate.

[4] The nature of marriage, regarded as a contract, is discussed in pp. 46, 47 of Poste's edition of Gaius; Hunter's R. L., 681-2, etc. But it must not be forgotten that marriage, as an institution, is older than even the earliest species of contract, Conveyance. Certainly in the earlier centuries of Rome there can have been no conscious identification of marriage with any kind of contract. Coemptio was a clumsy adaptation of civil law, but even with the plebs the true inwardness of marriage was sought in its religious aspects.

tion. Children conceived during the union were ex justis nuptiis and fell under the patria potestas. The only thing now needed to create marriage, when the parties were otherwise capable of intermarrying, was the consent of both parties; the only thing needed to dissolve it was the withdrawal of the consent of either spouse, and both were deemed to be proved by any act sufficiently demonstrative of the intention. It was therefore sometimes necessary to decide whether the circumstances in a given case had or had not actually operated to constitute a marriage (just or non-just), and where the question was in doubt the presence or absence of a dos might serve as the test whether the union was marriage or concubinage: the law soon recognized the institution of the dos in connection with matrimonium juris gentium, as well as just marriage. Cohabitation without the affectio maritalis was neither matrimonium justum nor juris gentium, and remained a criminal offence until the toleration of a latitudinarian society overcame the scruples of the ancient law, and led to its regulation under the name of concubinage. The woman who condescended to an illicit albeit enduring union had been branded by the ancients with the opprobrious epithet of pellex; she now received the gentler name amica, and in certain circumstances concubinage was deemed the only proper association.[1] But cohabitation during an appreciable period

---

[1] The issue of such unions were not entirely without rights as against the father. Concubinage, though a lower form of union

of a man and woman in the same station of life was usually held conclusive of the affectio maritalis.

Dissolution of a marriage was similarly effected by manifestation of will. The most unmistakable was re-marriage with another party, which of itself dissolved the former union, so that the offence of bigamy was unknown to the criminal law of Rome.[1] A usual

than marriage, was assimilated to it in some respects. Sohm, Inst., 274, goes the length of describing it as "eine Ehe minderen Rechts," and Pothier, Traité du Mariage, in vol. iii, 131, says practically the same. No man could legally have two amicae, nor a wife and an amica, at the same time. Ulpian's dictum (Dig., xxv, 7) "cum honestius sit patrono libertam concubinam quam matremfamilias habere," illustrates how the moral and social tone of the Imperial civilization had changed for the worse.

[1] Causeless repudiation is said, though on doubtful authority, to have been penalized in very early times. Statesmen of the late Republic attempted to check changefulness and caprice by laws which they themselves too often disregarded; and even the more strenuous efforts of Christian emperors were but moder-ately successful. The vagaries of wealthy women, in particular, in the eighth and ninth centuries of the City must have been extra-ordinary. Yet we may not accept, as of general application, the statement that in lieu of the practice of calling the years after the Consuls, ladies kept count of time by the tally of their divorced husbands. And some exaggeration may be suspected when a pro-fessional castigator of society writes:

> Imperat ergo viro; sed mox haec regna relinquit,
> Permutatque domos, et flammea conterit; inde
> Advolat, et spreti repetit vestigia lecti.
> Ornatas paulo ante fores, pendentia linquit
> Vela domus, et adhuc virides in limine ramos.
> Sic crescit numerus; sic fiunt octo mariti,
> Quinque per auctumnos: titulo res digna sepulcri.
>
> (Juvenal, Sat. vi.)

formula of repudiation began: tua res tibi habetur ("take away thy property"), and ended with a demand for return of the house keys.

We have already seen that under the earlier law a father could divorce his daughter in potestate against her own and her husband's will by an action against the latter for the recovery of her person, a right which he, of course, lost if manus had been acquired by usus. Marriage was also dissolved *against* the will of both the spouses if either of them suffered capitis deminutio maxima, losing both citizenship and liberty. If the minutio, being media, entailed only loss of citizen rights, the marriage, though no longer just, was juris gentrum, provided the affectio maritalis on the man's, and uxoris animus on the wife's part continued to subsist.

With the weakening of the religious sentiment, and increase of luxury, there arose among the men of the comfortable classes a growing unwillingness to incur the responsibilities of matrimony, which excited among the leaders of the State the same apprehensions which similar phenomena have aroused in the modern world. In the last century of the Republic we find the Censor, Q. Caecilius Metellus, anticipating the strictures of President Roosevelt,[1] and appealing to the patriotism of his

[1] Aul. Gell., Noct. Att., i, 6. Quoniam ita natura tradidit, ut nec cum illis (*i.e.*, women) satis commode, nec sine illis ullo modo vivi possit, saluti perpetuae potius, quam brevi voluptati consulendum. The composite lex Julia et Papia (about the middle of the eighth

hearers to undertake an admittedly disagreeable duty. It is significant that neither Metellus nor his critics ventured to assert that marriage was a desirable object in itself, though some of the latter thought he spoke truth too boldly.

SOCIAL POSITION OF THE MATERFAMILIAS

Religious nations and trading nations entertain peculiarly strict notions of wedlock, and the Romans were both. But underlying this seriousness of view we may also trace a noble and elevating female influence. "It is in the interest of the woman that the law of marriage should be strict, and that marriage should be single."[1] We have already seen that, in contrast with other racial groups, polygyny seems never to have been practised to any considerable extent among Western Aryans, and certainly never at all by the Romans. Yet monogamy was by no means an inevitable result of the association of the man and woman at the house-altar. Avowedly the sole purpose of marriage was to perpetuate the

century of the City) annulled or curtailed the right of most " celibate " or childless persons to take as legatees under a will. Any man between twenty-five and sixty, or woman between twenty and fifty, for the time being unmarried, was " coelebs," though he or she might have been married previously. For an instructive list of laws and ordinances framed with the like object, see Voigt, R. RG., ii, 48 ff. For the State to bring pressure upon widowers and widows to make them re-marry would have appeared monstrous to Romans of the old school.

[1] W. E. Gladstone, Juventus Mundi, p. 406.

sacra, and where it was thought, as there is some reason to believe was the case, that the male alone possessed the faculty of active propagation, a plurality of wives might have appeared in harmony rather than antagonistic with that end. But the earnest dignity of the patriarchal house-mother maintained the old-Aryan notion of the fundamental equality of the sexes, and disdained to. share either the privileges or the burdens of her estate. The very impressiveness of the Roman marriage ceremony discouraged its multiplication.[1] So hallowed was the nuptial tie, that the ancient law forbade the remarriage of flamens and widows. The latter were afterwards freed from the prohibition, provided a space of ten, later twelve, months intervened between the first husband's death and the remarriage, to prevent confusion of the bloods, turbatio sanguinis. But the initiation of the woman into successive cults continued to shock the sense of religious propriety, and the old-Roman nicety disrelished the presence of children born of the same mother to different fathers. A woman's second nuptials were celebrated without ostentation, as it were shamefacedly, and lacked most of the solemnly-joyous ceremonial of her first. No widow or twice-married woman could be a pronuba. The objections to the remarriage of

[1] F. de Coulanges, La Cité Antique, 48. La cérémonie des noces était si solonelle et produisait de si graves effets qu'on ne doit pas être surpris que ces hommes ne l'aient crue permise et possible que pour une seule femme dans chaque maison. Une telle religion ne pouvait pas admettre la polygamie.

widowers were less pertinent, as they did not change
cult; yet a bimaritus never became eligible as rex
sacrorum, flamen dialis, or pontifex maximus, and a
flamen whose wife died during the term of his office
was compelled to resign it for lack of an associate.
For the "house of him who has married a wife is
entire and perfect, but his house who once had one
and now has none is not only imperfect but also
disabled."[1]

Marriage was therefore a highly honourable estate,[2] so much so that the privilege was altogether
denied to slaves, whose cohabitation as man and
wife was respected by the masters, and, in later
times, in some degree protected by law,[3] but never
attained even to the dignity of matrimonium juris
gentium, however long and faithfully continued. On
the other hand, the vestal virgins, out of regard for
their sacerdotal quality, were co-ordinated with married women, and wore the red veil to symbolize, in
their case, devotion to the City altar. The title of

---

[1] Plutarch, Q. R., 50. So, also, children could not actively
assist at the marriage-rite unless both parents had been "justly"
married and were alive. At least, this is the most probable
meaning of patrimi et matrimi. The aversion with which the early
Christian church regarded second marriages sprang, of course, from
a different order of ideas. To the pagan Roman, marriage was so
sacred that it was profaned by repetition; the Christian reluctantly
tolerated *one* union as a deplorable but necessary concession to
the weakness of the flesh.

[2] Nuptiae sunt conjunctio maris et feminae et consortium omnis
vitae, divini et humani juris communicatio. Dig., xxiii, 2, 1. Uxor
socia humanae rei atque divinae. Cod., ix, 32, 4.

[3] Lecky, i, 304; Cod., v, 3; Dig., xxi, 1, 35.

materfamilias was denied to the wife not in manu, and in any case it was lost on the husband's death.

Thus the woman of the old-Roman family system offers, at first sight, the glaring anomaly of a position of undoubted dignity and esteem, coupled with an almost uncontrolled subjection to a house-tyrant. We have already seen that religion, custom, the supervision of the gens, and the support of the wife's cognates tended to check exorbitant abuses of marital power. But when all allowances are made, that power remained real and imminent, and even venial wifely indiscretions might be and were occasionally visited with almost grotesque severity.[1] It is true that the wife's subjection to the family head was but an incident of a system which bore equally upon all persons in potestate. Yet the XII Tables demonstrate conclusively that the early Roman law did in practice differentiate the sexes to the disadvantage of females. At no period of her life was a woman entirely withdrawn from male control. Subject in her girlhood to the potestas, and during coverture to the manus, a woman on becoming a widow or spinster orphan was still amenable to tutors, whose authority was

---

[1] See instances mentioned, Valerius Max., vi, 3, 9-12. But rhetoricians of a lax age, who regard effect more than accuracy, are prone to exaggerate the rigour of their forebears, and to accept any anecdote which will colour their text. Pothier, writing under the Ancien Régime, goes quite as far as the most autocratic of Roman husbands: La puissance du mari sur la personne de la femme consiste, par le Droit naturel, dans le droit qu'a le mari d'exiger d'elle tous les devoirs de soumission qui sont dûs à un supérieur (iii, 455). This is not the spirit of the Roman law.

required to validate every important transaction of her life.

Nevertheless, the subjection of the woman was free from any intentional obloquy or abasement.[1] We must distinguish questions of principle from those of expediency. To the latter belonged the law-assumed inferiority of women, which, accordingly, disappeared with the political and social conditions upon which it was founded. Rome's early politics were so mixed up with warfare, her very existence so often staked upon the issue of desperate venture, that the helm of State perforce remained entrusted exclusively to the hardier and more actively courageous moiety of the nation. Nature and the circumstances of the then world combined to assign the woman to the domestic sphere. The Roman wife was not, indeed, condemned to the seclusion of the hareem, or even of the gynaeconitis. But custom, which denied to her neither freedom of movement nor the amenities of social intercourse, withdrew public affairs and most private business from her orbit of activity, as unbecoming the modesty of the sex.[2] Except as a vestal, flaminica, or consort of the pontifex maximus, no woman could hold a position in the public service. Midwifery may have been practised by freewomen at all periods, and in Imperial times princesses may have employed female secretaries.[3] Apparently teaching as a profession was entirely in the hands of men; and isolated instances of women who scan-

---

[1] Cf. Gide, Etude, 108, 125, etc.   [2] Cf. Dig., III, i.
[3] Suetonius, Vespasian, iii.

dalized society by pleading at the Bar are naturally attributable to a sophisticated age.[1]

· Women's direct influence in public life was therefore infinitesimal. Yet it is probably no exaggeration to say that the whole social fabric was moulded by the forceful character of house-mothers in the serene atmosphere of the home,[2] and that the decline of the State dates from the active intervention of women in the bustle of public affairs.[3] In the household, the materfamilias barely yielded in dignity to the master, with whom she was associated as chief priestess for the purposes of the family ritual, and in whose absence the government of the family devolved upon her. Though she superintended the household and kept the keys, her duties did not extend to services which savoured of the menial. Spinning was the constant and seemly occupation of a Roman lady[4]; it was left to inferiors to dress the

[1] Val. Max., viii, 3; Plut., Lycurgus and Numa; Livy, xxxiv, 1-4.

[2] Rossbach, 36. Je weiter wir in das Altertum zurückgehen, desto abhängiger ist zwar das Weib vom Manne, aber auch eine um so würdigere Stellung nimmt es in der Familie ein, desto grösseren Einfluss hat es auf die Gestaltung der gesellschaftlichen Verhältnisse. Dieser Satz muss als ein allgemein gültiger für den ganzen indogermanischen Stamm aufgestellt werden.

[3] Roman women have on occasion displayed a breadth of mind which politicians might envy. Verginia, a patrician lady of stainless reputation, who had espoused a distinguished plebeian, was, because of her marriage, denied access to the Patrician Women's Temple of Chastity. She nobly revenged herself by erecting at her own expense a new Temple for chaste plebeian women, whom she invited to emulate the virtue of their sisters.

[4] Ovid, Fast. ii. (Lucretia) Nebat, ante torum calathi, lanaque mollis, erant. Wool was constantly worn by the Romans, who

meat and grind the corn.[1] Unworldliness did not
excuse ignorance, and the mother was expected to
educate her children. Their respect remained unimpaired by the knowledge that the letter of the law
ranked her with themselves, and even subjected
her, as widow, to the tutelage of her own sons.
Swayed by the habit of filial reverence, warriors and
statesmen have been turned from their purpose by
a mother's admonitions.[2] Not contempt for supposed defects of character, but solicitude to protect
unworldly habits, and shield from contact with the
rougher sides of life, prompted the political and
contractual disabilities of the early law. The retire-
ment of women from public life was honestatis
privilegium. The levitas animi feminarum is a mis-
description of the jurists.[3] There was little levity of
mind among those matrons of ancient Rome, whose
hard-favoured virtue the poets of a gentler civilization would pertly ridicule[4] for the amusement of
lady friends who were nothing if not "Graeculae."

introduced the habit into Britain (Tacitus, Agric., c. 21). The
swampy plains of Latium made warm clothing advisable; moreover, it is thought that the Italian climate was colder than nowadays. Silks were not worn in the early Republic.

[1] Plut., Q. R., 85.

[2] For instance, Coriolanus, or (a more authentic case) Gaius
Graccus.

[3] See Gaius, i, 144, 190. Cicero, pro Mur. 12, speaks of in-
firmitas consilii; Ulpian, xi, 1, et propter sexus infirmitatem et
propter forensium rerum ignorantiam.

[4] For instance, Ovid, Amores, i, 8. Forsitan immundae, Tatio
regnante, Sabinae noluerint habiles pluribus esse viris. Or again,
ii, 4, Aspera si visa est, rigidasque imitata Sabinas.

Speaking broadly, and admitting the possibility of not unimportant exceptions, it may be said with some confidence that the standard of any nation's civilization is determinable by the degree of esteem in which it holds its womankind. But though this be conceded, the generalization is of small value where the degree of esteem is sought to be ascertained by bringing modern habits of thought to bear upon a radically different perception of life and its problems. Certainly the state of the law regarding women at any given period is less apt to instruct than to misguide. It will not, I think, be asserted that English-women of the early Victorian period, for instance, stood in slighter personal regard with men than since the passage of the Married Women's Property Acts. Whatever be the state of the law, when salvation hangs upon the numbers, and the physical and mental vigour of its citizens, no enlightened community will depreciate its women. The proud acceptance of wifehood and motherhood was the glory and reward of the Roman matron. In the heyday of manus and tutela she may have commanded a deeper respect than at the end of her successful struggle for emancipation, when women aspired to elegance without usefulness, substituting a voluntary and genuine self-abandonment for the fictitious abjection of the law.[1]

[1] Gide, Etude, 147. Les progrès de la corruption dans Rome ont été plus rapides chez les femmes que chez les hommes: les Bacchanales ont précédé de plus d'un siècle la conjuration de Catilina.

CHAPTER XI

THE constitution of the primitive patriarchal group had its roots in the remotest epochs; and its earliest stages are but dimly surmised, though its later developments may be followed with tolerable confidence. Originally the patriarch's ascendancy over his kinsmen, as over his slaves, can scarcely have rested in the last resort upon other sanction than brute force, and, unless voluntarily surrendered, authority and life itself were liable to violent termination by the same agency when physical decay set in. Various causes, but above all the reverence begotten of ancestor-worship, in the course of ages softened and moulded manners to the elder's advantage. On the other hand, the subtle influence of a humanizing cult by slow gradations transformed the group-tyrant into a true father, and intensified a sentiment of solidarity and interdependence which became accustomed to behold in the head less the ruthless master and oppressor than the responsible Administrator and just Judge. And the limitations followed the power when the gentes began to fall asunder, and each eldest ancestor gradually assumed to himself exclusive authority over the persons of his descendants, leaving to the head of the gens (or a committee of its seniors) a few disciplinary powers, the care of the gentile sacra, and the representation of the group towards other groups, and, latterly for a time, the State.

It has already been pointed out that by the time Rome had become consolidated into a State there was no longer any effective head of the gens. The civil unit of the State was the Agnatic Family, or group of related individuals under the headship of the living common ancestor. Agnation, or relationship (natural or adoptive) through males, was, generally speaking, the sole relationship recognized by the early civil law. Agnates were all individuals subject for the time being to the same patria potestas, or who would have been so subject were the common ancestor alive. Brothers and sisters, with their uncles, aunts, nephews, nieces, and other collaterals, not having been received by adoption or marriage into another family, if related through males, were each other's agnates, whether patrician or plebeian. Gentiles, the patrician members of the same gens, were each other's agnates; towards their clients they were gentiles only, since no agnation was possible between patron and client. Agnation (where not artificially created, as by marriage, adoption, or arrogation) presupposed cognation, or natural relationship by blood; cognates who were not agnates (as the sons of one mother by different husbands)

were not civilly related, for they had no common
family altar. But cognation was effective as a bar
to marriage within the prohibited degrees, and was
recognized by the custom of summoning all the
blood relatives of the inculpated wife to witness
the trial of their kinswoman before the domestic
tribunal.[1]

The strictly agnatic character of the Roman family
was a consequence and a necessity of its internal constitution. Civilly, the State knew only patresfamilias
and those (if any)[2] subject to their power. It would
have been subversive of the principles upon which
society was built to subject the same individual to
two different powers at the same time, and, accordingly, a female remained only so long under the
power of her ancestor as she had not by marriage
entered another family, and come under the power
of the new paterfamilias, who might or might not
be her own husband. Such females were deemed
to have entirely renounced their natural family;
the release from the power under which they had
hitherto lived was as complete as their subjection to
the newly-acquired allegiance, under which their
children and descendants likewise fell. Thus the
family constantly absorbed within itself the wives
introduced by its males. Descent, therefore, was

---

[1] Extenuating circumstances could be pleaded on her behalf.
In public trials the only defence was Not guilty.

[2] Unmarried males and childless husbands, if sui juris, were
also in law patresfamilias.

never traced through females. Mulier familiae suae et caput et finis est. (Ulpian.)

The vitality of patria potestas was probably due to the fact that it responded to the temper and needs of the early City. Even if stripped of its religious element, the Roman Agnatic Family would still appear a military and political necessity. The Home afforded, and the Camp emphasized, the teaching of discipline and obedience; and within the City walls the responsibility of a family Head for those under him was a better guarantee of order than our own Frank-pledge or Ten men's tale. As the continuance of the system appeared to correspond with, so its chief limitations were dictated by, considerations of public efficiency. It formed no part of the jus publicum. In the seclusion of the family the chief was supreme; in field and forum father and son exercised their civic privileges, or discharged their duties to the State, upon a footing of equality. As citizen, the son voted if he listed contrary to his ancestor in the Comitia.[1] As military officer, he commanded, and where necessary punished, the soldiers committed to his leadership, including perchance his

---

[1] I know no sufficient reason why male adult citizens in potestate should not have voted in the comitia curiata; and the centuries, as originally constituted, would naturally comprehend them, unless they were specially excluded for legislative purposes. The fact that the amount of his property determined the century of each citizen, and that sons in potestate owned none, is not cogent, if we keep in view the original conception of property as belonging to a group rather than to an individual.

own father. As magistrate he might give judgment in a suit to which his father was a party, and even sit in criminal jurisdiction over him.

As employed by classical writers, the word familia has various significations: (1) Usually it denotes the Agnatic Family or group of free persons in the potestas of a living male Ancestor; or (2) such Agnatic Family, plus slaves and persons loco servorum, and clients attached to the family. In a wide sense (3) familia may include every human being and every movable and immovable for the time being under the power or dominion of a citizen sui juris, together with all rights of action acquired by himself directly or through his dependants. But familia is also used to denote (4) only the slaves of a household, or (5) generally the objects of dominium, as land and slaves or other chattels, as distinct, for instance, from objects of potestas, as children. (6) Sometimes the last signification is narrowed by contradistinguishing familia and pecunia; in this sense familia would mean that part of the family estate which in early times was expected to remain permanently in the family possession, as the ancestral habitation, the land appurtenant to it and the slaves and animals necessary for cultivation; whilst pecunia denoted those objects of property, such as grazing herds (pecus), which were regarded as eminently merchantable and constantly changing. (7) Occasionally familia is synonymous with gens, or (8) a branch or stirps of a gens.

In Rome, private law regarded the familia, both persons and things, as a mere appendage of the paterfamilias. A filiusfamilias was not, indeed, disabled from performing certain acts capable of producing legal effects. He had connubium, and could contract just marriage, though his wife and offspring fell under the power of the ancestor. He had also commercium and could validly take by mancipation, though the property thus acquired vested in the ancestor. He had testamentifactio to the extent that he could be witness to a will, libripens or even familiae emptor; though he could make no will himself, since he had no property within his disposition, and was unable even to dispose of his future interest in the patrimony. If he took under a will as heir[1] or legatee, the succession or legacy vested in the ancestor. Originally he could not sue or be sued, and although the practice of a more enlightened age enabled him if necessary to bring an action in his own name, when he had suffered such injury as seemed to cast a slur upon his honour, it was again to the ancestor that pecuniary damages were payable. He could not incur a debt, or other contractual obligation, for failure to satisfy it would, under the early law, have involved bondage to the creditor, depriving the ancestor of his dependant's services. Thus he could by his acts improve the condition of his ancestor;

---

[1] The Roman instituted heir was of course a very different person from the heir of English law. He united, among other qualities, those of the English executor and residuary legatee.

he could not worsen it, save in the case of delict involving his surrender to an injured party, as to which I shall have more to say later.

The denial of proprietary rights to the citizen for perhaps the greater part of his life was not consonant with the character of a progressive and trading community, and custom mitigated the harshness of a deprivation in which the first formal breach was not made by the law until after the dissolution of the Republic.[1] It was usual—no doubt from very early times—for a father to set aside portions of his stock, and assign them to the exclusive control and use of his grown-up and married sons. In primitive Roman society wealth most usually took the form of cattle (pecus), and the son enjoyed his quasi-property under the name of peculium.

The authority of the Roman paterfamilias was exercisable in five different forms:

[1] Under Augustus, filiusfamilias became the absolute master of what he had acquired through military service (peculium castrense). Analogous rights, though not, until Justinian, quite so far-reaching, were subsequently conferred upon officers of the palace, and later upon certain other functionaries, persons in the liberal professions, and ecclesiastical dignitaries, over their emoluments or earnings (peculium quasi-castrense). Another kind of peculium, called adventitium, which was introduced under Constantine, consisted of everything received by a filiusfamilias from his mother at her death, and of this the father had the usufruct only. Under subsequent Emperors the scope of the peculium adventitium was gradually extended until, under Justinian, it included every kind of property (other than castrense and quasi-castrense peculium) which had not been derived from the paternal estate.

1. Marital power, of the Hand, manus, over his own wife;

2. Parental power, patria potestas, over his unmarried female descendants,[1] his male descendants, married or not, and their wives;[2]

3. Mancipium, or temporary power over free persons not being kinsmen by birth or adoption;

4. Dominica potestas, or power over slaves;

5. Dominium, or ownership over cattle, land,[3] and all other non-human property, animate and inanimate.

The earliest Romans, indeed, cannot have scientifically appreciated the distinctions implied in this enumeration. "Manus," afterwards employed to denote only the power over a wife, had originally served to sum up the totality of authority as husband, father, master, and (using the expression very loosely) proprietor. The family head, anciently called herus, was, as the name indicated, monarch of his little kingdom. Even in much later times the control of paterfamilias over his cattle is, in theory, hardly more complete and far-reaching than over his slaves, or his children and children's children. He is entitled to enjoy and turn to account the services of all. Until well into Imperial times his proprietary right is carried out to its logical conclusion in the jus (in early law, potestas) vitae ac

[1] If not in manu, married female descendants would also remain under the patria potestas.
[2] Married with manus.
[3] Land originally vested in the gens, and could not be freely disposed of like movables.

P

necis. Having the power of life and death, he has complete control and disposition over their living persons for purposes of profit or chastisement. The XII Tables contain the statutory confirmation of his right to imprison, scourge, keep to agricultural labour in chains, sell and slay his children, and this even though they might hold high office of State. It is true that the law did not permit a Roman citizen to be divested of his freedom in his own country, unless he had forfeited it by crime, and, therefore, free persons in potestate could only be sold as slaves beyond the Roman territorial boundaries;[1] but this restraint appears to have been prompted by considerations first of religion and then of public policy, rather than any desire to limit the patria potestas.

Nevertheless, though unexpressed and unexpressible by the simple terminology of archaic ages, religion had long guided the Aryan instinct to differentiate between rights of Persons and rights of Things. The Roman paterfamilias derived his authority over man, and over beast and chattel, from two distinct sources: the sacred law of ages immemorial, and the law which resulted from the permanent attachment of tribal communities to the soil,

---

[1] Cod., viii, 46, 10. Libertati a majoribus tantum impensum erat, ut patribus, quibus jus vitae in liberos necisque potestas olim erat permissa, eripere libertatem non liceret. But this only held good within Rome itself. That the paterfamilias could send his son into a foreign country as a slave appears indubitable. Cf. Cicero, De Oratore, i, 40, 181.

the rise of settled polities and increasing inter-communication of their citizens. The latter law, indeed,
at first claimed to be sacred also. But it was visibly
moulded by human intellect, or at least by human
agency acting upon alleged divine inspiration, and
it was enforced not by an outraged Ancestor but by
a King or Consul, whom the citizens themselves had
elected. The human or temporal aspect of the law
of the City constantly asserted and distinguished
itself from the spiritual law of the pre-Roman family.
Closely considered, the dual capacity of the Roman
father, as Family Head and Master of the House, is
still discernible in historic times. His authority as
the former, however liable to abuse, was not, according to prevailing notions, absolute, but rather
subject to conventions[1] which, apart from their
divine sanction, received materiality from the voice
of kinsmen in family council. By virtue of the fas,
backed by the sentiment of the family and by public
opinion generally, the paterfamilias was the trustee
rather than the arbiter of his kinsmen dependants.
But all early Trusts, by whatever name they may be
known, are binding only upon the conscience, and
unenforceable at law. The earliest law of the Roman
State was itself chiefly founded upon religious practices, but the State interfered with great reluctance

---

[1] Patria potestas in pietate debet, non atrocitate consistere,
Dig., xlviii, 9, 5. The father whom Hadrian punished could
surely plead intolerable provocation, but the killing of the son was
irregular: latronis magis quam patris jure eum interfecit.

in internal matters pertaining to the family cult, and patria potestas was of the very essence and the mainstay of the latter. Only some of the more atrocious excesses were checked by the State, ostensibly on religious grounds, in reality because they were contrary to public policy. There was no public tribunal to protect a son against the harshest of fathers. No person under power could sue in his own name for any cause soever, and far from possessing a right to own separate property, children, however mature their years, as we have seen, were themselves, in the City law, virtually the property of their eldest living ancestor.

It is desirable for the better understanding of primitive Roman society to keep in view this double character of the paterfamilias as head of the family and master (dominus) of the house. In leaving wife and child at the mercy of their lord, the policy of the State was not deliberately to deny to all minors the elementary rights of human beings. But in the earliest ages the Roman consistently shrank from curtailing by any compulsitor of law an authority with which every fibre of his intellectual being was intertwined. Moreover, the machinery of archaic government, working slowly and clumsily, is the more effective the less frequently it is set in motion. The law of primitive societies is often extremely technical, but usually Procedure has nearly monopolized the legislator's attention. Substantive law must content itself with a few principles of sweeping application: it is impatient of distinctions and qualifications. And among men emerging from barbarism it cannot, without challenging resistance and jeopardizing the existence of the State, attempt to enforce artificial rules of conduct not sanctioned by a prevalent superstition.

The State therefore tolerated the merger of the individual in the group, for the purposes of the private law, because it was not yet prepared to substitute its own authority for the time-consecrated authority of the ancestor, and because it trusted to other forces than that of the law for good administration within the home. Considering how decisively the immigrant elements influenced the career of the City in many directions, it might have been expected that the plebeians, most of whom had no distinguished family connections to boast of, would soon have undermined the foundations of the patria potestas. In reality, they seem upon the whole to have aided in its preservation, since we know that the father's power, though it naturally declined in the course of ages, remained to the last strictest in Rome, a proof that the patrician spirit of conservatism, when non-political, was not uncongenial to the commoners.[1]

---

[1] Ferrero (Greatness and Decline of Rome, p. 5) says: " Ancient Roman society may perhaps fitly be compared to life in one of the monastic orders in the Middle Ages. Both systems display the same methodical combination of example and precept, of mutual vigilance and unremitting discipline. Both show us

Imperfect human nature will occasionally disregard dictates of religion and precepts of law, and
in large communities the ultimate safeguard of
all good government lies in the power and will
of the governed to revolt when tyranny reaches a
certain point. But in the miniature Roman family-
kingdom, natural affection[1] and the influence of

a community in which the individual is entirely at the mercy of
the feelings and opinions of his fellows, and where it is impossible
for him to become emancipated from the tyranny of the group.
Both succeeded in drawing out from their numbers, in the narrow
sphere allotted to their labours, an energy, a devotion, and a self-
control far greater than could be expected from anyone of them
in his individual capacity. In early Rome everything conspired
to maintain and increase among the upper classes the influence of
this powerful and minutely organized system. We find it in the
distribution of wealth, in religion, in the public institutions, in the
severity of the legal code: we find it in a public opinion which
demanded a relentless exercise of authority by fathers against
their children, or by husbands against their wives. We find it
above all in the family, which gave the earliest and most deep-felt
lessons in this stern and difficult discipline of the spirit. . . . It
was the family which taught even the richer Roman, from the
days of his youth, to be content with small enjoyments, to keep
pride and vanity in check, to own submission, not to another man
like himself—for monarchy he abhorred with a fanatical loathing
—but to the impersonal authority of law and custom." Perhaps
there is a tendency to exaggerate the early Roman austerity. At
least we know that public opinion did not always support father
against child (cf. Livy, vii, 4).

[1] Mr. Gladstone, in Juventus Mundi, 396-7, says : " The point
in which the ethical tone of the heroic age stands highest of all is,
perhaps, the strength of the domestic affections." " Perhaps even
beyond other cases of domestic relation, the natural sentiment, as
between parents and children, was profoundly ingrained in the

daily personal contact, impossible between a territorial ruler and the generality of his subjects, supple-
mented by religion, habit, and the family council,
appear to have sufficed to render the family tie
tolerable to the early Romans, though later ages
considerably relaxed it.

A further powerful check to family misrule arose
incidentally at an early period in the institution of the
censura, a creation of law originally exercised by
King or Consul, and subsequently made a distinct
office of State. It is in so far related with our modern
notion of the census, as one of its objects was the
careful enumeration of the citizens, though chiefly
with regard to their right (and duty) to serve in the
army and vote in the comitia. But the Censor exercised another less positive but indirectly perhaps
more influential jurisdiction, the regimen morum. He
watched over the morals of the citizens, investigated
cases of misconduct, and visited with graduated
marks of censure (notae censuriae), in grave cases
with expulsion from Senate or Comitium, delin-
quencies which could not be reached by the arm of
the law.[1] Although the lighter reproofs of the Censor

morality of the heroic age." Though the period alluded to is
prior even to earliest Rome, the words are not inapplicable to the
latter.

[1] Cuq, Inst. jurid. des Romains, p. 11. L'observation des devoirs qui en résultent [from fas and mos] n'a d'autre sanction que
la colère des dieux ou la crainte de l'opinion publique, parfois
une peine religieuse, et, à partir d'une certaine époque, le blâme
du censeur.

were of moral effect only, they were always dreaded, and exercised a salutary influence over the conduct of a too arbitrary or an unconscientious paterfamilias.

CREATION AND EXTINCTION OF PATRIA POTESTAS

Patria potestas could be acquired or lost *naturally*, by events happening in the ordinary course of nature; *voluntarily*, by acts done by a paterfamilias, with or without the concurrence of the person in potestate, having that object in view; and it could be lost *adventitiously*, by acts done or suffered by a paterfamilias, or person in potestate, not having such object in view. The other kinds of power over free persons were Manus and Mancipium. The former has been dealt with in the chapter on Marriage; mancipium is incidentally considered below so far as is necessary for our purpose.

Loss or Gain of Patria Potestas in the Course of Nature

1. The death of a paterfamilias operated to transmit his power to his sons, ex justis nuptiis or adopted, each of whom was henceforward paterfamilias over his own descendants and acquired in his own right such portion of the parent's property as he inherited, or took under the latter's will when the power of testamentary disposition had become established. One family thus might split up into

several, but all the members remained agnatically related to each other through their whilom common subjection to the deceased.

2. The birth of offspring conferred patria potestas upon the father, if himself paterfamilias; if not, upon the ancestor having power over him. This, however, was subject to the following conditions:

(*a*) The marriage itself must be matrimonium justum. If this condition were satisfied it was immaterial that the wife was not in manu, as although the latter remained either sui juris or in potestate of her own ancestor, her children were nevertheless in potestate of their father or eldest male paternal ancestor. All children conceived out of wedlock, or the offspring of some form of marriage not recognized in Roman civil law, were born sui juris. The law gave the father no power over them, and the mother was incapacitated by her sex from exercising it. This was the case, for instance, with the children of unions between patricians and plebeians before the lex Canuleia. Plebeian citizens could, of course, always contract just marriage with each other. Before they had conquered full political rights, plebeians cannot have been held, in strict law, capable of acquiring patria potestas, which was the prerogative of a Roman citizen, but it is to be assumed that custom remedied the law's deficiency.

(*b*) The child must have been *conceived* during the marriage. For this reason the legitimacy of children born before the one hundred and eighty-second day after the marriage was assailable.

Although *conception* during the marriage was necessary, actual *birth* was not, provided it happened within ten months of the dissolution of the marriage. In the latter case, the father's ancestor, if living, would have power over the child. If there were no living ancestor, the child was under no power, and thus himself paterfamilias. A posthumous child, whose father had been a paterfamilias, did not enter the family, and was consequently unable to inherit. This injustice was afterwards removed by the interpreters of the XII Tables.

(*c*) The child lawfully born under the above conditions must be formally recognized by the family chief, at whose feet the babe was laid. The act of recognition was marked by his raising the child in his arms (tollere, suscipere).

(*d*) It then only remained to associate the child with the family sacra by the ceremony of purification (lustratio), involving a sacrifice to the family gods. A name was given to the child, if a boy on the ninth, if a girl on the eighth day after the birth.

A Roman citizen intermarrying justly with a foreigner (peregrina), with whom he had connubium, acquired potestas over issue begotten of the marriage. If married cum manu, the wife came under the Hand and became herself a Roman citizen;[1] if sine manu,

---

[1] Karlowa, Röm. Rechtsges., ii, 70; but *contra*, Muirhead, R. L., 108.

the children still fell under the potestas, but the wife became neither a citizen nor her husband's or children's agnate. If a Roman woman justly married a peregrinus, he did not acquire manus at Roman law, but only such rights as his own State gave him. Children born of just marriage followed the condition of the father and, in the case last noted, would be foreigners. If born of marriage jure gentium, or any other lower intercourse, they followed the condition of the mother;[1] until, in the sixth century of the City, through the operation of a special law (the lex Mensia or Minicia) children born of a Roman woman who had condescended to a lower form of marriage with a foreigner, were made to follow the status of the "inferior" parent (deterioris parentis conditionem sequi jussit[2]).

Voluntary Acquirement or Surrender of Patria Potestas

1. *Adrogation.* The primary care of the Roman citizen was to perpetuate his family. The horror of dying and leaving no one whose duty it would be to perform the religious offices due from the living to the dead was ingrained in the Roman character, and known to many other ancient, as well as modern nations.[3] But Rome did not recognize the practice of begetting successors vicariously by calling in a

---

[1] Dig., i, 5, 24; Gaius, i, 76 ff. [2] Ulpian, v, 8.
[3] Czylharz, Lehrbuch der Institutionen, 239. "Der Grundgedanke der adoptio ist bei den verschiedensten Völkern ein sacraler."

kinsman or stranger to cohabit with a wife, or by "appointing" a daughter to bear a "son" to her father, or by marriage of the widow with the kinsman of a husband who had died childless, devices common to other Aryan and non-Aryan races.[1] Before testamentary dispositions became usual, a childless man commonly supplied the want by adopting some young relative, or, failing that, a stranger as his son. If the person adopted were himself paterfamilias, the transaction was called Adrogatio, from having been originally [2] carried out by rogatio populi in comitiis calatis.

To guard against loss of the family sacra of the adrogatus, the pontifices had first to be satisfied that there were others to continue them. They then convened the comitia, which sat pro collegio, under the presidency of the pontifex maximus acting as rogator. He asked the adrogator: an velit eum, quem adoptaturus sit, justum filium sibi esse. On an affirmative reply, the question was put to the adrogandus: an id fieri patiatur. The rogatio was then made to the people in the following terms: Velitis, jubeatis uti L. Valerius L. Titio tam jure legeque filius sibi siet, quamsi ex eo patre matreque familias ejus natus esset, utique ei vitae necisque potestas siet, uti patri endo filio est, haec ita, uti dixi, ita vos,

---

[1] Cf. Maine, Early Law and Custom, 100 ff.

[2] Adrogation by will, if it existed at all before the second century B.C., must have been very rare. Caius Octavius (Augustus) was so adrogated by Julius Caesar.

Quirites, rogo.[1] The question was then put to the vote. All the property of the adrogatus went to his new paterfamilias, into whose power his children (if any) likewise came nepotum loco. For his and their torts the paterfamilias became henceforward noxally liable, but the personal debts of the adrogatus lapsed through the capitis deminutio, until the Praetor gave equitable relief to creditors.

The object of adoption, viz., the perpetuation of a particular family, was kept in view much more closely in adrogation than in the adoption of a person already in potestate, and therefore during the Republic and early Principate:

(*a*) Females were never adrogated, for they could not continue a family;[2]

(*b*) Only one person could be adrogated by the same adrogator;

(*c*) The adrogator must be at least sixty years old, *i.e.*, at an age when the birth of a natural heir had become improbable.

Moreover, under the old law, impuberes, when sui juris, could not be adrogated, for they had not the free disposal of their caput.

2. *Adoption* in its narrower sense, *i.e.*, of persons

---

[1] Aul. Gell., N. A., v, 19. A declaration by the adrogatus that he renounced the sacral association of his old family (sacrorum detestatio) was also made at some stage of the proceedings. It was an immemorial rule that no person could be deprived of the position of paterfamilias against his will.

[2] Apart from this reason, females were ineligible for adrogation on the ground that they had not the comitiorum communio.

alieni juris, was accomplished in one of the following modes:

(*a*) It is highly probable that originally the adoption of a person already in potestate could be effected comitiis calatis by a ceremony similar to that of adrogation. This method fell into desuetude as soon as jurists had invented, with the aid of the XII Tables,

(*b*) Datio in adoptionem. It was now possible by mancipation to withdraw the whole transaction from the control of pontifices and comitia, and make it a purely private bargain. The consent of the adoptandus was apparently at first not required, and there was no limitation of the number of persons who could be adopted.

It is here the place to consider Mancipation (mancipium) in connection with the device by which adoption was effected by a fictitious sale on the part of the natural father of the adoptandus.

For the purpose of bargain and sale all alienable property belonged to one of two classes,[1] res mancipi and res nec mancipi. The former comprised, and the latter excluded, all property which, to a citizen of the earlier times, would appear most essential to the subsistence, comfort, and dignity of a family: beasts of draught and burden, such as plough-oxen and horses, lands and houses (included in the familia when they became alienable), with appur-

---

[1] A distinction which, though in increasingly attenuated form, survived until Justinian.

tenances and servitudes, and slaves. Whilst res nec mancipi were transferable by mere tradition, res mancipi in quiritarian right could pass only by surrender in court (in jure cessio), or by mancipium, by means of the ceremony of the copper and the scales (per aes et libram).

The legal distinction between res mancipi and nec mancipi is probably no more recent than the time of Servius, or whichever legislator first *regulated* the practice of Mancipation. Doubtlessly the latter was of high antiquity, however, and referable to an age when separate property in immovables was unknown, and the only commodities were things (chiefly slaves and animals) which could be grasped with the hand.[1] Originally, therefore, mancipation could suitably be applied to all things capable of being merchanted, which in time came to include immovables, and no doubt habitually took place in large transactions, because, when performed before witnesses, it was a convenient mode of securing notoriety to the bargain, and fixing in the memory of disinterested parties the fact that the purchaser had lawfully acquired possession, and the liability of the vendor to be vouched to warranty in respect of the title. For the purposes of the census, when it became of importance to ascertain with some precision the private

[1] Muirhead, R. L., 59-60, derives mancipium from manum capere (to acquire dominion or ownership) rather than manu capere (to grasp with the hand). But this is by no means conclusive, and the procedure forms in real actions are scarcely explainable except on the more generally received theory.

fortune of each citizen, an enactment attributed to Servius Tullius demanded the use of the copper and scales, the presence of witnesses, and the utterance of set forms of speech, whenever there was a transfer of property in those objects which, in the then estimation, were of the highest importance. Subsequently, it appears to have been assumed at Rome that those objects alone were capable of mancipation.

Mancipation had probably had its vogue throughout Italy during the period when trade among the recently-settled communities had developed beyond the stage where cattle formed the sole or predominant currency, whilst coined money still remained an unknown or exceptional medium of exchange. During that period, raw copper and, later, rough ingots of the same metal, sometimes guaranteed by a Government stamp, provided a general and comparatively convenient standard of value. The price was accordingly not counted, but weighed out to the seller.[1] After the use of coined money had become general, the weighing of the purchase price was represented by striking the scales with a single coin symbolizing the price, and handing it to the seller. Even in earlier times the purchase price, when large, must have been frequently weighed beforehand, and the ceremony of weighing before witnesses merely

---

[1] I know no reason for supposing that mancipation was confined to Rome or Europe, though the legal incidents would of course differ. The weighing of the purchase price and the presence of witnesses would suggest themselves anywhere under similar circumstances. Cf. Genesis, xxiii, 16; Jeremiah, xxxii, 9 ff.

denoted by touching the scales with a piece of metal.

We have already seen that paterfamilias could not at his discretion wholly divest himself of authority over his child. The law of the City, indeed, repudiated any general duty to protect child against parent, and sanctioned duly solemnized bargains disposing of the former's person.[1] But religion, safeguarded by the pontiffs and the domestic tribunal, forbade the arbitrary extinction of a child's birthright, and heinous crime against his kin would alone justify the permanent exclusion of the offender from the family sacra. By the copper and the scales à child could be transferred like a commodity to a strange master, but the new relationship was civil, not sacral. For religious purposes he was still a member of his father's, not of his master's, family. If by any means he became released from his bondage, his natural ancestor resumed the full potestas over him, and until 303 urbis this might happen again and again. But whether to confirm an already existing custom, or to introduce a new principle of law, the XII Tables enacted that if a father sold his son three times the son should be free from the father

---

[1] It is doubtful whether by the law of the City a man might mancipate his wife or daughter-in-law in manu, and such transactions are said to have been prohibited in regal times. Even without any express prohibition it must have constituted a hideous violation of the fas, and have been visited accordingly. It is possible, also, that a father was immemorially unable to mancipate a married son, or any child born of confarreate marriage.

(si pater filium ter venum duit, filius a patre liber esto). The precise object of this enactment is obscure. Sales by fathers of their children were not uncommon where the parents were poor, and the decemviri may have had it in their minds to punish an unnatural father who cared for his son only as a source of commercial profit.[1] Having regard, however, to the general trend of the decemviral legislation, it is not improbable that the enactment was meant to serve merely the object which it purported to intend, namely, to permit the irrevocable destruction, after the deliberation necessitated by a threefold transaction, of the hitherto indissoluble bond of union between father and son. The ancient authority of family sacral institutions had by this time become seriously impaired, and it may be assumed that the procedure indicated by the secular law now for the first time enabled the connection between Ancestor and Descendant to be entirely severed by the sole volition of the former.

As no freeman could be sold for a slave in Rome,

---

[1] "Venumduit" is generally rendered "sold." Cuq is of opinion that "hired out" is more correct, that the mancipation of a son (contrary to the ordinary rule of property transferred by the copper and the scales) was ad tempus only, and that the term of hiring came to an end with each lustrum. The object of the enactment was to allow the father to exploit his son's marketable services for a maximum term of fifteen years and no more. In support of this theory it is plausibly urged that if the sale were out and out the enactment would be mostly inoperative, and therefore meaningless.

a free person in mancipio was not servus but servi loco. We have already seen that the bondage was probably not indefinite, and the bondsman only suffered capitis deminutio minima (not maxima, as with slavery, nor media, which entailed the loss of civic rights), but in most other essentials the incidents of his position followed the law relating to slaves. He was not agnatically related with the children of his dominus, and far from sharing in the inheritance on the latter's death, he was himself part of the estate, and became the property of the heirs for the residue of the term of his servitude. A legacy left to him, like one left to a slave, was valid only if at the same time he were manumitted by testament. Like the slave he could also be manumitted vindictâ by a fictitious action claiming that he was in reality free; or, since the institution of the census, by his master acquiescing in the enrolment of his name as a free citizen. The restrictions subsequently imposed upon the manumission of slaves by the leges Aelia Sentia and Fufia Caninia did not apply to him.

If a person in mancipio had children born to him, they fell with him into his father's power upon his manumission, provided of course that (subsequently to the XII Tables) he had not been mancipated three times.

When the ancestor's right to divest himself of the whole of the potestas had become established, resort to the comitia, where the adoption of a child in potestate was in question, became unusual, and the object was accomplished by the means furnished by the XII Tables. A father having arranged for the adoption of his son would mancipate him in the first instance to a friend. The friend immediately manumitted the son, who relapsed under the father's potestas. Second sale and second manumission, and then a third sale followed, when the father's power was destroyed, the son remaining in mancipio of the friend. The adopter now appeared upon the scene as plaintiff in a fictitious lawsuit, in which (as with our old English Recoveries) judge, litigants, and onlookers joined in a solemn farce. The adopter claimed the son as his own from the friend by the formula: Aio hunc hominem ex jure Quiritium filium meum esse. The friend admitted that he had no answer to the claim, whereupon the son was awarded (addictus) to the adopter, under whose potestas he thenceforward remained. By adding one stage to the transaction the co-operation of a friend could be dispensed with. The son would be mancipated each time to the adoptive father. The latter, after the third mancipation (which destroyed the patria potestas), remancipated the adoptandus to the natural father, who, instead of a friend, became the defendant in the fictitious action which was thereupon brought.

A plebeian might by adrogation or adoption enter a patrician family and acquire gentilitas. Conversely, there appears to have been no legal hindrance to the adrogation or adoption of a patrician by a plebeian.[1] But in the earlier ages both events would be regarded with disfavour. Particularly the passing from a patrician to a plebeian family would be distasteful to old-patrician notions, and the pontiffs would, save in very special cases, refuse their concurrence, where such concurrence was necessary. During the latter half of the Republic, however, translations from the higher to the lower order became more frequent, as a convenient mode of rendering the scion of a patrician house eligible for the tribunate.

In addition to subserving the purposes of an adoption, the transaction creating the relation of mancipium[2] between a free person in potestate and a stranger was usually entered into with one of the following objects:

(a) Where a father sold his son (or rather hired out his services) in Rome for purposes of gain. The son's bondage lasted only until the next census, when he was entitled to reinstatement as a full freeman,[3] subject of course to the father's right to sell him again, unless (after 303 urbis) such right

---

[1] Mommsen, Römische Forschungen, i, 74 ff.

[2] A distinction between mancipium and nexum seems to be indicated by the passage in the XII Tables: Cum nexum faciet, mancipiumque, uti lingua nuncupassit, ita jus esto. Nexum was apparently a contract for the repayment of a money loan, the security for which was the debtor's own person. We have already seen how the treatment of prisoners for debt was among the foremost causes of domestic strife during the early Republic.

[3] Cuq, Inst. jur., 56.

had already been exercised three times, when he became sui juris.

(*b*) To effect a noxal surrender (*infra*).

(*c*) It was very usual for a child to be placed in the family of a friend for the purpose of education. This was especially the case with clients, who sent their children to be brought up as alumni in the houses of their patrons. In such cases the child was generally given in mancipio, and manumitted on leaving the house of his foster-father.

We have already seen that a son given in mancipio did not thereby become agnatically related with his new master's family,[1] and it seems that he could complain to the magistrate if subjected to ill-treatment by his master. A person in mancipio remained (as has already been said) a citizen, though what became of his political capacities during bondage is uncertain. Though in bondage to his master, he was free in respect of the rest of the world. The status of mancipium was relative, whereas the status of slavery was absolute, since a man might be a slave without an owner, as when condemned to slavery for a capital crime, or abandoned by his master.[2]

(*d*) With a view to emancipating the son (*infra*).

3. *Noxal surrender* (*noxae deditio*). We have already noted the responsibility of the head for the

---

[1] Nor of course a nexus, or paterfamilias whose person had been seized in default of satisfaction of a debt.

[2] Poste's edition of Gaius, p. 76.

torts of the members of his family; but it is probable that the original nature of this responsibility had become profoundly modified. The early law distinguished but dimly Breach of Contract from Tort, or private wrong; Tort from Crime, or offence against the State; and Crime from Sin, or offence against the gods. It made no difference in principle whether a citizen broke his contract or his neighbour's head, and it was immaterial that the breach or fracture had been unwilling or inadvertent. Probably the consequences of default, trespass, murder, and sacrilege in each case had their root in the notion of Expiation.[1] The religious element must certainly have predominated in the practice of surrendering to the enemy a representative who had concluded a treaty which the Senate refused to ratify, since treaties were sacrosanct. The duty to avenge a kinsman's wrongs was part of the sacred fundament upon which had rested the primitive group. The duty had a double aspect: the group had not only to satisfy its own rough sense of justice, but was the instrument designated to exact retribution for an outrage against the gods. The blood-feud, though certainly a part of the gentile tradition, could not long have been tolerated in an orderly community.[2]

---

[1] Cf. Florus, Epit., ii, 18 (deditione Mancini); Livy, viii, 39, cited in Holmes, Common Law, c. i, but Holmes seems to have held that redress was only due for intentional torts.

[2] Among the turbulent German tribes the talionic law died hard, and the Frankish kings followed it constantly, though

Yet though the State stepped in to substitute its
own regulated justice for the unregulated vengeance
of the injured party or his relatives, the punishment
long retained its character as an expiatory act, and
authors of crimes accounted serious, who were put
to death, or became civilly dead by voluntary ban-
ishment, were considered to have been sacrificed to
the gods. But in the case of private wrongs and
defaults which were not directly subversive of the
State or of religion, the notion of expiation was relegated to the background by an ordered administration, solicitous above all to prevent a breach of
the peace by appeasing the anger of the injured
party. Mutilation of a freeman was, by the law of
the XII Tables, still visited by similar mutilation of
the aggressor, but the parties might agree to a compromise, and later a fine became substituted for the
lex talionis. The defaulting debtor, or thief caught
upon the spot,[1] was handed over as a bondsman to
his creditors, or the person robbed. A wrongdoer,
who was paterfamilias, if he had the means, could
in most other cases be compelled to offer, and the
injured party to accept, money compensation for
the trespass. But the object sought was retribution
of some kind upon the offender personally: slaves
and animals, and originally persons in potestate,

---

probably from mixed motives. " Deadly feud " was recognized in
England till Canute's time at least.

[1] Gaius, iii, 184. A slave, however, under similar circumstances
suffered, after scourging, death.

had no property of their own, and money paid on their behalf constituted only a vicarious punishment. Accordingly, where a son,[1] slave, or animal,[2] had committed injury, the father or master, unless he were himself the author of, and actionable for it, was obliged to surrender the delinquent into the hands of the party injured. In course of time advancing civilization allowed the father or master to save his son or property from the claimant, on making good the damage, but still left to the former the option of surrender, if the liability were more than he could or cared to discharge.[3] The liability (failing payment of damages) to be surrendered still clung to

[1] Daughters were similarly liable, and I do not know that the law placed wives in an exceptional position. The alleged prohibition, in the regal period, to mancipate a wife in manu may have referred to voluntary mancipations only. Cuq, Inst. jur. des Romains, 111. But women in early Rome had small opportunity to bring themselves into conflict with strangers. In some cases penalties threatened by the State were mitigated when the offender was a child of tender years.

[2] The same may have applied even to inanimate objects from which a person had received bodily injury. The idea of satisfying a desire for revenge is not incompatible with such a course, for (1) primitive man can scarcely conceive anything as otherwise than sentient, and (2) even if he did, his instinct would still be to mutilate or destroy the tree or other object which had raised his ire. The same reason would prompt the surrender of the offender's dead body, or part of it, although a distinction seems to have been observed between the body of a human being and that of an animal. Cf. Poste's edition of Gaius, p. 524; Cuq, Inst. Jur. des Romains, 114.

[3] Holmes, Common Law, p. 9: The right of surrender was not introduced as a limitation of liability, but, in Greece and Rome

the tortfeasor, even though he meanwhile changed his master, for the obligation to surrender or compensate lay with his superior for the time being (noxa caput sequitur). Thus, if a paterfamilias, after commission of a tort, by adrogation fell under the power of another, the direct action for damages, which would have lain against him, now lay against the adrogator, who could only absolve himself by payment, or surrender of the adrogatus; conversely, where filiusfamilias, after commission of the act, had become paterfamilias, a direct action lay against himself.

A slave who had been noxally surrendered merely changed his master; a filiusfamilias became in mancipio, but, under the later law, was entitled to his release after having by his work and services given adequate compensation for the injury which had caused his surrender.

It is probable that one single noxae deditio, and not three, sufficed to free the son from the father's potestas.[1]

In the transactions so far examined, an existing power has been merely transferred from one person to another without being extinguished. The only exception is the obvious one of death, which destroyed absolutely the power of the deceased over his sons, transferring, however, to the latter power over their respective descendants. Abdication attenu-

---

alike, payment was introduced as the alternative of a failure to surrender.

[1] Gaius, iv, 79.

ated, sale as a slave and emancipation destroyed, the power in one without vesting it in another.

4. *Abdication, Repudiation.* Short of selling the child abroad as a slave, the most ancient law knew no means of destroying the rights of the ancestor by voluntary act. A paterfamilias could, however, as a punishment banish from his house[1] a member of his family, and thus exclude him from participation in the private sacra. This was called abdicatio where the culprit was a male, and repudiatio where she was a female, for instance a daughter-in-law in manu, her husband being powerless to forbid her repudiation. Legally the act was inoperative, the chief retained even against his will his proprietary rights, and the child his quality of suus heres. This method of punishment became obsolete when the law made emancipation possible.[2]

5. In ancient times a father could sell his son as a slave[3] "beyond Tiber"—that is, into a foreign State having no sacral connection with Rome. According to the original notions, it was not in any mortal's discretion to confer freedom upon a slave, or impose slavery upon a freeman, otherwise than by a fiction. A slave could only achieve liberty through a fictitious action brought at the suit of a citizen, and postulating that he was in reality free. A child sold abroad was reputed civilly dead: his subsequent fate was no longer a matter of solicitude for the

---

[1] Val. Max., v, 8, 3 : "protinus e conspectu meo abire jubeo."
[2] Cod., viii, 46, 6.   [3] Cic., De Orat., i, 40, 181.

State, and unlike one who, having fallen a prisoner into the enemy's hand, had escaped back to his countrymen, a cast-off son recovered none of his rights on returning to Rome.

6. *Emancipation.* Though it be open to doubt whether the conservatively-inclined Decemvirs ever intended a father to be enabled either to give his son in adoption without the concurrence of the comitia, or to make him sui juris under any circumstances, yet both these results were achieved by the instrumentality of the enactment already noticed: Si pater filium ter venum duit, filius a patre liber esto. The first case of emancipation is said to have taken place in the year of the City 398, when C. Licinius Stolo, in order to evade his own law prohibiting the holding of more than 500 jugera of land by one person, emancipated his son, and then conveyed the surplus land to him. He was fined for it, on the legally not very sound ground that emancipando filium fraudem legi fecisset,[1] but the transaction itself could not be upset.

The father desiring to emancipate his son went three times through the form of giving him in mancipio, by the copper and the scales, to a friend in the manner already described, the son being each time manumitted. The friend was called, in respect of the fictitious purchase, parens fiduciarius, in respect of the manumission, extraneus manumissor. By the act of manumission, the manumittee became his

---

[1] Livy, vii, 16.

client, and in order to reserve to the father the privileges of patronage over his son, it became usual for the parens fiduciarius, after the third sale, to re-sell him to the natural parent, who now acquired power in mancipio over the son in place of the patria potestas, which he had irrevocably lost. The father then himself manumitted the son, whereby he became the son's patron, and the expectations of succession to each other's property were to some extent reversed.

The emancipation of a daughter, grandchild, or great-grandchild was accomplished by a single sale only, followed by manumission by the extraneus manumissor, or by re-sale to and manumission by the natural parent. With the object of simplifying the procedure, the enactment of the XII Tables, which mentioned a son (filius), but not a daughter (filia), was construed to mean that the treble sale in the case of daughters and other descendants not being sons, was unnecessary ; and that these, having been once sold, could not again automatically relapse into the power of their natural ancestor.[1] Whatever may be thought of this construction, there was some reason for it. The State being based upon the family system, public interest could not brook frivolous or capricious changes of the family status, and the compulsory treble sale insured that degree of deliberation which must accompany so important a trans-

---

[1] Gaius, i, 132a. Possibly the decemviri purposely neglected daughters and grandchildren as unimportant, leaving them under the old law.

action. But females were incapable of perpetuating or initiating a family, and their emancipation might reasonably be carried out more summarily. For instance, a daughter, who was promised in marriage to a Roman living in one of the colonies, might be emancipated with a view to rejoining him in the new home and marrying him there; or a daughter-in-law might, under similar circumstances, be emancipated to follow an already emancipated son. When grandchildren, male or female, were alienated from the ancestor's power it would usually be for the purpose of transferring them to the power of their already emancipated natural father, and in this case also a single sale might conveniently be deemed to satisfy the law.

Through the severance from the family the emancipatus lost all agnatic rights, including that of inheritance. Instead of being his father's heir, the latter, if (as was usually the case) he had manumitted him, now, in certain circumstances, became his, by virtue of the patronage. Through the change of status he suffered capitis deminutio, and therefore, if a patrician, lost gentilitas. For the same reason, he did not by his emancipation acquire patria potestas over children already born to him. So long as the patrician privileges retained their importance, and fathers did not freely use their testamentary power of appointing as heirs persons outside their family (*e.g.*, an emancipatus), emancipation entailed serious consequences for the son. But with the advance of civilization the fetters of sonship must have been felt to be increasingly galling, and emancipation no doubt in time became the reward and privilege of a dutiful or distinguished son.

The acquisition of patria potestas by legitimation of illegitimate offspring as a consequence of the subsequent marriage of the parents, or, in the case of Latini Juniani, as a corollary to the acquisition of citizenship, belongs to a much later epoch.

Adventitious Loss of Patria Potestas

1. A paterfamilias might suffer loss of citizenship, and even of liberty, from various causes: by way of punishment at the hands of the State; by capture on the part of a foreign enemy; by surrender to a foreign State upon non-ratification of a treaty in the manner already mentioned; by neglect to perform his military duties or to register himself on the census; or by being sold into slavery by his creditors. Loss of citizen rights extinguished the potestas, but a Roman prisoner of war who was fortunate enough to escape back to his country became reinstated in his former position by virtue of the jus postliminii. Conversely, the ancestor's power over a descendant who had been captured by the enemy was similarly paralysed.[1]

2. Where a filiusfamilias had been guilty of violence to a tribune, he could be summoned before the

---

[1] Gaius, i, 129.

comitia tributa and punished for treason. And a filiusfamilias guilty of manifest theft, after being beaten,
was delivered into the bondage of the injured party.[1]
In these cases the State exceptionally over-rode the
father's private jurisdiction.

3. Flamens used to have the assistance of their own
children in performing the public rites. If left childless, they appear to have been permitted to take for
the purpose the children of other parents, who must
be living at the time,[2] even against the will of the
latter. Similarly, unmarried girls could be impressed
as vestals. In such cases, the ancestor's power was
suspended so long as the child remained consecrated
to the service of the gods, but revived when the
service terminated. The vestal, although freed from
the ancestral power, was not strictly sui juris, but
under the power of the pontifex maximus. She was
not subject to wardship.

WARDSHIP (TUTELA) AND CURATEL

Children became sui juris upon the death of their
father, if paterfamilias, and remoter descendants
upon the death of their ancestor, if their more immediate ancestors had predeceased him. Where
they were still of tender years something was required in the place of the expired potestas, and this
was partially supplied by Tutory or Guardianship
(tutela). Tutory was a trust of great sanctity, which

---

[1] Gaius, iii, 189.   [2] Rossbach, Römische Ehe, 140.

the incumbent was expected to discharge reasonably and honestly. Originally the gens (where the ward was a patrician), and later the censor, no doubt exercised some supervision, but regular legal remedies for a tutor's maladministration probably did not exist in the first few centuries.

A tutor's duties were twofold. He assumed the ancestor's potestas to this extent, that he was entitled and bound to care for the proper nurture and education of his young ward (pupillus) and to exercise the amount of personal control necessary to that end, though the ward did not usually reside with the tutor if his mother still lived. In addition, he acted in circumstances which could not have arisen whilst the child was alieni juris. He brought and defended actions on behalf of the ward, administered his affairs, and by concurrence enabled him where necessary to enter into valid business transactions. The tutor could not in such transactions represent the ward: it was necessary that the latter should himself go through the prescribed forms, and if unable to do so through extreme youth (infans[1] or infantiae proximus) the tutor could only validate a bargain which was unmistakably to the ward's benefit.[2] In all other transactions the will of the tutor was not substituted

---

[1] Infans was a child who was not yet able to speak plainly, and consequently could not pronounce the requisite formulas. In time the period of infantia came to be arbitrarily fixed as the first seven years of life.

[2] Gaius, iii, 109.

for the will of the ward; the tutor by his concurrence merely increased (augebat) the measure of the pupil's will to the extent legally necessary to bind him.

Tutory, as we know it, probably did not become a well-defined institution, nor did the need of it arise, until the ancient gentile constitution was in an advanced stage of decay. Originally, tutory was probably exercised either by the gens as a corporate body, which perhaps delegated the duty to one or more kinsmen, or as of right by the nearest adult male agnate or agnates of the ward, and the latter were the persons designated by the XII Tables (and hence called tutores legitimi), failing contrary directions on the part of the deceased parent. But the latter's right to choose a guardian was acknowledged long before his right to choose an heir, and the appointment of tutors by a father (tutores testamentarii) was no doubt the earliest and, to ancient notions, the most legitimate of mortis causa dispositions. The appointment, however, only held good for those descendants who became sui juris on the death of the appointor : a grandson, for instance, on the death of his grandfather came under his own father's power if the latter were then alive. As guardianship was deemed a public office, filiifamilias were eligible as tutors.

Tutelage over a male ward ceased with the advent of puberty, which, though afterwards fixed at the completion of the fourteenth year,[1] was

---

[1] Just. Inst., i, 22.

originally determined by the family after bodily inspection.

Tutelage over adult women sprang from a different order of ideas. A girl's normal destiny was to remain under the ancestral potestas until nubile, when she was provided with a dos out of the family stock and married. Her kinsmen were then considered to have done their duty by her, and she lost her agnatic relation and quality of sua heres; since as we have seen, in early times marriage invariably meant for the woman the exchange of one family for another. Her sphere of activity—and it was often a large one—was in any case the home; all serious transactions with the outside world fell to her father or husband, and at no period did the Roman law encourage women to engage in business affairs.[1] But a wife might at any time be widowed, and, however infrequently, an adult girl might become fatherless whilst still unmarried. There is no reason to assume that either was considered intellectually inferior, or deficient in strength of character. Neither need we follow those who would derive the necessity for perpetual wardship over females from the woman's

[1] Dig., xvi, 1. Velleiano senatus consulto plenissime comprehensum est, ne pro ullo feminae intercederent. Nam'sicut moribus civilia officia adempta sunt feminis et pleraque ipso jure non valent, ita multo magis adimendum eis fuit id officium, in quo non sola opera nudumque ministerium earum versaretur, sed etiam periculum rei familiaris. The date of the senatusconsult is A.D. 46, but the same object had been aimed at by older edicts.

inferior physique and courage; for Rome was a well-
ordered community, and property was far more secure
there than in Plantagenet England. But in addition
to ordinary prudence and intelligence, technical skill
and experience were required for all important business in an age when ignorance of a mere form might
entail the gravest legal consequences, which, however iniquitous, the administrators of the law were,
strictly speaking, powerless to avert.[1] And in early
times the breach of a solemn covenant was visited
with such terrible effects that we can well understand
the general desire of men to lift their womenfolk
altogether above the perils which lurked in most
business transactions.

Thus (apart from certain technical sex-disabilities)
the dangers involved in worldly inexperience, and
the old-Roman delicacy at the frequent appearance
of women in public, pointed to the necessity of a
protection similar to that extended to children when
dealing with strangers. Originally, no doubt, another
reason may have been the desire of the brothers,
who in any case had to provide for their sister on
their father's death pending her marriage, to prevent
her from dissipating her share of the common stock
by ill-considered gifts, or transferring it elsewhither

[1] The Praetors did, however, sometimes stretch the law on
purely technical points for the benefit of women, young persons,
soldiers, and illiterate peasants. In fact, the indulgence allowed
women became in after ages so unfair as to require restriction by
Imperial Ordinance.

by an undesirable alliance; but to this consideration too much weight should not be given.

A husband could by will appoint a tutor to his widow, or confer upon her the right to choose her own tutor, thus ousting the kinsmen from the privilege. A slave could be appointed tutor by a will whereby he became enfranchised. Where a woman had neither testamentary nor statutory tutor, which would happen, for instance, where a female slave had been manumitted by her mistress, a tutor appointed under the lex Atilia (the date of which is uncertain), and named after it, was nominated by the magistracy.

The tutor of an adult woman did not administer her property, but he was bound to represent her before the courts, and his auctoritas was necessary to validate transactions per aes et libram. A woman could not marry coemptione without the auctoritas of her tutor, and if subject to a testamentary or statutory tutor could not (until Imperial times) make a will even with it,[1] a disability which will be further considered in the following chapter. There was an exception in this latter respect in the case of a freedwoman under the tutory of her patron, the latter being enabled to validate by his authority the will of a liberta made per aes et libram.

In later times, with the change of the social atmo-

---

[1] Gaius, i, 115a. This view is widely, though not universally, accepted. Cohn (Conrat), Beiträge zur Bearbeitung des römischen Rechts., 1-17.

sphere and increasing liberality of the law, tutory
over adult freeborn women lost what justification it
may have originally had, and by the invention of
fiduciary tutorship the law, whilst obeyed in the letter, came in time to be more or less satisfactorily
evaded. The ceremony of coemption broke the
tutory by placing the woman in the manus of the
husband: the woman, therefore, with her tutor's
auctoritas (which in course of time she became entitled to enforce), went through the ceremony of a
coemptional marriage with one who had promised
not to claim any marital privilege but forthwith to
remancipate her to a person of her own selection—
perhaps the very tutor from whose control she was,
with his consent, about to escape. The latter thereupon manumitted her. Thus she again became sui
juris and her manumittor her quasi-patron and, as
such, her tutor. The tutory of the quasi-patron permitted, and a trust previously undertaken bound, him
to sanction any acts of his nominal ward. Gaius
mentions that such a coemption might be for the
general purpose of avoiding the guardianship, coemptio fiduciaria tutelae evitandae causa (i, 114), or
for the special purpose of making a will, testamenti
faciendi gratia (i, 115a).[1] By hiring an old and frail

[1] We are informed (Cic., Pro Murena, xiii, 27) that fiduciary
coemption was sometimes employed by a female heir to an estate
to extinguish the sacra attaching to it (interimendorum sacrorum
causa). Apparently this was done by mock coemptional marriage
(followed by mancipation and manumission) with a destitute,
heirless, and aged trustee, who thereby acquired the universitas

man (senex coemptionalis) in humble circumstances, perhaps a slave freed for the purpose to act the bridegroom for a reasonable consideration, the lady obviated the danger of awkward consequences which might have arisen out of a breach of faith on the part of the nominal husband. The ultimate effect of this indecorous practice, which evidently belongs to a more sophisticated age than that which has claimed our chief attention, was to bring tutelage over adult females into contempt and desuetude.

Curatel originally denoted the power of the gentiles or agnates to administer the affairs of a kinsman sui juris and of the age of puberty, whom lunacy, imbecility, a recklessly wasteful disposition, or bodily infirmity rendered unfit to control his own property. Any male not so disqualified, and being sui juris, attained on puberty full contractual capacity, and when manners became less simple, men of business—especially, we may imagine, usurers—would not scruple to exploit the follies of youth. Legislation of the sixth century A.C. penalized those who overreached inexperienced young men, and it then became usual for the Praetor to appoint a person—who was called a

of the estate, including the sacra, and was bound by his trust to return the property to her in instalments. The trustee was then left quiritary owner of the bare universitas with the sacra. Upon his death the sacra became extinguished, since there was no heir to succeed him. The woman was not his heir, as the fiduciary coemption had not the effect of making her his filiafamilias, and even if it had, the mancipation would have destroyed the technical relation.

Curator—to advise a minor in respect of a particular contemplated transaction. Under the Empire, curatorship in this sense was made general, and to endure until the minor had completed his twenty-fifth year (perfecta aetas). So long as tutelage over women was permanent, a woman might have both a tutor and a curator at the same time, since their functions were considered to be distinct.

CHAPTER XII

SUCCESSION

THE old-Aryan family was an economic, as well as a religious, entity. The family estate was inseparable from the sacra, and co-associates in the cult of the family were necessary co-partners in its worldly assets and liabilities, or rather their individualities were merged in and formed an integral part of the joint and undivided family, whose chief managed the joint possessions. The family fortune and the family sacra formed an agglomeration of rights and duties which remained stable, though its administrators shifted.

The establishment of States by the coalescence of considerable numbers of gentes entailed a gradual decay of the gentile system, and the recognition of the Family in the narrower sense grouped under the eldest living male ancestor. But even the latter was never regarded as an owner of the family property in anything like the modern meaning of the word. The irresponsibility of the Roman head in the eye of the secular City law only masked the character of his sacred Trust; and paterfamilias, who, in his lifetime, could not capriciously deprive his dependants of their right to worship at the family altar, was also precluded from arbitrarily influencing the devolution of the patrimony upon his death so as to prefer some at the expense of others. Filiusfamilias was heres suus et necessarius [1]—the expression suus heres may be considered equivalent with sibi heres or heres sui ipsius: "self-successor." He was said to assume, or sustain, the ancestor's persona, though what is exactly meant by the phrase has never been established with certainty.[2] It is evident that at no time in Rome, nor, so far as I know, with any of the Aryan races, did a successor assume the deceased's personality to the extent of standing in his shoes for all purposes whatsoever. Magistracy in Rome, even in the regal period, was never heritable. No heir was obliged or expected to marry the defunct's widow,[3] even if there were no bar of blood-relationship, and the control which a son might as tutor

[1] Cf. Gaius, ii, 157; Voigt, XII Tafeln, ii, 387.

[2] Hoelder, in an article, Ueber die Stellung des römischen Erben (Zeitschrift d. Savignyschen Stiftung für Rechtsgeschichte, vol. xxix), disputes that the heir represented the persona of the defunct, and considers that the phrase was applicable to the inheritance as a connecting link between its dead and its living possessor.

[3] To the ancients, however, such a suggestion was by no means inherently absurd, and, but for the objection against mating a woman with her nearest blood-relative, might have been considered eminently desirable of realization. Where the patriarchal system and ancestor-worship were still in full force, women could not be continuers of the cult, and so could not become heirs. Therefore the best way of providing for a girl whom her father had not portioned and given in marriage during his lifetime, was to marry her to the heir, whom, if already married, the old law of

exercise over his mother, sisters, and younger brothers was more indirect than direct, and very different from manus or potestas. The word persona itself suggests a double explanation. It meant, among other things, a mask as worn by stage actors to personate the characters they represented, and also the waxen impression which it was usual to take of the face of a dead man, to be preserved by his posterity and displayed at the funerals of his descendants. The heir might be said to sustain the persona of the deceased, in that upon the stage of life he represented him in his character of dominus, creditor, and debtor against the outside world. But a more likely explanation seems to be that the heir, who in the most ancient times was invariably

Athens obligingly permitted to divorce his wife for the purpose. Where a son and a daughter were left, the same law even went the length of permitting their union if they had been born of different mothers. The idea that a man's womenfolk went with his property, however alien from Roman law, may have widely prevailed in remoter ages. Absalom was advised to take his father's concubines, apparently that he might irrevocably commit himself to an act of usurpation (2 Samuel, xvi, 21), and the prohibition of Deut., xxii, 30, may indicate that the practice of espousing a father's wife had at one time been not uncommon. Moreover, Solomon's indignation when asked to bestow Abishag, his father's widow, upon Adonijah, was evidently political, not moral. He perceived in the request a manœuvre to advertise his brother's claim to the throne in the eyes of the people. "Ask for him the kingdom also, for he is my elder brother" (1 Kings, ii, 22), is his bitter retort, and he proceeds instantly to arrange for the removal of one who had before intrigued for the throne (1 Kings, i), and has now again convicted himself of treasonable intent.

a natural or adoptive son, literally took and set up in the ancestral abode the image of his father's dead features. On the other hand, the inheritance itself, as an aggregate of rights and duties, might equally well be said to represent the persona of the deceased. However this may be, in taking over the deceased's property, the heir became charged with all his debts, as well as the obligation to continue the family cult. Far from being a necessary beneficiary, an heir might be called upon to assume an empty honour, or even a grievous burden (since the estate might conceivably represent a minus quantity), from which the most ancient law offered no escape, even if it had occurred to him to seek one.

Sui heredes were all those persons in the power of the deceased at his death, who thereby became sui juris. Grandchildren whose father had predeceased their grandfather, were therefore sui heredes, as well as any living children of the defunct. In a still primitive community one would have expected each of the sui to take the same share, for as all had been equally subject to the power, so all might have been deemed equally interested in the heritage. But the XII Tables—which cannot be supposed to have changed the law on so important a point—declared that descendants of the defunct took per stirpes, not per capita. Thus grandsons whose father had predeceased the defunct only divided their father's portion among themselves, instead of sharing equally with their uncles.

The women of the family, the widow, unmarried daughters, and widowed daughters-in-law, were accounted to rank with the men as sharers in the patrimony.[1] Yet in practice they were subjected to rules which effectually deprived them of free disposition over their fortunes, as well as to some extent even over their persons, and the anomaly of their position suggests that the earliest known canons of succession among the Romans represented modifications of a yet older system. Perpetuation of the sacra could not have been realized through daughters, who were unable to continue them beyond their own lifetime at the most, since upon their marriage they quitted for ever the paternal family, to which their offspring were born strangers. It is therefore evident that the primordial group constituted upon a patriarchal basis cannot have contemplated as a legitimate contingency the devolution of an estate solely to females. But so long as the ancient and indivisible gens remained the normal type of the social group, such a contingency could hardly arise. The original gens had a single head, perhaps designated by the rule of primogeniture,[2] perhaps by that of tanistry, or possibly in some cases appointed by the free will of his fellows, for it is unnecessary to assume a

---

[1] This was only fair to the widow, as she could not claim to receive back any part of her dos if it had become incorporated in the husband's or husband's ancestor's possessions. Voigt, XII Tafeln, ii, 388 n.
[2] F. de Coulanges, 90 ff., 120.

universal rule of succession for all gentes; and even if, among its usually numerous male members, the supply of eligibles threatened to run short, the remedy of adoption from another gens would be timeously applied.

When the gentile bond had become loosened by City association, new family units were constantly constituted, and each son on his father's death claimed an independent temporal and sacral head-ship over his own descendants, though he con-tinued a member of, and in many respects subject to, the control of his gens. Among these smaller groups, especially amid perpetual wars waged with the outside world, failure of natural male heirs be-came far more likely, and the practice of Adoption or (where a whole family was absorbed) Adroga-tion consequently more frequent. Thus there was a gradual breaking with the ancient rule of fixed devolution, and the choice of an adopted son, although no doubt it usually fell upon a blood relative, was, subject to the consent of the comitia, remitted to the adopter's discretion. But the persons adopted were invariably males, and female succes-sion, we are constrained to believe, was still a thing unknown.

TESTATION

It is doubtful whether, among the earliest Romans, even a limited power of Testation in the modern sense was exercised, save on very extraordinary occa-

sions. We know that in Rome patrician wills could
be made from very early times before the comitia
curiata, which sat in calatis twice yearly for the
purpose, or in procinctu, that is before one's comrades in arms, when ready to join battle with the
enemy ("procinctus est expeditus et armatus exer-
citus"; Gaius, ii, 101). But we are led to suppose
that the nature of such "wills" did not correspond
with what we now understand by that term. Moreover, it is highly probable that originally the express
consent (not a mere witnessing) of the comitia, or
assembly of citizens presided by the pontiffs as
guardians of the sacral law, was necessary to validate
the will, and this consent was by no means asked as
of right. The will upon the eve of battle was a con-
trivance to meet a specially urgent case, when a
citizen, desiring to appoint an heir, had been called
to arms before there was an opportunity of applying
to the comitia calata, or had neglected such opportunity as he had had. Even here some forms had
doubtless to be satisfied, including the taking of the
auspices.

From the point of view of the public interest, the
institution of an heir charged to continue the family
sacra was the vital element and primary object; the
disposition of the family estate (so far as competent
to the testator) and the appointment of guardians
over the females and minor male children of the
household, were only incidentally determined. Where
a paterfamilias had a suus heres, almost his only

object in going to the comitia at all (since he could not, save under very special circumstances, exheredate him) would be to ensure the due observance of some special duties, such as the payment of legacies or bringing up of infants, which he desired to impose upon the heir. But it is very probable that Testament in its earliest known form was most usually a mere modified Adoption,[1] which was resorted to by an aged paterfamilias, or by a youthful paterfamilias on active service, who, being sonless, and fearing, by reason of his age or imminent danger, to die in that condition, now besought his fellow citizens to sanction a publicly appointed heir. Such a successor would require no further proof of title to enter upon the deceased's estate, nor, if the estate fell short of his expectations, was he permitted to disclaim it and neglect the sacra.

Whilst our conceptions of the original gentile system drive us to reject both free testation and the capacity of women to inherit as original patrician institutions, the evidence is still stronger which leads us to recognize in them, at all events partly, the outcome of conditions in which the unattached plebeians found themselves in the primitive City. Undoubtedly many even of the earliest immigrant plebeians were or became men of some substance, who could not be indifferent to the manner of bestowal of their possessions upon their decease. But to them no law as yet applied. They or their ancestors had lost the citizenship of their vanquished or abandoned States

---

[1] Clark, Early R. L., 27 ff., 116 ff.

without gaining that of Rome, and public policy required the suppression of any quasi-gentile or other association calculated to crystallize the discontent of a subject population. The plebeian father already represented what the patrician father was only just becoming through the disintegration of his gens —an independent paterfamilias—and he was very willing to imitate within his own household patrician institutions like manus and potestas, whilst his freedom of action was untrammelled by the powerful checks of gentile custom. When such a man died, his dispositions, in the absence of legal sanction, would be followed as piety and interest dictated, and, failing special directions, his estate would be most naturally divided, according to the rough and ready rule that "equality is equity," among those who, in addition to natural right, had the first opportunity to handle it: his wife, and his children of both sexes, or failing such, among his nearest agnates, and possibly even his cognates also, since non-client plebeians were not bound by gentile rules. To such a course the City magistracy, who took no cognizance of plebeian sacra, could raise no objection founded on religion or public policy; and although in the beginning neither the unattached plebeians nor their belongings were technically under the wing of the law, in practice a man's nearest relatives would be treated as entitled to the enjoyment of his estate. Later, when plebeians had become full citizens, actual enjoyment, when continued a sufficient time, was converted into legal or quiritary ownership by usucaption.

But to such a man it would occur much more readily than to the disciplined mind of a custom-worshipping gentilis to innovate in regard to the distribution of his estate when fancy or seeming necessity so demanded. So long as he remained without the City law he could not secure the sanction of the comitia to his testamentary dispositions, and had to rely upon the interest or piety of his next-of-kin for their faithful observance. But when plebeians became liable to military service there was no ground for disputing their right of testation ·in procinctu; and when full citizenship had been achieved, I know no reason why a plebeian's testament should not have been considered and adjudicated upon even by a comitium in which he himself had as yet no right to sit. And it is extremely probable that in such cases more latitude would be given to the plebeian than to the patrician. There were no gentile interests to protect; the private sacra of a plebeian family scarcely challenged inquiry from such a body, and a plebeian estate which, upon intestacy, was suffered to pass in a manner contrary to patrician canons, might *a fortiori* be permitted to be so dealt with at the expressed wish of a testator. Hence it was that the Romans familiarized themselves with an ever-widening discretion on the part of the testator, a discretion which gradually extended to patricians. But it does not follow that the process was rapid, or even continuous. When the plebeians had secured for themselves an acknowledged and important place in the community, the wealthier elements, through closer intercourse with the patriciate, imbibed much of its conservatism, and the movement toward complete freedom of testation, instead of constantly progressing, may even have experienced a temporary set-back until the growing liberality of patrician sentiment enabled the nation to advance in one body towards a set of rules of universal application.

The relative enactments of the XII Tables mark a long step towards this goal, though they probably only legalized by statute what had already become recognized custom. By this time, among the patricians, the Agnatic Family had definitely ousted the gens in the prevailing social system. The gens still held corporate property, still celebrated religious rites, and still, as a body, was the repository of some potential rights in regard to individual members. Otherwise the patrician paterfamilias governed his family, and administered his (or its) property, as independently as his free plebeian fellow citizen. Special dispositions of property mortis causa had now become the rule rather than the exception, and the XII Tables recognized in every citizen a right to dispose of part of his estate independently of the assent of the comitia. I say part of the estate, for even now testamentary power does not appear to have been absolute. The intention of the new laws was not to aid the father to defeat the son's natural birthright. The enactment wisely enabled a testator to appoint whomsoever he considered most trustworthy to the guardianship of his wife and children, without reference to the relationship, and also allowed him to make bequests at his discretion. But such bequests could only be made out of the pecunia, or floating and transitory property of the family: flocks, herds, and other marketable chattels, and any interest in lands belonging to the State. He does not appear to have been allowed full discretion to will away the familia—that part of the estate which, as its name denotes, was more particularly identified with the family group, and had presumably been maintained by the combined exertions of all: the homestead, with freehold lands, and the instruments commonly employed for their cultivation. As to these latter, therefore, the last word still lay with the comitia calata.[1]

---

[1] Legare and testari were therefore two distinct functions; cf. Cuq. It must be confessed that the theory rests to some extent upon the assumed correctness of the rendering uti (paterfamilias) legassit *super pecunia tutelave* suae rei, ita jus esto, and would be more difficult to uphold if it could be shown that the words in italics were merely an interpolation or gloss of later interpreters (Muirhead, R. L., 117 n., 158 n.). And the view has failed to find favour in some authoritative quarters (*e.g.*, Voigt, XII Tafeln; Girard, Manuel de Droit Romain, 795 ff., who, however, favours the inclusion of the words super pecunia tutelave in the text). Nevertheless an absolutely unlimited right to exclude one's nearest relatives according to whim and caprice is, I think, almost confined to English law, and even in England the expression

The intention of the Legislature to protect the interests of persons in potestate was liable to be defeated by lavish gifts on the part of a paterfamilias during lifetime. It was probably to prevent as far as possible such a result that the XII Tables gave legislative force to an old gentile rule, by enacting that a spendthrift father might be placed, like a madman, under curatory, and his estate administered by kinsmen for the family's benefit. That the State should have ventured upon so decided an invasion of the father's privileges is proof of its anxiety to safeguard the natural rights of his helpless dependants, and perhaps also indicative of a rising tendency, under plebeian influence, on the part of fathers, to a more arbitrary bestowal of the property committed to their charge.

The XII Tables sought to establish as far as possible uniform rules of conduct for both orders, and the enactment which widened the patrician's testamentary liberty may have curtailed to some extent the freedom with which the plebeian in actual fact had been suffered to dispose of his property mortis causa. The expression—Si intestato moritur, cui

---

" to be cut off with a shilling " shows how hard the notion died that a father must leave *something* to his son. So complete a flouting of family sentiment as absolute freedom of testation is scarcely conceivable in a still primitive society founded upon patriarchism. That a testator was expected never to abuse his freedom is no answer to the objection. Communities will not legalize with their eyes open what they consider to be a heinous crime, however unlikely its perpetration.

suus heres nec escit, adgnatus proximus familiam habeto ("If a man die intestate without suus heres, let his nearest agnate have the familia ")—is sufficient evidence that among Romans generally the suus heres still succeeded as of course, failing express contrary disposition. It is allowable to suppose that the testament (as distinct from legacies) of a plebeian was now subjected to the same degree of scrutiny as that of a patrician, and that causeless disherison of a suus heres was liable to be opposed. Nor, when we remember the character of those sections of the plebs which were primarily affected, is it difficult to explain acquiescence in such a restriction, even on the part of men triumphantly emerging from a tremendous constitutional struggle. The small plebeian farmers, the toiling husbandmen, had remained poor, and how to bestow their property was the last of their anxieties. The richer plebeians, who controlled the popular movement, would not be predominantly freeholding farmers, but dealers and traffickers who depastured their cattle upon the comparatively extensive State lands—men who had risen to affluence by such rude commerce as was then practised in Latium and Etruria.[1] The bulk of their property was pecunia, the disposal of

---

[1] That commerce and trafficking was originally largely identified with a certain class of plebeians probably explains the unreasoning contempt affected by the Roman upper classes of later centuries for the trading and speculative occupations which they themselves so ardently pursued.

which the new law left entirely in their discretion.
But even plebeian landed proprietors might conceivably submit without reluctance to a curtailment
of their liberties. In England, where for upwards
of four centuries [1] the right of the tenant in tail to
bar the entail has been firmly established, an elaborate method of settlement has been devised, and from
time to time modified to suit shifting legislation, for
tying up property in land by which it is continued in
one family from generation to generation. In every
free community the tendency of each class is to approach as nearly as possible to that next above it.
Barbarous or semi-barbarous men will readily copy,
or bodily adopt in lieu of their own, an alien institution, or even an alien language, when stamped with
the prestige of a dominant class or race, with which
they have been compelled by circumstances to
familiarize themselves; and a plebeian whose homestead had been purchased by himself or his grandfather would not object to its being classed with the
heredia of families who claimed to have held them
since the building of the City.

Testamentum per aes et libram. — Originally a
testament could be made only before the comitia
sitting in calatis twice yearly; and when the necessity for a will arose, the best part of a year [2] might

---

[1] That is dating from Taltarum's case, temp. Edward IV, but
the practice is still older.

[2] The assemblies in calatis, though they took place twice
yearly, were not held at regular intervals of six months. Mommsen,
Staatsrecht, iii, 319.

elapse between intention and accomplishment, unless in the interim opportunity presented itself in procinctu. In these circumstances, a citizen who feared to die before his last dispositions could be declared, would supply the deficiency by transferring with the copper and the scales to a trusted friend, called a "purchaser of the familia" (familiae emptor) in the manner of an ordinary conveyance, the whole of his estate, familia pecuniaque, upon trust to deal with it on the death of the grantor in accordance with directions there and then orally given. The transfer was of the totality of the grantor's rights and obligations, considered as one aggregate (universitas), the pecunia, which comprised things non-mancipable when treated singly, being thereby carried along with the familia. The intention, of course, was that the familiae venditor should retain full control and disposition over his belongings during life, the conveyance only operating upon his decease. The intervention of a stranger, where the dispositions were for the benefit of a man's wife and children, was necessary because mancipation could not take place between a paterfamilias and those in his power.

The so-called testament per aes et libram may have been known as early as the regal period, but though patricians might avail themselves of it in emergencies, it must have appealed chiefly to plebeians as a preferable alternative to troublesome proceedings before an unsympathetic assembly. Originally its strict legal effect must have been to forthwith divest the grantor of the whole of his estate in favour of the alienee, whose acceptance was esteemed an adequate guarantee that he would not abuse the advantage to oust the grantor during life, or defraud the intended beneficiaries or creditors of the estate upon his decease. So tremendous a Trust seems to have been conferred without hesitation in those simple times, in reliance upon the Fides Romana and the moral atmosphere of the City life, with a minatory priesthood in the background.

In course of time, however, the missing legal protection came to be supplied by the enactment of the XII Tables: cum nexum faciet mancipiumque, uti lingua nuncupassit, ita jus esto. The directions to the familiae emptor contained in the nuncupatio, or public oral declaration (nuncupare est palam nominare, Gaius, ii, 104; Varro, De L. L., vi, 60), before five witnesses and a balance-holder, being all Roman citizens and puberes, now gave legal effect to the grantor's reservation of a life-interest and all dispositions to be observed upon his death.[1]

Both methods of quasi-testamentary disposition sanctioned by the XII Tables—the declaration of legacies in comitiis, and civil conveyance of the familia by copper and scales with reservation of life-interest and directions attached—failed in what to Roman

---

[1] Creditors apparently remained unprotected against fraudulent alienations inter vivos until the Praetor's equity furnished the remedy.

notions was the chief purpose and indispensable characteristic of a true Will—the institution of an Heir,
charged with the care of the family sacra. A legatee
under the statute was not an heir, a familiae emptor
was not an heir,[1] nor did a beneficiary, on whose
behalf the latter took, thereby become an heir.
Testamentum per aes et libram was therefore not at
first a satisfactory mortis causa disposition of the
family property where there was no suus heres. But,
contrary no doubt to the spirit and intention of the
statute, it was in time perceived that even if " uti
legassit . . . ita jus esto " still withheld from the
settlor the uncontrolled right of passing over his
natural heirs to the extent of leaving the familia away
from them, the words, "uti lingua nuncupassit, ita jus
esto," could be stretched to cover not only the uncontrolled bestowal of the whole family estate, but the
institution of any stranger as heir, without reference
to the comitia. The Decemvirs had overreached
themselves in their efforts to broaden the law.

Glaring abuse of the new complete freedom of
testation was probably rare in the earlier ages, for
in the then state of public opinion the publicity which
was still unavoidable might cause hesitation to an
unnatural father who contemplated defrauding his
children of their heritage. The introduction of the
Written and Secret Will swept away this last safeguard. Here the nuncupatio consisted merely of the

---

[1] Heredis locum obtinebat (Gaius, ii, 103) does not mean that
he was heir in the ancient sense of continuer of the cult.

usual formal transfer to the familiae emptor, with a reference to provisions declared to be inscribed upon tablets folded and tied up (codex) which the testator held in his hand and displayed to the witnesses.

The further development of the law relating to wills belongs to the maturity of Roman jurisprudence. The whole ceremony of mancipation was now meaningless, and whether it had been properly performed or not was immaterial, provided there was no reason to suspect the identity of the tablets produced. Of this, in time, the seals of seven witnesses [1] came to be considered sufficient evidence. Accordingly, by a change in the judicial procedure, it was made impossible for the opponent of a will so authenticated to inquire into the circumstances of its making. Thus, whilst professing to respect the strict legal right of an exheredated heir-at-law to upset a will on the ground of informality in the mancipation, magistrates practically defeated his claim by granting to the persons designated by the will beneficial enjoyment of the estate, which the heir-at-law was powerless to disturb, and which thus ripened by usucapion into full quiritary ownership.

As the civil law developed and moulded itself

---

[1] And, later, their signatures in addition. The number is supposed to have been made up from the five witnesses and the balance-holder required for a mancipation, plus the person who had originally represented the familiae emptor, but there is some doubt as to the last named. See Muirhead, R. L., 272 n., and the authorities there cited.

during the ensuing centuries, a mass of rules grew
up around the subject of testation. The latitude acquired by the testator had no doubt outrun the
intention of the legislators who were responsible
for the XII Tables. But in the growing community,
increasing fluidity of wealth had attenuated the ancient semi-sacred significance of the familia, as distinguished from pecunia, and progressive economic
conditions favoured a wide discretion in owners of
large fortunes. Yet, although the heir-at-law's
natural rights henceforward remained largely at the
mercy of the testator, they were never lost sight of
by legislature or judiciary. No exclusion of sui
heredes was suffered to operate unless pronounced
unmistakably, and in prescribed form, and disherison depended upon rules which, unless strictly
observed, might completely avoid the will, or at
least nullify the testator's intentions so far as they
were aimed against the interests of sui heredes.[1]
If these rules were observed, then indeed the clear
intention of the will must perforce prevail. But
even so, the ingenuity of later jurisconsults did not
permit matters to remain as they were. In the
course of time the doctrine of the Unduteous Will
stumbled into recognition under the equitable jurisdiction of the centumviral judges, and gave rise to a
special form of action, in which the unjust testator

---

[1] This benefit was subsequently extended to natural children
who, having been emancipated by the testator, had at civil law
lost their rights of agnation.

was treated as if he had been deranged,[1] unless good cause could be shown for the manner of his disposition. Out of this fiction grew the portio legitima. Countries which have adopted the Roman law still recognize in certain next-of-kin some indefeasible right to the family succession.

INTESTATE SUCCESSION.

"Where wills are recognized, it is necessary, upon each decease, to examine first whether a will exists, and then, whether it is valid. Only when one of these questions is negatived does the law proceed itself to designate the heir. The legal succession is then called hereditas ab intestato delata. It is a substituted succession, which only falls to be considered secondarily."[2]

Such was the position under the later Republic and the Empire. But when we deal with the first centuries of Rome, the statement is more correct in an inverted form. We have seen that "testation" in its earliest sense probably meant merely the public institution by a sonless man of an heir, as an alternative to adopting him outright, or at most the public confirmation of certain directions charging an heir-at-law, whose discretion would be otherwise unlimited.

---

[1] Actual insanity was not assumed, as that would have upset the will altogether, whereas the law only aimed at diverting some portion of the inheritance to the next-of-kin.

[2] Leonhard, Inst. d. röm. R., 370.

Such directions would generally refer to legacies payable out of the pecunia, and to the wardship of the testator's womenfolk and male children of tender years. The latter business was of frequent occurrence, for where an heir-at-law was himself disqualified by youth or defects of character, a paterfamilias would naturally desire to appoint as tutor a more distant agnate, or even a legal stranger, as for instance a kinsman of his wife's. On such matters it is permissible to suppose that the legislation of the XII Tables was contented merely to declare what was already law, or at least long-standing custom. Complete liberty of testation, if we have correctly apprehended the situation, was the result of accident, not a deliberately foreseen conclusion. Testation, when it first came to regulate heirship at all, represented an artificial succession as substituted for the natural succession of sui, and its consideration, but for reasons of convenience, should have been postponed to, instead of preceding, that of the latter.

The language of the XII Tables, " Si intestato moritur cui suus heres nec escit, adgnatus proximus familiam habeto," to which attention has already been drawn, is evidence that at the beginning of the fourth century urbis, testation was not uncommon, but at the same time the natural right of sui heredes to succeed, failing special provision to the contrary, is so firmly established as to be merely indicated by allusion as something self-understood.

Failing sui the nearest male agnate would most usually be a brother. The enactment was probably, like most of the provisions of the XII Tables, declaratory of existing law, or of custom,[1] which was itself the natural outcome of economic conditions. In regal times and the early Republic, the lands and herds, which formed the bulk of a family's property, were tilled and tended by all male members not disabled by age or infancy, whilst the women taught the children, spun, and managed the interior of a large household.[2] To break up what was virtually an extensive business organization each time a senior partner died would often have entailed loss and grave inconvenience, and it appears to have been usual on the ancestor's death for the new family heads to continue living and working together. If, then, one of the sons died childless, the association still endured; his interest went to the survivors by accrual, and they cared for the widow. The custom was, however, itself a development of the City, for under the older system it is difficult not to suppose that, in the rare event of a paterfamilias dying

---

[1] Muirhead, R. L., 118, mentions Ulpian's dictum that agnatic inheritance derived (descendit) from the XII Tables. I have several times shown cause for limiting the amount of innovation in that exceedingly cautious code.

[2] Cf. Cicero, De Off., i, 17. Prima societas in ipso conjugio est; proxima in liberis; deinde una domus, communia omnia. Id autem est principium urbis. . . . Sequuntur fratrum conjunctiones; post, consobrinorum, sobrinorumque; qui cum una domus jam capi non possint, in alias domos, tanquam in colonias, exeunt.

heirless, the gens would take as a corporate body. Moreover, it had already begun to lose its vogue with the growth of prosperity, and particularly the increased fluidity of wealth; and we find the XII Tables, which allowed great freedom of contract and testation, logically confirming in the co-heirs a right of partition enforceable at law (actio familiae erciscundae). Failing sui and testament, the adgnatus in the nearest degree[1] took, and this was interpreted strictly to mean *only* the nearest agnate, or agnates if more than one were in the same degree. Surviving brothers and sisters of the deceased took the whole of the inheritance, to the exclusion of any children of predeceased brothers and sisters; and in the event of refusal of the nearest agnates to enter upon an inheritance it was not open to remoter kinsmen to do so. Cognates, however near in degree, still remained entirely outside the circle of possible successors ab intestato.

It is a widely held view[2] that the subsidiary clause, Si adgnatus nec escit gentiles familiam habento (or words to that effect), was intended to refer to patricians having no agnates, and since all patrician members of a gens were actually or assumedly descended from a common ancestor, it is supposed that

---

[1] This could not be the father, for a son in potestate had nothing to leave, and an emancipated son was no longer agnatically related. But a father, whose emancipated son died intestate and heirless, might take as patron.

[2] Following Gaius, iii, 17.

"agnation," as then recognized by law, was already confined within certain degrees, or else that the enactment provided for those cases where, though the gentility was established, the exact degree or nature of the kinsmanship had in course of time become lost to sight. Both suppositions are difficult to reconcile with our view of the gentile association, and with the social conditions of the period. The classical jurists, writing at a period when the gens was but a memory of the past, are very uncertain guides. When the XII Tables were enacted, the privileged order was engaged in a passionate struggle for the defence of its political preponderance over the generality, and its social precedence before the wealthier, of the plebeians. It is not likely that at such a time artificial inner circles of kinsmen should have grown up within the gens in such manner as to confine rights of agnation to members of each circle *inter se*, whilst those outside were gentiles only. Neither is it very probable that at that period wider kinsman-ship should have been frequently lost to sight among patricians, proud, possibly to exaggeration, of their ancestry and connections.

A more probable explanation has been offered of the sentence, Si adgnatus nec escit, gentiles familiam habento, namely, that it was intended to cover the case of deceased clients and descendants of those who were known to have been freedmen. Clients certainly could own property in their own right from the moment they had achieved citizenship. A client also enjoyed rights of family. But if he died without sui or remoter agnates, his property upon intestacy went to his gentiles, from whom his own family derived its status, and whose name it bore. Where a client's family had remained from time immemorial in a state of clientage to a gens, the whole of the gentiles succeeded to his estate, probably as a corporate body. But after the gens had for most purposes become subdivided, a client might have originally commended himself to a patron who represented the head of one patrician family, or a branch (stirps) of a gens. Here only the patron and his descendants succeeded, in the circumstances related, to the client and his descendants; and only upon failure of the patron stirps was the entire gens entitled to the succession. Freedmen, who had been slaves of a patrician, and their descendants, were practically in the same position as those clients who derived from a particular gentile family or stirps. The freedman and his descendants became clients to the manumittor and his descendants. But since plebeians had become citizens, they also could own slaves and enfranchise them. To his freedman, a plebeian, whether himself a client or not, stood in the position of patron. If he predeceased the freedman the patronage vested in his descendants; but it did not devolve by operation of law upon collaterals, nor could it be bequeathed by testament.[1] But the

---

[1] When it became possible to enfranchise a slave by testament, the slave's patron was considered to be not the instituted heir

patronage was distinct from gentilitas; for whilst patricians were gentiles to their clients, no client or plebeian (at least in the earlier ages) could be gentilis to any one. Now, a man just released from slavery had no legal family, though he had the faculty of founding one, because in earlier times he became a citizen at once upon enfranchisement. Accordingly, a deceased freedman and former slave of a plebeian, who died leaving neither will, widow, nor children, was succeeded by his patron or patron's children. In the rare event of the plebeian patron family having itself become extinct during the freedman's lifetime, or whilst the patronage still subsisted over his descendants, it was necessary to look for successors among the gentiles of the patron family, who were considered to be derivatively gentiles of the freedman. Where the extinct patron family had been unattached to a gens there could be no gentiles; there was consequently total failure of succession and the estate was derelict.[1]

The manumittor's patronage over his freedman was continued in the former's children. But custom soon broke with the hereditary quality of the freedman's subjection, and by the fifth or sixth century of the City his descendants at least from his grand-

but the deceased testator. But the instituted heir might be directed by the will to enfranchise the slave, and he then became the patron by obeying the injunction.

[1] Upon the whole subject see Ortolan's Commentaries, Inst. de l'Empereur Justinien, vol. iii, pp. 30-49, and compare chapter, Die römische Clientel, in Mommsen's R. F., i.

children downwards had become entirely free and unattached plebeians.

As time progressed, the identity of individual families, save the most distinguished, became increasingly difficult to establish; and amid the turmoil of political dissensions it was impossible to preserve clientage or its incidents in their original form. Family ties became loosened or altogether broken. Many of the older gentes died out. New gentes and quasi-gentes emerged, some founded by immemorially free plebeian families, whilst others were of more questionable title. Towards the end of the Republic the relationship of gentilis and gentilicius had almost disappeared, and clientage was the name of a newer and baser association. Patronage over freedmen was longer lived, since the former enfranchisement of a still living man was easily remembered and provable. It was frequently regulated, mostly in the patron's interest, by later jurisprudents, and survived even the attentions of Justinian's reformers.

An inheritance vested in suus heres immediately upon the death of the ancestor—whether he had been instituted heir by will or had become so by operation of law, made no difference—and we have seen that it was not in his option to decline the succession with its attendant burdens.[1] Likewise, a

---

[1] This was remedied by later legislation. Under the praetorian practice, the beneficium abstinendi enabled suus heres to decline an insolvent inheritance, and the beneficium separationis entitled a slave-heir to retain his earnings made since the testator's

slave who had been instituted heir by his owner
was heres necessarius, though his compulsory succession to a probably insolvent estate was sweetened
by the gift of freedom.[1] The object of the latter
institution was usually to save a testator, whose
affairs were involved, from the possible disgrace of
post mortem bankruptcy, and it was customary to
mention the slave as heir in the will only after one
or more of the testator's kinsmen and friends, to
whom the hereditas was offered. A person not
being suus or necessarius heres, who succeeded by
virtue of agnation or testament, could decline an
inheritance, and consequently some act of acceptance (aditio) on his part was necessary to vest it in
him. Until this occurred the estate was hereditas
jacens.

A succession might be left derelict either because
no one was lawfully entitled to claim it, or because
the person so entitled, being neither suus nor necessarius heres, omitted or declined to do so.[2] There
would then be no one to continue the persona

death. Justinian's beneficium inventarii enabled an heir, whilst
taking over a doubtful estate, to keep it separate from his own,
so that he enjoyed any surplus of assets, but was not responsible
for any excess of liabilities. Beneficium separationis might also
be granted to creditors whose interests were threatened by merger
of a deceased's *solvent* estate into that of an *insolvent* heir.

[1] The enfranchisement was at first required to be express; later
it was implied. Just. Inst., ii, 14.

[2] Under the ancient law the State did not take over a deceased's
effects failing lawful successors.

of the deceased or attend to the sacra, and creditors would be unable to benefit by whatever assets there were. In such circumstances, the law permitted any stranger who cared to do so, to enter upon the estate; if he remained for twelve months in unchallenged possession, he was considered to have constituted himself the heir (usucapio pro herede), charging himself with the sacra and, no doubt, the obligation of compounding with creditors. Later, in the sixth and seventh centuries, to meet the case where the heir or heirs did not beneficially take the bulk of the succession, the duty of the sacra was made to devolve upon whichever legatee or usucapient had become possessed of the major part of the estate.[1] It is reasonable to suppose that the same person was answerable to the creditors, at least in proportion to the beneficial interest acquired.

In the foregoing chapter I alluded to the position of women under the early law of testation and tutelage, which gave right of testation by the copper and scales to the liberta, subject only to her patron-tutor's auctoritas, whilst withholding it altogether

[1] Qui majorem partem pecuniae capiat. The distinction between pecunia and familia was no longer preserved. A debtor to the estate who could not discharge his obligation was, in the last resort, burdened with the sacra, since he was rightly held to have benefited to the extent of the debt. Cicero, De Leg., ii, 19, 20, 21. The old principle, that the sacra followed the family property, was still maintained as far as possible, although the family property now so often went to strangers. The old religion, however, would not have permitted a stranger to perform the family rites.

from freeborn women (except vestals)—an anomaly
which further marks the haphazard growth of the law
relating to wills. In the most ancient times we are
obliged to believe that no woman could become heir
to an estate under a will or ab intestato, or dispose
of her own property by will. Both disqualifications
were necessary consequences of the social system,
which it would have been superfluous to enun-
ciate. No woman could have made good her title
to heirship, because to the heir fell the duty of
continuing the sacra; but the point never arose,
since care was always taken to secure male succession. In the absence of express prohibition, the
practice of tolerating women as co-heirs no doubt
afterwards crept in, as a consequence of the looser
plebeian ideas of succession and sacra, at a time
when the status of the plebeian was still in a transition stage. Then the citizen's subsequent, acci-
dentally-acquired freedom of testation enabled him
even to institute a woman as heir. Similarly, in
the first centuries of Rome, testation by a woman
was, apart from principle, impossible on practical
grounds, since no woman ever found herself in procinctu, and to publicly appear before the comitia was
an unheard-of proceeding. But when testation with
copper and scales had become general, it is not easy
to understand why any woman might not have made
her will with a tutor's auctoritas in the same way as
she could transfer property. The explanation that
the males were interested in retaining her property

in the family does not seem satisfactory. When a woman could become heir under a will or on intestacy, why should she not make a will herself? Female heirship continued, indeed, to be regarded as an abuse, and was discouraged by various enactments in the last centuries of the Republic.[1] Yet it may be asked why a woman, whose right to be instituted heir had become so well established that it required special legislation to curb it, apparently could at no time, until special legislation was brought to her aid,[2] herself dispose of her estate by will, unless (a further anomaly) she were a freedwoman, or a freeborn manumittee, acting with the concurrence of her patron.[3] The second contradiction forms the subject of one of Dr. Conrat's studies,[4] and he explains it by assuming that tutela over freeborn women being more ancient, was consequently stricter than that over libertae and manumissae e mancipio. Like emancipation, the former was undoubtedly older than the XII Tables which confirmed it, whilst the new tutela which flowed from the patronage of a manumittor, although also called legitima, was the work of the later jurists who interpreted the enactment (Gaius i, 165) at a time

[1] For instance, the lex Voconia, 585 urbis.

[2] Gaius, i, 115a; ii, 112, 113. There had always been an exception in favour of vestals.

[3] Such is the prevailing opinion, which is also adopted by Dr. Max Cohn (Conrat) in Beiträge zur Bearbeitung des römischen Rechts., 1-17.

[4] *Ibid.*

when the patron's power had become enormously attenuated. Dr. Conrat considers that the older tutela approached so near to potestas that a faculty of testation on the part of the ward would have been repugnant to its principles. Without adopting the explanation, I think the distinction he draws between the patron-tutor and other tutors may contain the solution of the whole question. But if we distinguish the various kinds of tutela, I am rather led to conclude that a difference had always existed, and that the patron's was the most, not the least, powerful. The liberta enjoyed her advantage, not because the authority of a patron-tutor was alone insufficient to withhold, but because it alone was sufficient to confer, the special privilege. A guardian was not necessarily even a kinsman, and without further proof I am not prepared to admit that his authority over his freeborn ward ever represented even a modified potestas or manus. On the other hand, it is reasonable to expect the lord's former authority over his enfranchised slave to have originally continued in a modified form; and we know that the old gentile patronage (which did not differ essentially from that of an enfranchising master), though it may have stopped short of the jus vitae necisque, exerted a wide authority over the client. A dominus could not, of course, have authorized his female slave to make a will, since she had neither property of her own, nor capacity to go through the legal forms. But when the ancilla had been converted by manumission into a freedwoman sui juris, there is no reason why the remnant of his authority[1] —the patronage—might not suffice to validate her will, and it is easy to imagine that this power was included among the functions with which the interpreters of the XII Tables invested the patron. By means of fiduciary coemption with a trustee, followed by mancipation to another trustee and manumission, in the manner already described, freeborn women afterwards contrived to reach the same position. By analogy with the patron-tutor (however different in reality) a manumittor-trustee was, like the former, held entitled, and he was by the terms of his trust bound, to validate by his auctoritas whatever will his nominal ward chose to make per aes et libram. The whole of the irrational procedure was swept away under the Empire, when the Legislature reconciled itself to the necessity of formally acknowledging in women the right of testation, which they had long exercised in practice.

[1] Cf. Sohm, Inst. d. röm. R., 77, Die Freilassung ist eine Art von Wiedergeburt. Der Herr (patronus) tritt daher zu seinem Freigelassenen in ein vaterähnliches Verhältniss.

INDEX

283

CHISWICK PRESS: PRINTED BY CHARLES WHITTINGHAM AND CO.
TOOKS COURT, CHANCERY LANE, LONDON.